C0-CFJ-174

Visual QuickStart Guide

CorelDRAW 5

Glen Waller
&
Paul Webster

Webster & Associates

 Peachpit Press

CorelDRAW 5: Visual QuickStart Guide
Glen Waller & Paul Webster

Peachpit Press
2414 Sixth Street
Berkeley, CA 94710
510/548-4393
510/548-5991 (fax)

Copyright © 1994 by Webster & Associates

Notice of Rights
All rights reserved. No part of this book may be reproduced or transmitted in any form by any means, electronic, mechanical, photocopying, recording, or otherwise, without the prior written permission of the publisher. For information on getting permission for reprints and excerpts, contact Trish Booth at Peachpit Press.

Notice of Liability
The information in this book is distributed on an "As Is" basis, without warranty. While every precaution has been taken in the preparation of the book, neither the author nor Peachpit Press, Inc., shall have any liability to any person or entity with respect to any loss or damage caused or alleged to be caused directly or indirectly by the instructions contained in this book or by the computer software and hardware products described in it.

ISBN 1-56609-167-5

9 8 7 6 5 4 3 2 1

Printed and bound in the United States of America

Why a Visual QuickStart?

Virtually no one actually reads computer books; rather, people typically refer to them. This series of **Visual QuickStart Guides** has made that reference easier thanks to a new approach to learning computer applications.

Although conventional computer books lean towards providing extensive textual explanations, a **Visual QuickStart Guide** takes a far more visual approach—pictures literally show you what to do, and text is limited to clear, concise commentary. Learning becomes easier, because a **Visual QuickStart Guide** familiarizes you with the look and feel of your software. Learning also becomes faster, since there are no long-winded passages through which to comb.

It's a new approach to computer learning, but it's also solidly based on experience: Webster & Associates has logged thousands of hours of classroom computer training, and have authored many books on computer applications.

Chapter 1 introduces you to the CorelDRAW basics, focusing on the CorelDRAW screen components.

Chapters 2 and 3 show you the tools you use in CorelDRAW.

Chapters 4 through **12** show the commands you use in CorelDRAW. These chapters are easy to reference and use screen shots to ensure that you grasp concepts quickly.

Acknowledgments

The authors wish to acknowledge the effort and dedication of the following people:

- Jenny Hamilton
- Catherine Howes
- Elwyn Williams
- Wayne Clarke
- Tony Webster

Contents

INTRODUCING CORELDRAW 5

STARTING CORELDRAW 5

Figure 1. To start CorelDRAW 5, double-click on the CorelDRAW icon in your Corel 5 Program Group.

When you start CorelDRAW 5, your screen looks like this. You are in a new, untitled CorelDRAW 5 file.

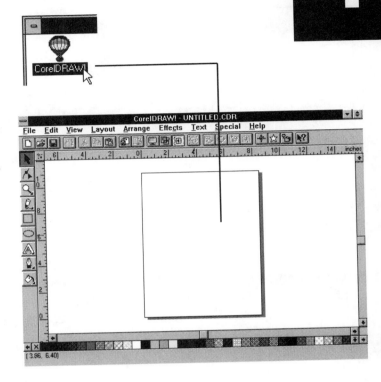

Figure 2. You can now open an existing file by selecting the *Open* command from the **File** menu. This brings up the *Open Drawing* dialog box.

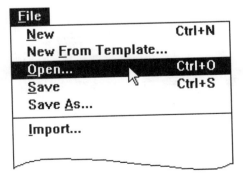

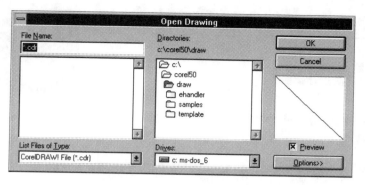

Figure 3. The *Open Drawing* dialog box gives you access to the computer's drives and directories. Find and select the file you want from the list of files in this dialog box, then click on the *OK* button. Alternatively, double-click on the filename to open the file.

For more information on the options available in this dialog box, see **Chapter 4, The File Menu.**

THE SCREEN

Figure 4. This figure shows the CorelDRAW 5 screen and its components.

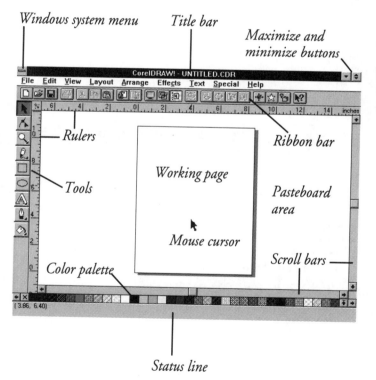

SCREEN COMPONENTS

TITLE BAR

Figure 5. At the very top of the screen is the CorelDRAW 5 title bar. The title bar contains the name of the current CorelDRAW 5 file. If you have not yet given this file a name, it reads *UNTITLED.CDR*.

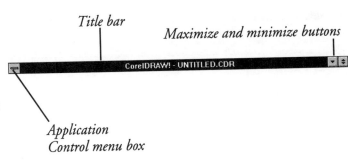

Title bar

Maximize and minimize buttons

Application Control menu box

MAXIMIZE AND MINIMIZE BUTTONS, AND APPLICATION CONTROL MENU

The maximize and minimize buttons on the title bar operate in the same way as standard maximize and minimize buttons in Windows applications.

Using the single down-arrow minimizes the window to an icon in the bottom left of the screen. You can double-click on this icon to reactivate the window. The Restore button (up and down arrow) restores the window to its pre-maximized size.

The Application **Control** menu, which you open by clicking on the Application **Control** menu box (see Figure 5), is common to all Windows applications. From this menu you can maximize, minimize, or close the current application.

MENU BAR

Figure 6. The menu bar is immediately below the title bar on the screen. When you click on a menu bar command with the mouse, a menu of options appears. Each option performs a unique function. Menus are used in most Windows programs.

Menu bar

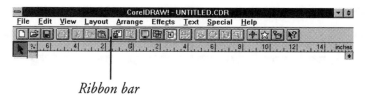

Ribbon bar

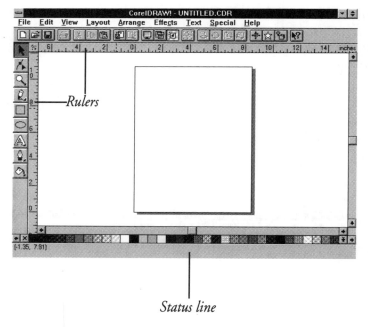

Rulers

Status line

RIBBON BAR

Figure 7. The ribbon bar sits immediately below the menu bar and contains a variety of icons that correspond directly with menu commands. These icons are a quick way of performing some of the most common CorelDRAW tasks.

For instance, clicking on the *To Front* icon is the same as selecting the *To Front* command from the *Order* submenu in the **Arrange** menu.

STATUS LINE AND RULERS

Figure 8. The status line in CorelDRAW 5 is the wide bar running along the bottom of the application window. The status line is in effect a bar of information that indicates what object you have selected, as well as its dimensions; the font and point size of selected text; outline and color of a selected object; the angle of rotation; as well as other vital pieces of information. The status line tells the position of the mouse on the page in relation to the rulers and also displays current information on what you are doing in CorelDRAW.

You use the rulers to measure distance and to accurately place objects on the page. For more information on the rulers, see **Chapter 6, The View Menu.**

WORKING PAGE AND PASTEBOARD AREA

Figure 9. The relationship between the working page and pasteboard area is similar to the relationship between a piece of paper and a desk. The pasteboard works like a desk area; you can place objects on it and they will save with the file but will not print unless you select the *Fit to page* option in the *Print Options* dialog box.

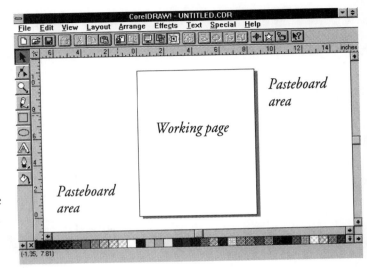

The working page represents the area of the page that prints.

See **Print** in **Chapter 4, The File Menu** for more information.

MOUSE CURSOR

Figure 10. The mouse cursor is the icon that moves around the screen as you move your mouse. The mouse cursor changes shape when you select a tool from the Toolbox.

(a)

The icon in (a) indicates that you have selected the Pick Tool.

(b)

The icons in (b) and (c) show the Shape Tool and Zoom Tool, respectively and the cross-hair icon shown in (d) indicates that you have selected one of the various drawing or text tools.

(c)

(d)

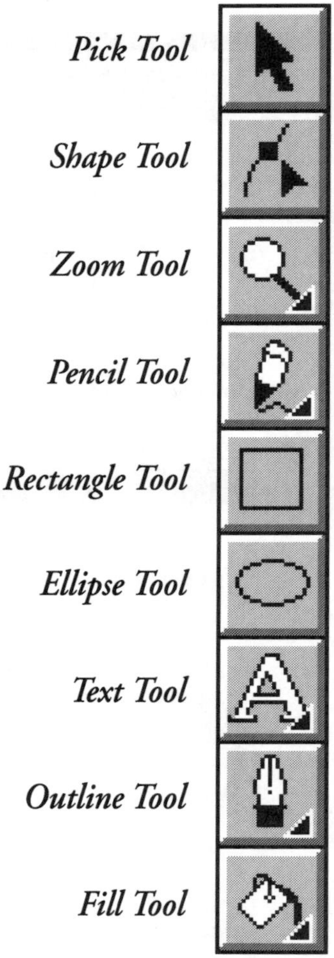

TOOLBOX

Figure 11. You can select the tool icons in the Toolbox with the mouse. These different tools have a wide range of functions and uses which we explain in detail in **Chapters 2, The Utility, Drawing, and Text Tools** and 3, **Outline and Fill Tools.**

Pick Tool

Shape Tool

Zoom Tool

Pencil Tool

Rectangle Tool

Ellipse Tool

Text Tool

Outline Tool

Fill Tool

SCROLL BARS AND THE COLOR PALETTE

Figure 12. You use the scroll bars with the mouse to move different parts of the screen into view. Scroll bars are common to most Windows applications.

The Color palette is a bar, running along the bottom of the screen, which lets you apply colors to selected objects quickly. For more information, see **Chapter 6, The View Menu.**

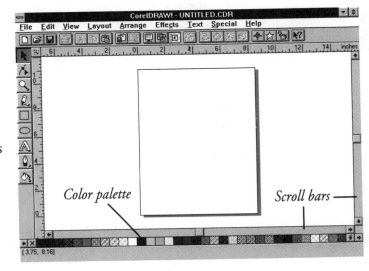

Color palette   *Scroll bars* —

THE HELP MENU

Figure 13. The **Help** menu provides you with online help on how to use CorelDRAW 5.

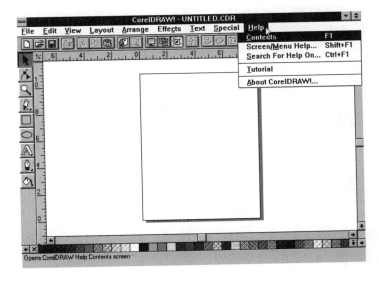

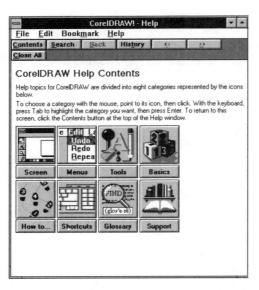

Figure 14. You can activate this *Help* screen through the *Contents* command from the **Help** menu; alternatively, you can use the F1 key. Follow the instructions in the *Help* window to find information on any topic related to CorelDRAW 5.

Pressing the Shift+F1 keys, when there is no *Help* dialog box on screen, activates this icon: ▶?. Clicking with this cursor on any menu item or screen component gives you context-sensitive help for that menu item or screen component.

VIEWING MODES

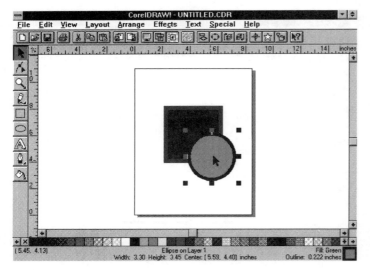

Figure 15. By default, CorelDRAW 5 works in editable preview. This view displays all objects in full color. To select a filled object in this view, click inside the object (on the filled part).

The other option is *wireframe* view. *Wireframe* view is much faster, as it displays only the outlines of the various objects. To move between the two views, select the *Wireframe* command from the **View** menu. Alternatively, press the Shift+F9 keys or click on the *Wireframe* icon on the ribbon bar. For more information, see **Chapter 6, The View Menu.**

DIALOG BOXES

Dialog boxes give you access to a number of different options to do with a particular command. You can select and activate dialog box options in a number of different ways.

Figure 16. Tabs in dialog boxes are a way of navigating through sub-groups of options that affect a given command. For instance, the *Page Setup* dialog box is broken into three tabs, each of which determine a different aspect of controlling the page setup.

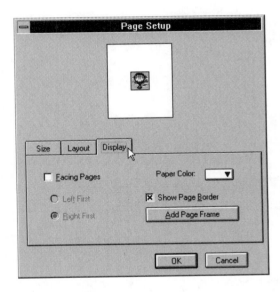

To select a tab, click on the tab heading with your mouse. The dialog box then changes, displaying the options available for that tab. In this example we have selected the *Display* tab of the *Page Setup* dialog box to display the options available for changing the display of the page setup.

Figure 17. You use radio buttons to select mutually exclusive options—you can select only one option at a time from each section containing these kind of buttons.

To activate a radio button, simply click on the button next to the option you want to select so that it becomes filled as shown.

This section of the *Page Setup* dialog box shows an example of radio buttons. You can select the *Portrait* or *Landscape* option for the orientation of your page, in this case we have selected the *Portrait* radio button.

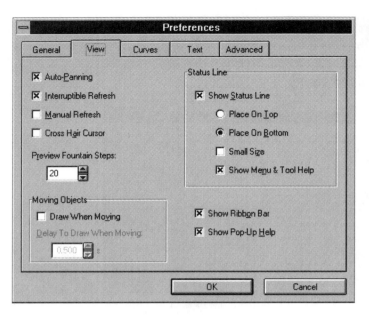

Figure 18. Check boxes allow you to choose between applying or not applying an option in a dialog box. To mark and unmark check boxes, you click on them with the mouse. An active check box has a check mark in it. You can select as many check boxes as you want.

This example shows a variety of check boxes in the *Preferences* dialog box. We have selected the *Auto-Panning* and *Interruptible Refresh* check boxes at the top left of the dialog box.

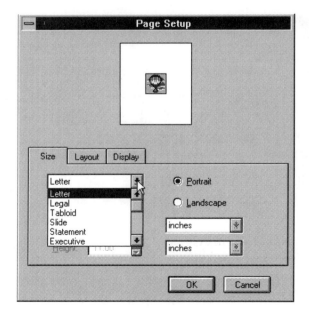

Figure 19. A drop-down list in a dialog box gives you access to a list of options. Clicking on a down-arrow (⬇) in a dialog box activates a drop-down list. In this example, we have clicked on the page size option in the *Page Setup* dialog box. This displays a drop-down list of options from which you can select a page size.

Figure 20. Some dialog boxes, such as in the *Display* tab of the *Page Setup* dialog box, have buttons that open pop-up palettes or quick-pick palettes, from where you can select a color or an item.

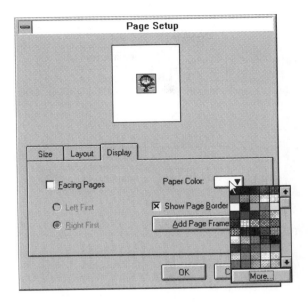

Figure 21. Also, certain buttons in dialog boxes open a further dialog box. These buttons are indicated by an ellipsis (three periods) after the button command name.

Figure 22. This dialog box shows two additional features—a text box and a list box. You enter or edit text within a text box, much like any text editing procedure. You can delete existing text with the Delete or Backspace keys. You can also highlight text by dragging across it with the cursor.

List boxes let you select an item from a group of items. Use the scroll bars if you need to view the item you want to select.

Text box

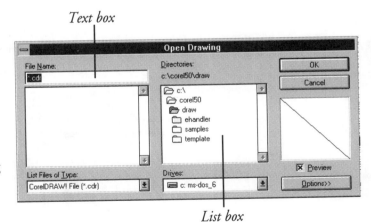

List box

(a)

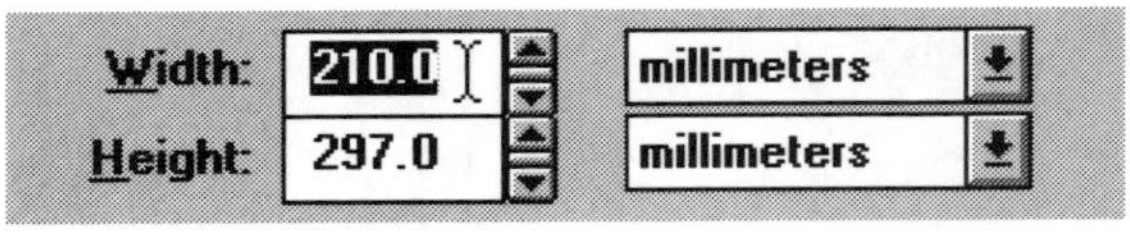

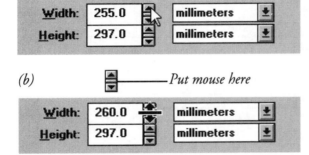

Figure 23. You can change certain dialog box options by selecting the numeric value with the mouse (a) and typing a new value directly over the top (b).

(b)

(a)

Figure 24. You can also use the up or down arrows to the right of the frame to increase or decrease the value (a).

(b) *Put mouse here*

Alternatively, hold the mouse down on the bar between the up and down arrows (b) and move the mouse up or down to change the value.

The *OK* button confirms your dialog box selections and returns you to the editing screen. Click on the *Cancel* button if you want CorelDRAW 5 to ignore any changes you have made within a dialog box.

ROLL-UPS

Figure 25. Roll-ups can have all the features of a dialog box. They are constant dialog boxes that remain on screen until you remove them.

Many commands in CorelDRAW 5 use roll-ups. For more information on each roll-up, see the specific command.

Figure 26. To reduce screen clutter, you can roll up or down the roll-ups (hence their name) at any time. To do so, click on the arrow in the top right of the roll-up.

Figure 27. You can move a roll-up around the screen by holding the mouse down on the title bar of the roll-up and dragging it to a new position.

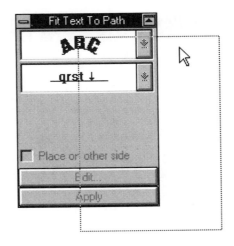

Figure 28. Clicking on the icon in the top left of a roll-up window displays this menu. Use the *Arrange* or *Arrange All* commands to arrange one or all of the roll-up windows currently on the screen.

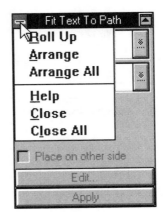

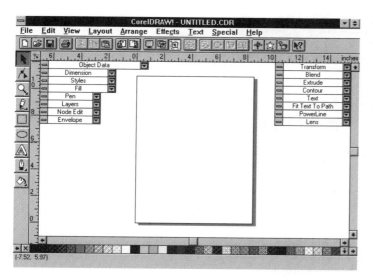

Figure 29. Selecting the *Arrange All* command from the menu of Figure 28 arranges all roll-ups currently active.

This example shows most of the available roll-ups in CorelDRAW arranged using the *Arrange All* command.

ON-SCREEN HELP

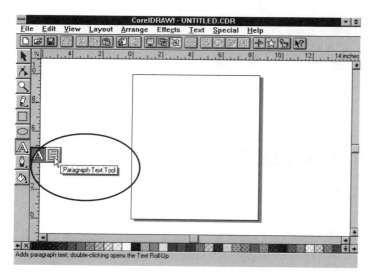

Figure 30. Corel also has an on screen help feature that brings up balloon help prompts when you position the mouse cursor over any tool.

Figure 31. Similarly, the status line displays information about any tool or menu item that you select with the mouse cursor.

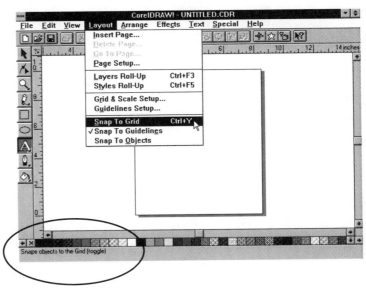

Figure 32. You can turn either of these options on or off through the *View* tab of the *Preferences* dialog box. For more information on this dialog box, see **Chapter 11, The Special Menu**.

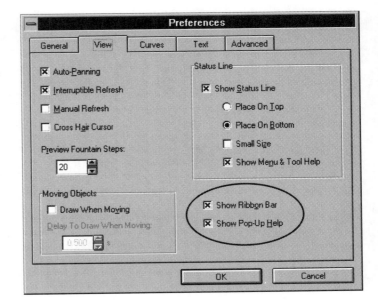

THE UTILITY, DRAWING, AND TEXT TOOLS

2

USING THE TOOLS

The CorelDRAW Toolbox contains all the tools you need to draw and manipulate objects. In this chapter you will learn the various functions of all tools except the Outline and Fill tools. You will also learn how to use the various tools in conjunction with each other, and with the menu commands.

Chapter 3 describes the Outline and Fill Tools.

Figure 1. The Toolbox, at the left of the screen, contains all the CorelDRAW tools. Once you select a tool, it remains active until you select another from the Toolbox.

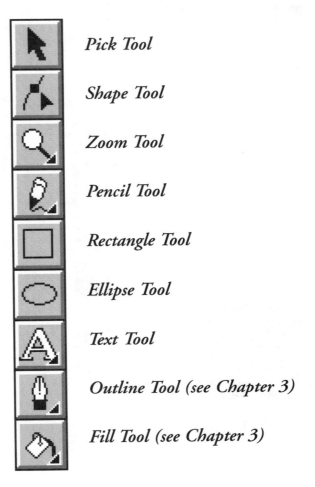

Pick Tool

Shape Tool

Zoom Tool

Pencil Tool

Rectangle Tool

Ellipse Tool

Text Tool

Outline Tool (see Chapter 3)

Fill Tool (see Chapter 3)

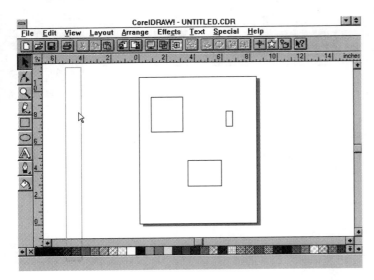

Figure 2. You can tear the Toolbox from its normal position and make it a floating palette. To do this, hold down the Shift key and then click and drag the Toolbox into the editing window.

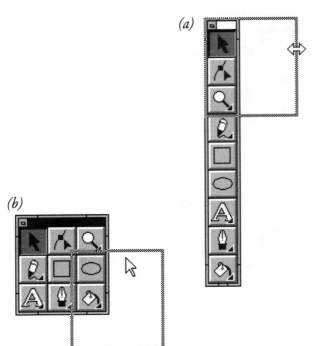

(a)

(b)

Figure 3. You can then resize this Toolbox palette by dragging its sides (a), or you can move the palette around the screen by dragging its title bar (b).

Figure 4. To return the Toolbar to its original position, double-click its title bar, or activate the Toolbox **Control** menu and de-select the *Floating* option.

Figure 5. You can also use the commands in the Toolbox **Control** menu to group or ungroup all of the subsets of each tool. Ungrouping the tools makes all of the available tool options appear at the same level in the Toolbox palette.

Figure 6. If you close the Toolbox through the **Control** menu command, you can reopen it by selecting the *Visible* command from the *Toolbox* submenu of the **View** menu.

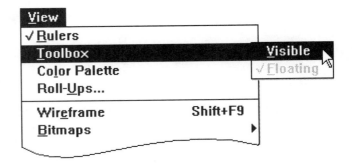

THE PICK TOOL

You can use the Pick Tool (➤) to select, resize, move, rotate, and skew objects. This is the tool that you use most of the time. If you are using a different tool from the Toolbox, press the Spacebar to select the Pick Tool.

SELECTING OBJECTS

(a)

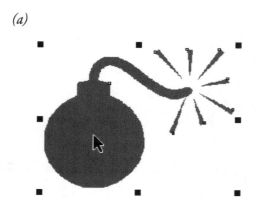

Figure 7. With the Pick Tool, click anywhere on a filled object to select that object (a). If the object has no fill, you click anywhere along the perimeter of the object to select it.

(b)

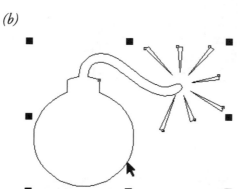

If you are in *wireframe* view, you have to click on the edge of the object to select it (b).

Once selected, an object displays eight small handles around its edge. This is known as a highlight box. When you select an object, the status line indicates what sort of object it is, as well as its size, position, fill, and outline. To select more than one object, hold down the Shift key while clicking the Pick Tool on the objects you want to select. Choose *Select All* from the **Edit** menu to select everything on the screen at once.

Use the Tab key to select the objects on the screen in turn automatically.

MARQUEE SELECTION

Figure 8. To select one or more objects as a whole, hold the mouse down and drag it over all the objects. This procedure selects all objects that fall entirely within the selection marquee (a).

(a)

When you have marquee selected multiple objects, all the objects are included in the one highlight box (b). You can now apply the same options to these multiple objects as you apply to a single selected object.

(b)

When you have more than one object selected, the status line indicates how many objects you have selected.

MOVING OBJECTS

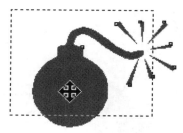

Figure 9. In *editable preview*, you can move a filled object with the Pick Tool if you hold the mouse button down when the cursor is anywhere on the object's interior, and drag the mouse. The object moves to where you release the mouse button.

If the object has no fill, or you are in *wireframe* view, hold the mouse down on the border of the object, and then drag the mouse to the new position and release it. See also the **Nudge** section in **Chapter 11, The Special Menu,** for another way of moving objects.

ROTATING AND SKEWING OBJECTS

Figure 10. Click twice on any object (or once on any object you've already selected) with the Pick Tool, to activate the rotate and skew handles (a).

To rotate an object, hold the mouse button down when the cursor is on any corner handle, and move the object in the direction you want it to rotate (b).

A cross-hair appears when you put the cursor over a rotate handle

(a)   *(b)*

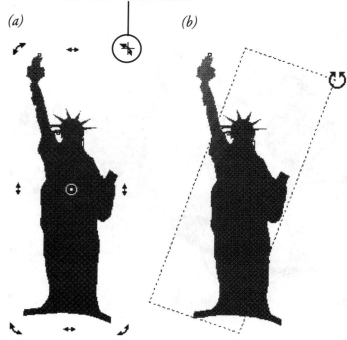

After releasing the mouse, you have rotated the object (c).

(c)

Figure 11. To skew an object, hold the mouse down on any middle handle and move it in the direction you wish to skew the object (a).

The result of skewing an object is shown in (b).

(a)

(b)

CENTER OF ROTATION

The (⊙) symbol that appears in the middle of an object when you activate the rotate and skew handles, shows the center of rotation. You can move this symbol if you drag it to a new position.

Moving this symbol changes the center of rotation of an object. The center of rotation symbol remains in the new position until you change it. See **Chapter 9, The Effects Menu,** on how to rotate and skew using the associated menu commands.

RESIZING OBJECTS

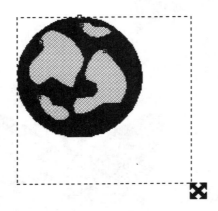

Figure 12. To resize an object, hold the mouse button down with the cursor on one of the eight selection handles and drag the mouse toward, or away from, the center of the object. The object then resizes accordingly.

Using one of the four corner handles to resize an object, as shown in this example, scales the graphic, keeping it in its true proportion.

(a)

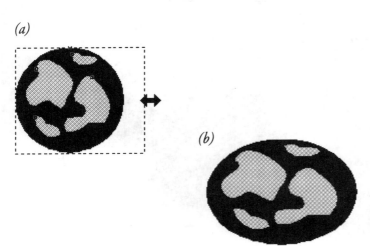

(b)

Figure 13. Using any of the four remaining handles (a) stretches or distorts the object, as in (b).

Clicking on the right mouse button as you move, rotate, skew, mirror, or resize objects leaves a copy of the original object behind.

MIRRORING OBJECTS

Figure 14. To mirror an object horizontally, hold the mouse down on either side handle (a), press the Ctrl key, and drag the mouse across the object (b). Release the mouse before releasing the Ctrl key to mirror the object (c).

To mirror an object vertically, follow the same steps, but use either the top or bottom center handle.

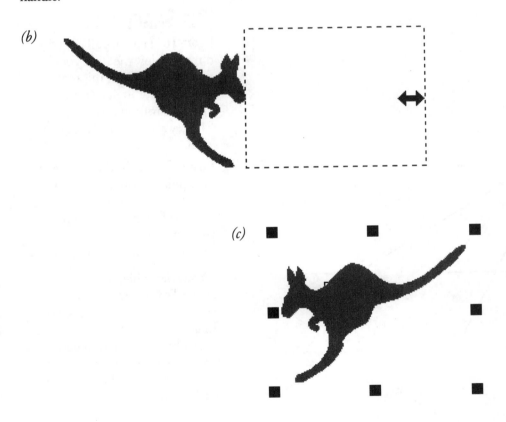

Edit	
Undo Delete	Ctrl+Z
Redo	Alt+Ret
Repeat Delete	Ctrl+R
Cut	Ctrl+X
Copy	Ctrl+C
Paste	Ctrl+V
Paste **Special**...	
Delete	Del
Duplicate	Ctrl+D
Clone	
Copy Attributes **From**...	
Select **All**	
Insert O**bj**ect...	
Object	▸
Links...	

DELETING OBJECTS

Figure 15. To delete an object, first select it with the Pick Tool, then press the Delete key on the keyboard; alternatively, select *Delete* from the **Edit** menu.

THE SHAPE TOOL

Figure 16. The Shape Tool (⚲) is directly below the Pick Tool in the Toolbox. Once this tool is selected, your mouse cursor looks like the cursor in this figure. The F10 key also activates the Shape Tool.

Figure 17. Use the Shape Tool to manipulate existing objects. Once you select an object with this tool, a series of nodes appears on it; you can move and manipulate these nodes and their properties.

You select objects with the Shape Tool the same way you select objects with the Pick Tool. In *wireframe* view, and when the object has no fill in *editable preview*, click on the outline of the object. If the object has a fill, click anywhere on the object.

Nodes ———

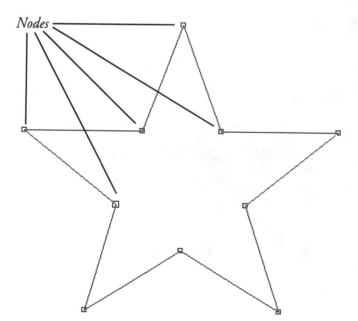

To deselect an object selected with the Shape Tool, click on another object. Alternatively, you can select the Pick Tool and then click away from the object.

You can also use the Shape Tool to crop bitmaps, and modify rectangles, ellipses, and text.

MODIFYING RECTANGLES

Figure 18. To modify a rectangle with the Shape Tool, select one of its four corners (a) and move it along the rectangle side to create the round-cornered rectangle shown in (b).

(a)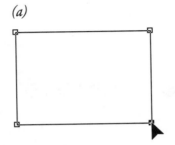

(b)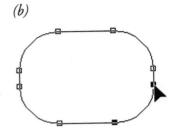

MODIFYING ELLIPSES

Figure 19. To modify an ellipse with the Shape Tool, move the node on the circumference of the ellipse to make an arc or a wedge (a).

If you drag the mouse inside the ellipse, you will create a wedge shape (b).

If you drag the mouse outside the ellipse, you will get an arc (c).

(a)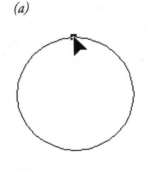

(b)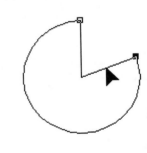

(c)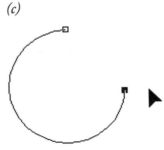

CONVERTING TO CURVES

Arrange	
Align...	Ctrl+A
Order	▶
Group	Ctrl+G
Ungroup	Ctrl+U
Combine	Ctrl+L
Break Apart	Ctrl+K
Weld	
Intersection	
Trim	
Separate	
Convert To Curves	**Ctrl+Q**

Figure 20. You can't change text, rectangles, and ellipses with the Shape Tool the same way as objects you have created with the Pencil Tool (see **The Shape Tool and Text** section later in this chapter). You must convert them to curves first. To do this, select the object with the Pick Tool and choose *Convert To Curves* from the **Arrange** menu, or click on the *Convert To Curves* icon on the ribbon bar.

You can convert Artistic Text to curves, but not Paragraph Text. Once you do this, a series of nodes appears along the object, which lets you change the shape of the object. Once you have converted an object to curves, you cannot change it back (unless you immediately choose *Undo* from the **Edit** menu). For more information, see **Convert To Curves** in **Chapter 8, The Arrange Menu**.

SELECTING NODES

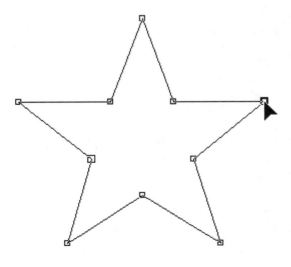

Figure 21. To select an individual node of an object selected with the Shape Tool, simply click on the node.

Figure 22. To select more than one node, hold down the Shift key and click on each node in turn (a).

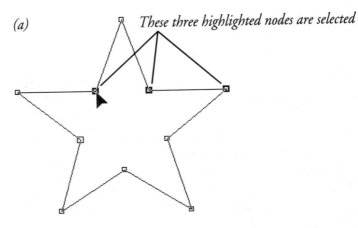

(a)   *These three highlighted nodes are selected*

Alternatively, use the Shape Tool to draw a selection rectangle around the nodes you wish to select. This procedure selects and highlights all nodes that fall inside this square.

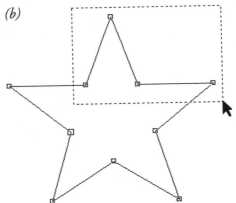

(b)

MOVING NODES

Figure 23. To move a node with the Shape Tool, hold the mouse down on a node and reposition it. Notice that some nodes, when selected, have control points attached to them, which you can also select and move when manipulating curves.

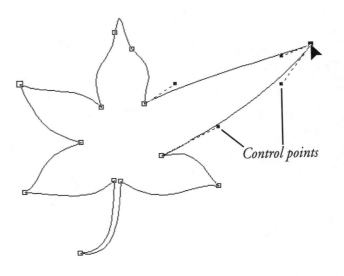

Control points

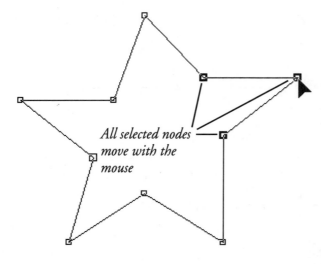

*All selected nodes
move with the
mouse*

Figure 24. You can move multiple nodes by selecting all the nodes you want to move and dragging one of the highlighted nodes to a new position. All the selected nodes then move with the mouse.

You can also move nodes using the directional arrow keys on your keyboard. For more information on this procedure, see the *Nudge* option in the *Preferences* dialog box, from the **Special** menu.

MOVING CONTROL POINTS

Certain nodes have control points connected to them, which display when you select them (see Figure 23). Curved segments' nodes have control points, while straight (line) segments do not.

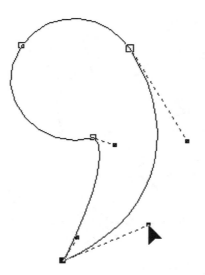

Figure 25. You can move a control point with the Shape Tool to change the shape of a curved segment. How this affects the shape of the object is determined by the type of node attached to the segment (see **Editing nodes** on the next page).

MOVING CURVED SEGMENTS

Figure 26. You can change the shape of the line by dragging the line segment with the mouse. The way the segment moves depends on what sort of curve it is.

For more information see the **Cusp**, **Smooth**, and **Symmet** sections later in this chapter.

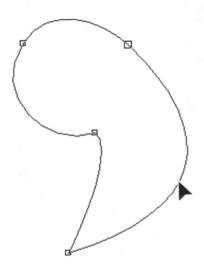

EDITING NODES

Figure 27. To change the properties of one or more nodes in an object, double-click on the object, or one of its nodes, with the Shape Tool. This activates the *Node Edit* roll-up.

This option does not work with text, rectangles, or ellipses.

ADDING NODES

(a)

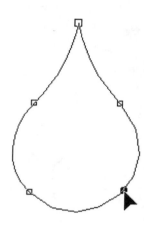

Figure 28. If the *Node Edit* roll-up is not active, double-click on the segment where you want the node to appear. This places a black dot (●) on the line where you clicked the mouse and opens the *Node Edit* roll-up (a).

If the *Node Edit* roll-up is already open, click once on the line to add the black dot in the position you want to add the node.

(b)

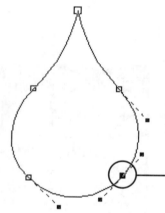

Click on the **+** button in the *Node Edit* roll-up to add the node; this adds the node where the black dot originally appeared.

Alternatively, you can use the + key on the numeric keypad on your keyboard to add nodes where a black dot is.

You have now added a node to the object

If you click on the **+** in the *Node Edit* roll-up when you have a node selected, this adds a node midway along the segment adjacent to the selected node.

You can add several nodes to an object simultaneously by selecting the nodes next to the segments you want to add the nodes to, then clicking on the **+** button in the *Node Edit* roll-up.

DELETING NODES

Deleting nodes in an object is sometimes necessary to smooth out the object. The less nodes you use to create an object the better.

Figure 29. If the *Node Edit* roll-up is not active, double-click on the node you want to delete, and then click on the — button when the *Node Edit* roll-up appears.

If the *Node Edit* roll-up is on, click on the node with the Shape Tool, and select the — button.

If you have multiple nodes selected, the — option in the *Node Edit* roll-up or the Delete key on your keyboard removes all selected nodes.

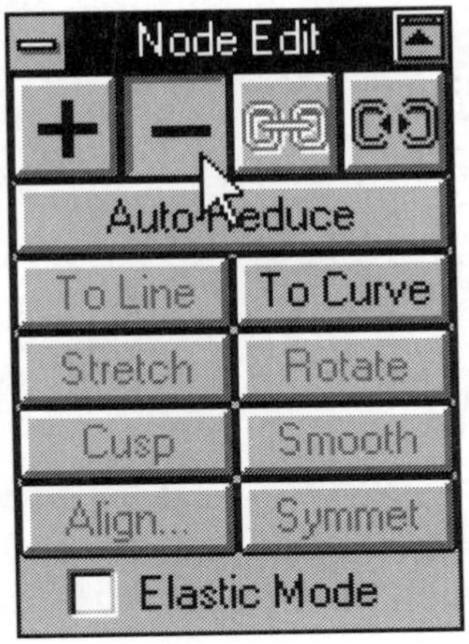

JOINING NODES

You use the chain links icon in the *Node Edit* roll-up to join two nodes.

Figure 30. Select two nodes with the Shape Tool (they must be the last or first nodes of the same path), double-click on one of them to activate the *Node Edit* roll-up, and then click on the chain links icon to join the nodes (a).

If the *Node Edit* roll-up is already active, select the two nodes and choose this option.

(a)

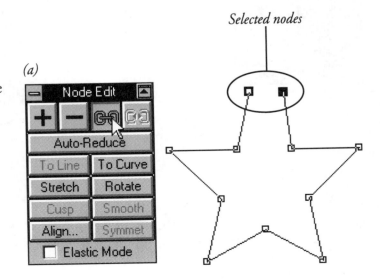

Selected nodes

(b)

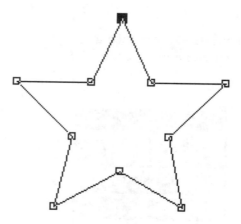

You have now joined the two nodes (b).

(a)

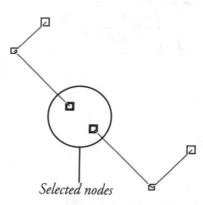

Selected nodes

Figure 31. You can also join starting or ending nodes that belong to different subpaths of a path. All objects in CorelDRAW are known as paths. A path can contain several subpaths. When you select an object with the Shape Tool, the status line indicates how many subpaths (if any) are included in the one path.

The selected nodes in (a) belong to different subpaths of the same path. When you click on the chain links icon, the nodes join and the two subpaths become one path (b).

(b)

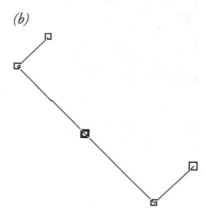

Figure 32. To join two separate paths (which differ from subpaths), first select them both with the Pick Tool. Then, choose *Combine* from the **Arrange** menu (a).

(a)

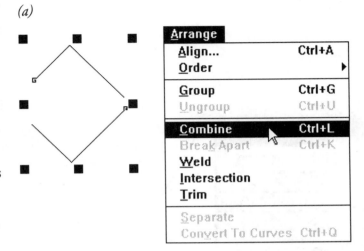

Now select the two nodes you wish to join with the Shape Tool and choose the chain links icon from the *Node Edit* roll-up. If this roll-up is not active, double-click on one of the selected nodes to activate the *Node Edit* roll-up (b).

This procedure joins the selected nodes (c).

(b)

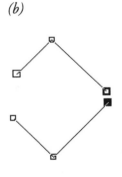

(c)

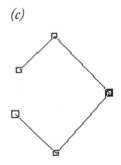

BREAKING NODES

Use the broken chain option in the *Node Edit* roll-up to break a line or a closed object.

(a)

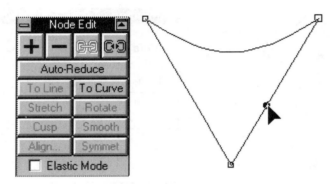

Figure 33. If the *Node Edit* roll-up is active, click once on the node or line segment where you want to break the object (a). If the roll-up is not active, double-click on the node or line segment to activate it.

Click on the broken chain icon in the *Node Edit* roll-up (b).

This breaks the section of the line where you clicked the mouse (c). You can then move these nodes independently with the Shape Tool.

(b)

(c)

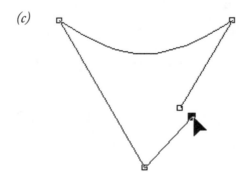

AUTO-REDUCE

Figure 34. You can use the *Auto-Reduce* option to have CorelDRAW remove any unnecessary nodes from an object that has too many nodes.

Marquee select the object with the Shape Tool to select all the nodes (a).

Click on the *Auto-Reduce* option in the *Node Edit* roll-up (b).

CorelDRAW then removes all the nodes from the object that aren't necessary to maintain its shape (c).

(a)

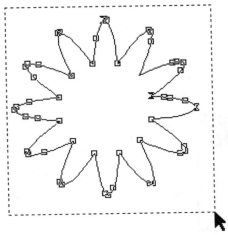

(b)

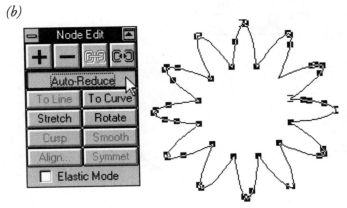

(c)

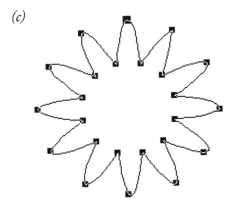

TO LINE

The *To Line* option converts the distance between two nodes from a curve to a straight line. You can access this option only if the selected segment is a curve.

(a)

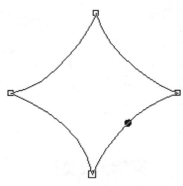

Figure 35. If the *Node Edit* roll-up is not active, double-click on the segment that you want to convert to a straight line. This adds a black dot along the line and activates the *Node Edit* roll-up. Now, click on the *To Line* option (a).

If the *Node Edit* roll-up is active, click on the segment that you want to convert to a straight line, and then choose the *To Line* option.

(b)

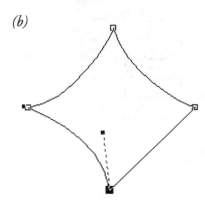

CorelDRAW converts the curved line to a straight line (b).

If the line is actually concave, as in this example, you will see the change in the line from curve to straight. If the line is a curve but is in a straight position, you will not necessarily notice any change in the line.

What will happen though, is the control points of the nodes connected to this line disappear because straight lines do not have any control points attached to their nodes.

TO CURVE

The *To Curve* option changes the distance between two nodes from a straight line to a curve.

Figure 36. Double-click on the straight line to activate the *Node Edit* roll-up and choose the *To Curve* option (a).

(a)

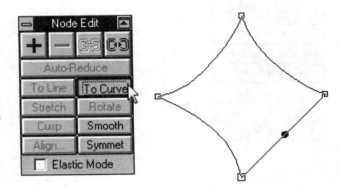

If the *Node Edit* roll-up is already active, click once on the straight line you want to convert to a curved line, and then click on the *To Curve* option.

You can now manipulate the line as a curve. Notice the control points attached to the nodes on either side of the line (b).

(b)

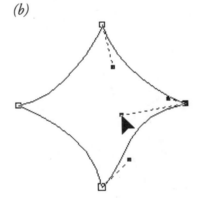

STRETCH

You can resize sections of a curved object using the *Stretch* option in the *Node Edit* roll-up.

(a)

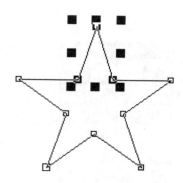

Figure 37. Select two or more nodes with the Shape Tool and click on the *Stretch* button. Eight selection handles appear around the selected nodes as though you had selected an object with the Pick Tool (a).

(If your *Node Edit* roll-up is not active, double-click on one of the selected nodes to open it.)

Use the mouse to resize the section that has the selected nodes in it (b).

The segments with the selected nodes resize accordingly (c).

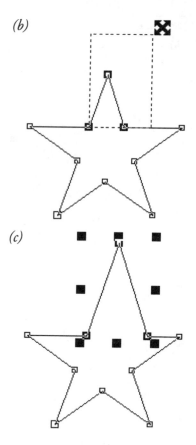

(b)

(c)

ROTATE

You can rotate and skew sections of a curved object using the *Rotate* option in the *Node Edit* roll-up.

Figure 38. Select two or more nodes with the Shape Tool and click on the *Rotate* option in the *Node Edit* roll-up. Rotate and skew handles appear around the selected nodes (a).

Use the mouse to rotate (b) or skew (c) the area containing the selected nodes.

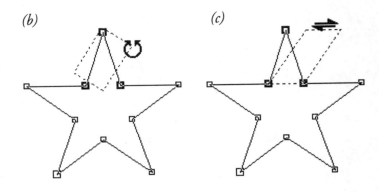

(a)

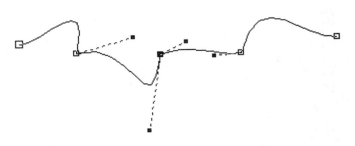

(b) *(c)*

CUSP

Figure 39. You can use the *Cusp* option in the *Node Edit* roll-up to change a selected node's attributes. This allows you to move the control points on either side of the node independently without affecting another part of the line. A cusp node lets you make a sharp change in direction in a line.

SMOOTH

Figure 40. The *Smooth* option converts a sharp point to a smooth point. Unlike the *Cusp* option, the control points of a *Smooth* node, when you move them, affect the lines on both sides of the node. This allows the control points to run along a straight line on either side of the node.

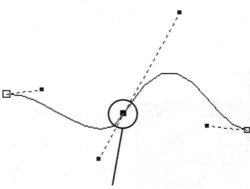

We applied the Smooth option to this middle node, causing the control points on either side of the node to run in a straight line. Moving one of the control points now affects the other control point.

SYMMET

Figure 41. The *Symmet* option is similar to the *Smooth* option, but the control points move the line in opposite directions of equal distance.

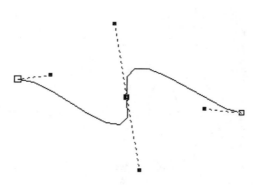

The control points of a node which you have given the *Symmet* option to (in this case the middle node), move in the opposite direction but at an equal distance. This option also moves the line on either side of the node the same way.

ALIGN

Figure 42. To use the *Align* option in the *Node Edit* roll-up, you must first have two nodes selected with the Shape Tool. Then double-click on one of the selected nodes, and click on the *Align* option.

In this example, we selected the top and bottom nodes on the left-hand side of the object. We then double-clicked on one of the nodes to open the *Node Edit* roll-up, and then on the *Align* option to activate the *Node Align* dialog box of Figure 43.

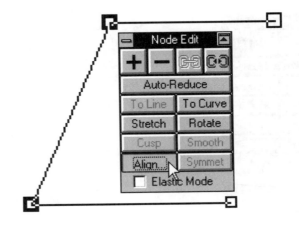

Figure 43. In the *Node Align* dialog box, you can align nodes horizontally, vertically, or by their control points. This is useful for technical drawings where you need a high degree of accuracy. For this example, we chose the *Align Vertical* option for the two selected nodes in Figure 42.

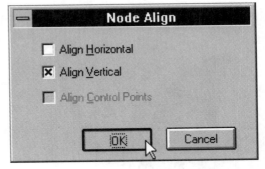

Figure 44. The above method has now vertically aligned the two nodes.

You can also use the *Align* option to line up the edges of objects. You can align objects from different paths if they are first combined through the **Arrange** menu.

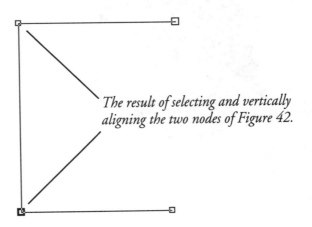

The result of selecting and vertically aligning the two nodes of Figure 42.

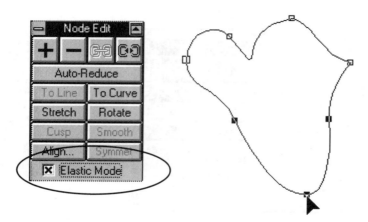

ELASTIC MODE

Figure 45. Choosing the *Elastic Mode* option when you have two or more nodes selected affects the way you can move the selected nodes. As you move any one of the selected nodes, the other selected nodes move in different amounts.

CROPPING BITMAPS

Figure 46. To crop a bitmap, select it with the Shape Tool; selection handles appear around its edge (a).

(a)

Hold the mouse down on any handle and drag it towards the center of the bitmap (b). You may reverse this procedure to reveal any part which you have covered.

In this example we are cropping the bitmap from the bottom middle handle.

(b)

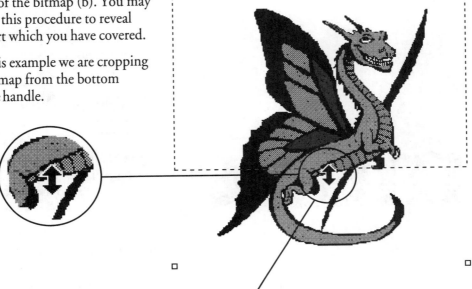

Drag a selection handle toward the center of the bitmap to crop it.

The result of cropping the bitmap from the bottom (c).

(c)

THE SHAPE TOOL AND TEXT

You can use the Shape Tool with text in various ways.

MOVING INDIVIDUAL LETTERS

(a)

Figure 47. If you select text with the Shape Tool, each letter displays a node to the bottom left (a).

(b)

You can move each letter independently by selecting a node and dragging the letter with the mouse (b). You can move more than one letter at a time by first holding down the Shift key and selecting multiple nodes.

Alternatively, you can select multiple nodes using marquee selection.

Figure 48. You can move individual letters with both Artistic and Paragraph Text.

MODIFYING KERNING AND LEADING

Figure 49. To modify the kerning or inter-letter spacing of a text string, first position the Shape Tool over the right arrow marker (a).

(a)

move

Then, drag the marker to the right to increase the spacing, or to the left to decrease the spacing. We are dragging the marker to the right (b).

(b)

move

You increase the spacing between the letters when you drag to the right (c).

(c)

m o v e

If you hold down the Ctrl key as you drag the right arrow marker, you change the inter-word spacing instead of inter-letter spacing.

You can move the arrow marker at the left of the selected text block up or down (d). This modifies the leading (line spacing) of the text. This works only if there is more than one line of text.

(d)

move me

move me

Modifying kerning and leading works with both Artistic and Paragraph Text.

CHANGING SINGLE CHARACTER ATTRIBUTES

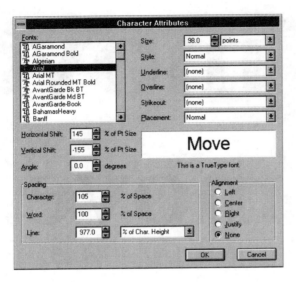

Figure 50. If you double-click on any node to the left of a letter with the Shape Tool, you activate the *Character Attributes* dialog box. Here you can change font, point size, position, and angle of any letter or letters. For more information, see **Chapter 10, The Text Menu.**

Figure 51. In this example, we changed the font, point size, and character angle of the letter "o."

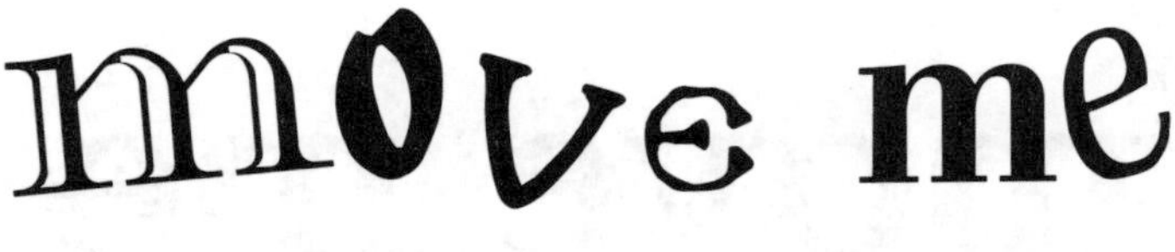

Figure 52. In this diagram, we have changed all of the characters in this text string.

Figure 53. Changing single character attributes also works with Paragraph Text.

Figure 54. You can also change the outline and fill of individual letters. By selecting a single letter with the Shape Tool, as previously described, you can then change the fill and outline of this letter without affecting the rest of the text.

For more information on outline and fill options, see **Chapter 3, Outline and Fill Tools.**

THE ZOOM TOOL

Figure 55. Use the Zoom Tool (🔍) to change the viewing size and position of the screen. Selecting the Zoom Tool activates the *Zoom Tool* fly-out.

The *Zoom Tool* fly-out contains six different options as shown here.

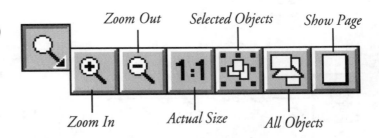

Figure 56. You use the *Zoom In* tool to view a section of your screen more closely. You select the area you want to zoom in on by dragging it with the *Zoom In* tool. You can also press the F2 key to activate the *Zoom In* tool.

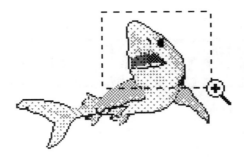

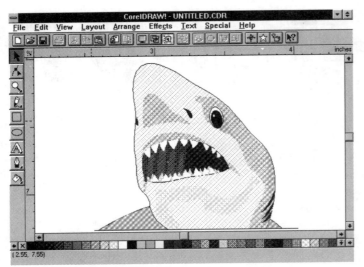

Figure 57. The section defined in Figure 56 now fills the entire working screen. You may use this tool as many times as you need to enlarge an area you wish to view more closely.

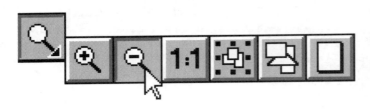

Figure 58. Selecting the *Zoom Out* option in the *Zoom Tool* fly-out takes the page view back to the size it was before you last magnified it. If there was no previous zoom in, it zooms out by a factor of two each time you select it. You can also activate the *Zoom Out* tool by pressing the F3 key.

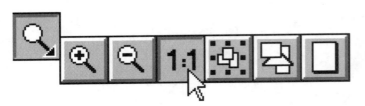

Figure 59. When you select the *Actual Size* option, the screen displays the drawing at the size it prints.

Figure 60. Selecting the *Selected Objects* option zooms in to the maximum size so that all of the currently selected objects fit in the screen.

Figure 61. Choosing the *All Objects* option displays all objects in the current file, even if they are outside the working page. You can also use the F4 key for this.

Figure 62. Selecting the *Show Page* option displays the whole working page, taking you back to the default view size. Alternatively, you can use Shift+F4.

THE PENCIL TOOL

Figure 63. The Pencil Tool (ℓ) is the drawing tool; you operate it in either *Freehand* or *Bezier* mode. By default, *Freehand* mode is active when you first select the Pencil Tool.

You can also use the F5 key to activate the Pencil Tool.

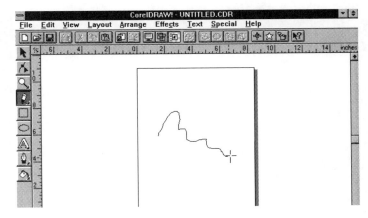

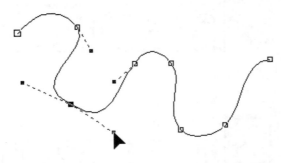

FREEHAND MODE

Figure 64. To draw curved lines in this mode, hold the mouse down and drag it on the page the same way you would with a pencil. When you release the mouse, the line displays a series of nodes; you can then manipulate these nodes with the Shape Tool.

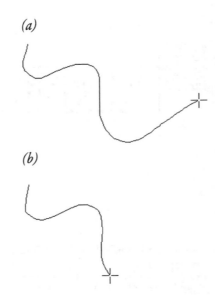

(a)

(b)

Figure 65. When you are drawing lines with the Pencil Tool in *Freehand* mode, you can erase what you have drawn before you release the mouse. If you are not happy with the curves you are drawing (a), hold down the Shift key and drag the mouse back over the line you have just drawn.

The line disappears as you drag the mouse back over it (b). Stop dragging the mouse when you have erased the part of the line you don't want.

STRAIGHT LINES

Figure 66. To draw a straight line in *Freehand* mode, click the mouse once on the page, move it to the end point of the line, and click the mouse once more to end the line.

You can continue drawing from this line by connecting a new line to it. To do this, click the mouse (with the Pencil Tool still active) directly over the last node of the line. CorelDRAW assumes you want to connect the lines and joins them up for you. The *AutoJoin* option in the *Curves* tab of the *Preferences* dialog box lets you adjust how close to the node you have to click for CorelDRAW to assume you want to connect new lines with existing lines.

Figure 67. To change the direction of straight lines, double-click the mouse at the point you want to change direction. This adds a node in the spot you double-clicked while still allowing you to continue drawing straight lines with the Pencil Tool.

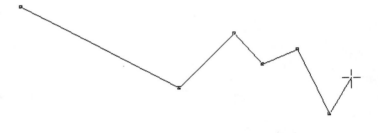

CLOSED OBJECTS

Figure 68. To create a closed object in *Freehand* mode, begin drawing as if you were creating a straight line and create your shape through the method shown in Figure 67. Create as many nodes as you need for the shape of the object.

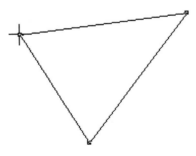

To close the object, click the mouse once on top of the starting point. If you didn't close the object, the right side of the status line reads *Open Path* when you select the object with the Pick Tool. If this is the case, you can join the start and end nodes using the *Join* command from the *Node Edit* roll-up.

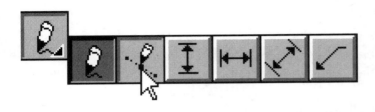

BEZIER MODE

Figure 69. To activate *Bezier* mode, hold the mouse down on the Pencil Tool in the Toolbox until the fly-out menu appears. Select the *Bezier* option as shown. This remains active until you change it back to *Freehand* mode. Drawing in *Bezier* mode gives the nodes slightly different qualities, making it easy to draw curves.

Note: You may find it easier to draw an object using straight lines, as previously described. You can add the curved sections later using the Shape Tool and the options in the Node Edit roll-up.

DRAWING CURVES

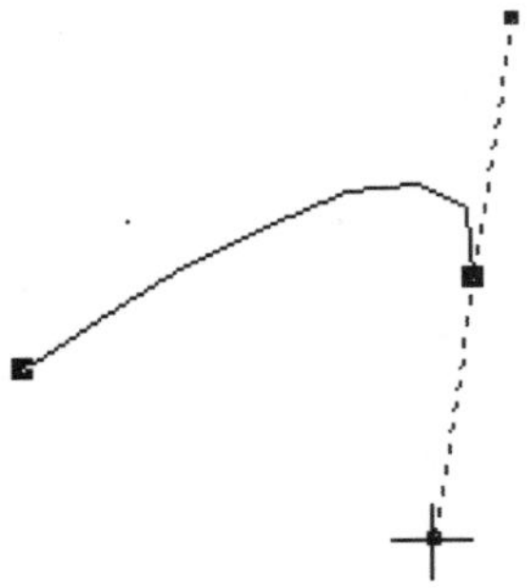

Figure 70. Click the mouse to begin your curve and then click and hold the mouse down on the first editing node for your curve. As you do so you can manipulate built-in control points in order to define the direction and angle of the curve (a).

Click once somewhere else to continue this curve. Repeat this to draw any shape you like (b).

To draw a straight line in *Bezier* mode, click the mouse button at the starting point, move the mouse cursor elsewhere on the page, and click the mouse button again.

(a)

(b)

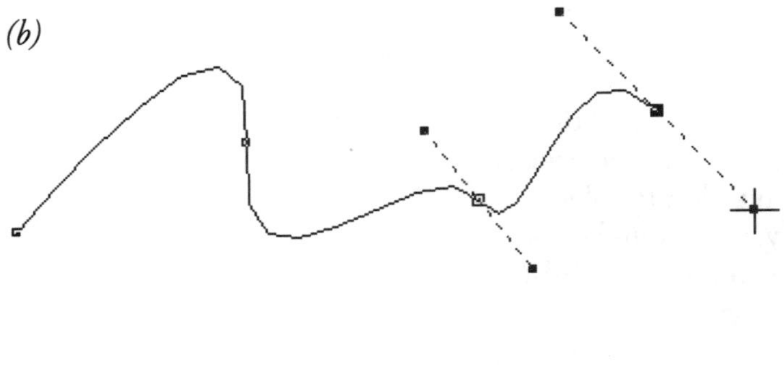

When drawing a closed object in *Bezier* mode, you click the mouse once only at each change of direction. To close an object, click on the beginning node, as in *Freehand* mode. To stop drawing an object that is not a closed object, click once again on the Pencil Tool in the Toolbox.

AUTOTRACE

With the Pencil Tool, you can trace TIF, PCX, GIF, and BMP images imported into CorelDRAW. Do not confuse this feature with CorelTRACE, which is a separate tracing utility that comes with CorelDRAW.

You can trace bitmaps in *editable preview* or *wireframe* view, with either *Freehand* or *Bezier* mode active.

Figure 71. In this figure, we are looking at a bitmap file in *wireframe* view. You may find it easier to trace the bitmap in this view, because if it has a black outline or fill (*editable preview*), it may be hard to see where you are tracing.

Figure 72. Select the bitmap with the Pick Tool, and then choose the Pencil Tool. Note the new shape of the mouse pointer (⊹). This indicates you can now use the Pencil Tool for tracing.

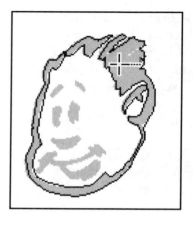

Figure 73. Click the mouse on the section of the graphic that you want to trace. After a few seconds, this procedure displays an outline around the selected area.

Repeat this process until you are satisfied with the results. Once you have finished, you can move or delete the underlying bitmap, and also edit and color the traced image like any other drawing in CorelDRAW.

DIMENSION LINES

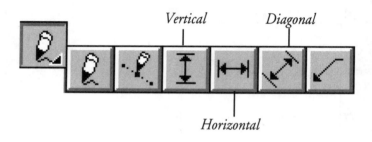

Vertical   *Diagonal*

Horizontal

Figure 74. The next three options on the *Pencil Tool* fly-out are for drawing dimension lines. You can use these tools to draw lines for technical drawings to measure and label vertical (⬍), horizontal (↔), and diagonal (⤢) distances.

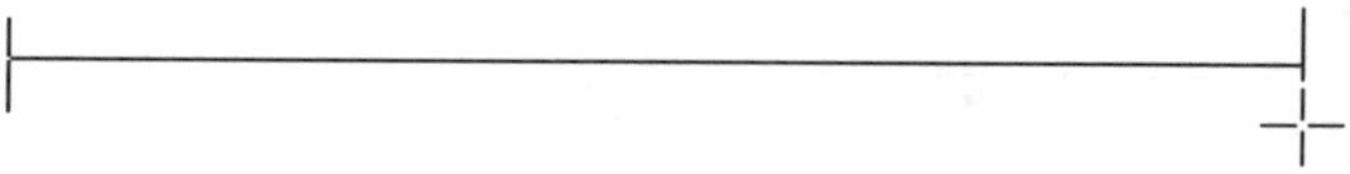

Figure 75. To draw a line with any of the dimensional line drawing tools, first select the tool from the *Pencil Tool* fly-out. Then, click the mouse where you want to start drawing the line and move the mouse either horizontally, vertically, or diagonally (depending on the tool you have selected).

A line extends from where you first clicked the mouse as you move it. In this example we used the *Horizontal* tool.

Figure 76. Click the mouse once again when the end of the dimension line is in the position that you want to end it. You can then drag the mouse to establish the extension line height.

The extension lines appear at opposing ends of the dimension line. Then, click the mouse once more to finish the line. The dimension text appears along the line where you clicked the mouse.

You can also select and edit this text independently of the dimension line through the commands in the **Text** menu. For more information on formatting this text, see **Chapter 11, The Special Menu**.

Figure 77. The *Callout* tool allows you to add callout labels to your illustrations.

Figure 78. To use this tool, click where you want your callout to point to, and then move the mouse to where you want the text label and click the mouse again (a).

Then slide the text box horizontally until it is in the position you want and click the mouse button again (b).

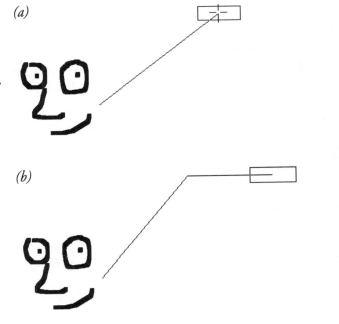

(a)

(b)

(c)

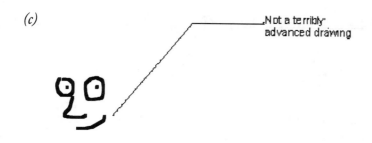

Once you have done this, CorelDRAW places the insertion point at this position. You can now enter the text for your callout label (c).

THE RECTANGLE TOOL

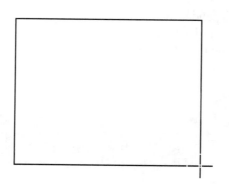

Figure 79. Use the Rectangle Tool (▣) to create rectangles and squares. To draw a rectangle with this tool, click and drag the mouse diagonally in any direction. Release the mouse button to stop drawing the rectangle.

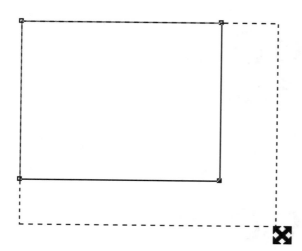

Figure 80. You can resize and move a rectangle with the Pick Tool. Note that the status line always reflects the width and height of a selected rectangle.

DRAWING SQUARES

To draw a perfect square with the Rectangle Tool, hold down the Ctrl key while drawing, and do not release it until you release the mouse button.

THE ELLIPSE TOOL

Figure 81. Use the Ellipse Tool (◉) to create circles and ellipses. To draw an ellipse, select the tool, then click and drag the mouse diagonally to complete the ellipse and release the mouse button.

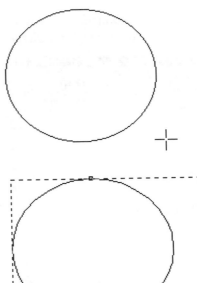

Figure 82. You can resize and move an ellipse with the Pick Tool. The status line reflects the width and height of a selected ellipse as you resize it.

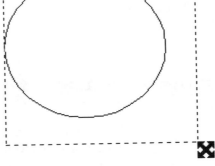

DRAWING CIRCLES

To draw a perfect circle with the Ellipse Tool, hold down the Ctrl key while drawing and do not release it until you release the mouse button.

THE TEXT TOOL

You use the Text Tool in CorelDRAW (𝔸) to add text to the page. You can then go on to edit, manipulate, and format this text using the Pick Tool, the Shape Tool, and the options in the **Text** menu (see **Chapter 10, The Text Menu**).

You can add text to the page in two different ways: Artistic Text and Paragraph Text. In this section we discuss the differences between Artistic Text and Paragraph Text and how you apply them to your documents.

ARTISTIC TEXT

We will look at Artistic Text first. You use Artistic Text when you want to create a special effect with your text.

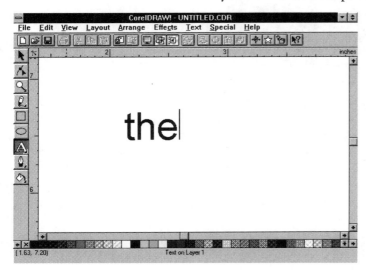

Figure 83. When you have selected the Text Tool, click anywhere on the page. The text entry cursor appears on the screen where you clicked with the mouse. You can now type and edit text directly on the screen.

You can also select any existing Artistic Text by positioning the mouse over the text with the Text Tool selected, until the cursor changes into an I-beam. You can then select and edit the text as you want.

When working with Artistic Text, you have a limit of 8000 characters in each text block, however, if you are going to use the Artistic Text for special effects like fitting text to a path, then you have a limit of around 250 characters per text block.

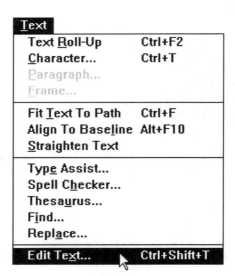

Figure 84. To edit the text attributes, position the insertion point in the text string you want to edit, or select the text string with the Pick Tool. Then select *Edit Text* from the **Text** menu to open the *Edit Text* dialog box.

Figure 85. You can now edit the text in the text entry window of the *Edit Text* dialog box. If you want to change the character attributes of your text, select the text you want to change and then select the *Character* button at the bottom of this dialog box. This opens the *Character Attributes* dialog box.

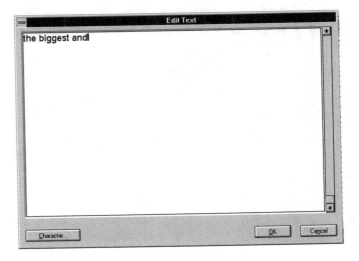

Figure 86. The *Character Attributes* dialog box offers a range of choices for changing the attributes of your text. You can select a new font, size, style, alignment, and spacing for your text from the various parts of the dialog box.

For more information on the options available in this dialog box, see **Chapter 10, The Text Menu.**

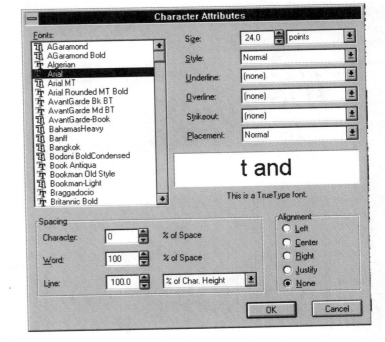

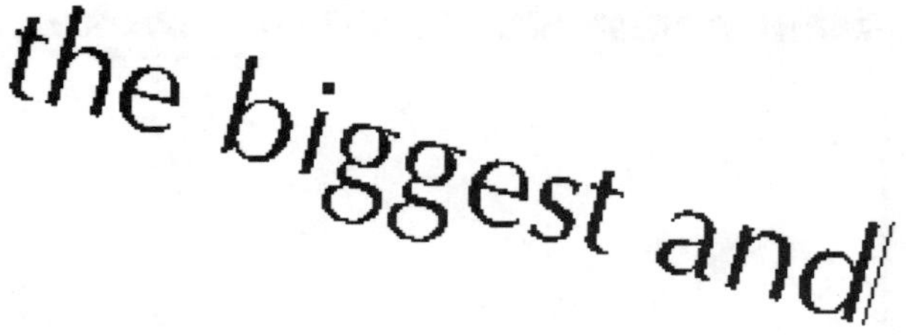

EDITING ARTISTIC TEXT

Figure 87. You can still directly edit Artistic Text that you have manipulated. Note the insertion point at the end of this rotated text block.

To put the insertion point back into a text block after working with another object, click anywhere on the text block with the Text Tool. You can also select the text with the Pick Tool, then choose the Text Tool from the Toolbox. This automatically inserts the text cursor at the end of the text block.

If you have applied an envelope, extrusion, or perspective to your Artistic Test, you can edit it through the *Edit Text* dialog box. When you click the Text Tool on text that you have applied any of these effects to, it automatically activates the *Edit Text* dialog box.

Figure 88. You can also highlight text with the Text Tool (in the same way you would in a word processing program). You do this by holding the mouse down (with the Text Tool selected) and dragging across the text. You can then directly edit the text.

Figure 89. You can (a) move, (b) rotate, (c) skew, and (d) resize Artistic Text with the Pick Tool in the same way as you manipulate other objects in CorelDRAW.

To change the shape of text with the Shape Tool, the same way you can for other curved objects, you must convert the text to curves. For more information see **Convert To Curves** in **Chapter 8, The Arrange Menu.**

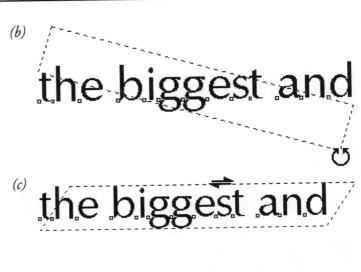

(b)

(c)

(d)

PARAGRAPH TEXT

Use Paragraph Text to add lengthy blocks of text to a CorelDRAW file. Paragraph Text has an advantage over Artistic Text, in that you have more formatting options available.

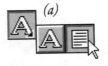

Figure 90. To place Paragraph Text on the page, hold down the mouse on the Text Tool in the Toolbox and select the *Paragraph Text* tool (a).

Once you have selected the *Paragraph Text* tool, you can click the tool on the page to add a paragraph text frame (b).

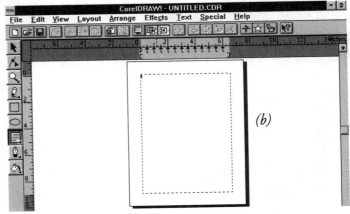

(a)

(b)

Figure 91. Another way of creating a Paragraph Text frame is to drag the mouse to outline the text frame, releasing the button to create the text frame in the outlined box.

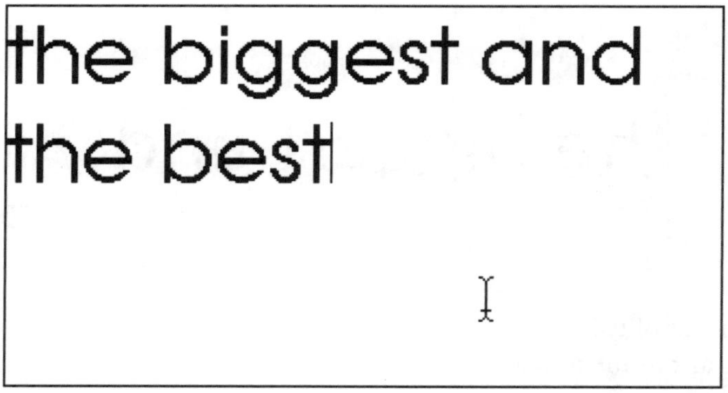

the biggest and
the best

Figure 92. Both the Paragraph Text frames created in the previous two figures are the same except for the size. You can now type the text directly into the Paragraph Text frame, no matter how you created it.

You can edit the text directly on the screen, as with Artistic Text, or through the *Edit Text* dialog box. To activate the *Edit Text* dialog box, make sure the insertion point is still in the text, or that you have selected it with the Pick Tool. Then, choose *Edit Text* from the **Text** menu.

Edit Text
the biggest and the best
Character...
Paragraph...
OK
Cancel

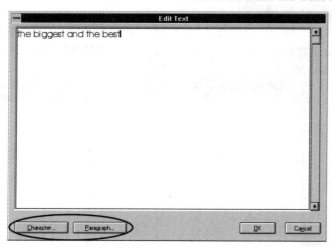

Figure 93. The *Edit Text* dialog box for Paragraph Text works the same way as for Artistic Text, but in addition to the *Character* button that allows you to change the character attributes of your text (as in Figure 86) you also have a *Paragraph* button. This button allows you to alter the paragraph attributes of your text through the *Paragraph* dialog box. For more information on the *Paragraph* dialog box, see **Chapter 10, The Text Menu.**

EDITING PARAGRAPH TEXT

Figure 94. To edit Paragraph Text on screen, insert the text cursor back into the text block and edit it directly (a).

You can also drag across Paragraph Text with the Text Tool to highlight it before you start editing (b).

(a)

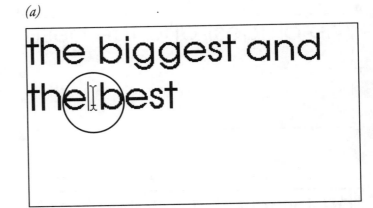

(b)

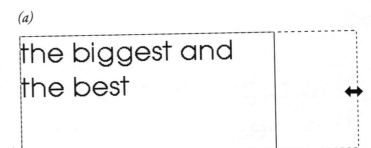

Figure 95. Unlike Artistic Text, you cannot directly resize Paragraph Text, but only the Paragraph Text frame (a).

Resizing the Paragraph Text frame with the Pick Tool resizes the text frame only, and can change the layout of the text (b). You resize the text through the *Character* button in the *Edit Text* dialog box (Figure 93), or through the *Character* command in the **Text** menu.

(a)

(b)

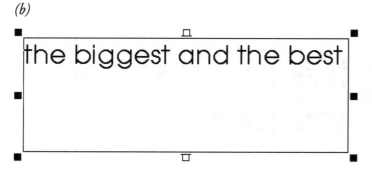

Note that the text size itself has not changed, only the frame size has altered, changing the layout of the text.

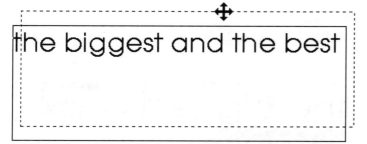

Figure 96. You can move a Paragraph Text frame with the Pick Tool by holding the mouse button down when the cursor is on the border of the frame, or on the actual text, and dragging it to a new position.

If you press the right mouse button or the + key on the numeric keypad on your keyboard while you are moving Paragraph Text, the original text block remains behind and you make a copy of it.

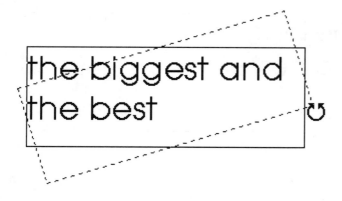

Figure 97. You can also rotate Paragraph Text in the same way you rotate all other objects in CorelDRAW. You can still edit rotated Paragraph Text on screen.

Figure 98. You can also skew Paragraph Text. However, when you skew Paragraph Text, the actual text frame skews but the text itself does not. The text simply reformats to adjust to the new shape of the text frame.

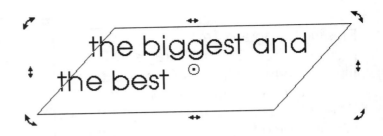

FLOWING PARAGRAPH TEXT

Figure 99. You can flow Paragraph Text into separate text frames. These text frames can be on the same page or on different pages. This lets you resize frames without losing text, because if you shrink a text frame, the text then flows into the next connected frame.

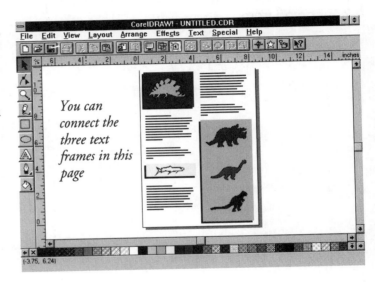

Figure 100. When you select a Paragraph Text frame that has not flowed into another frame, you will see a hollow box at the top (□) and bottom (▢) of the text frame.

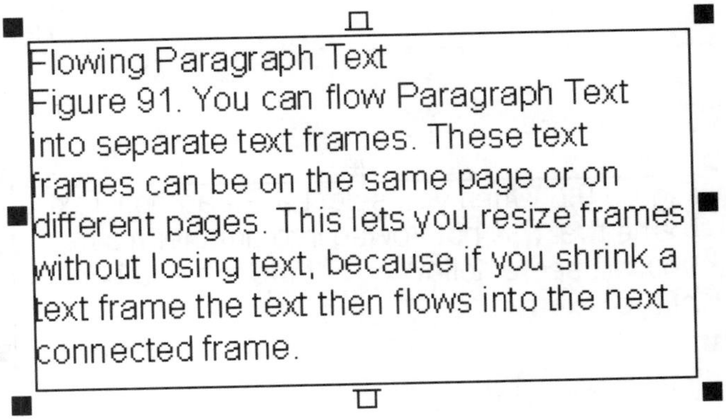

Flowing Paragraph Text
Figure 91. You can flow Paragraph Text into separate text frames. These text frames can be on the same page or on different pages. This lets you resize frames without losing text, because if you shrink a text frame the text then flows into the next connected frame.

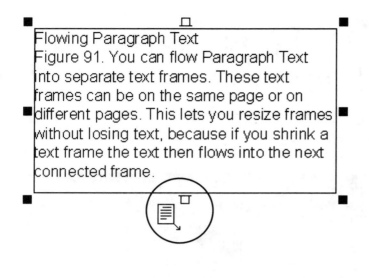

Flowing Paragraph Text
Figure 91. You can flow Paragraph Text into separate text frames. These text frames can be on the same page or on different pages. This lets you resize frames without losing text, because if you shrink a text frame the text then flows into the next connected frame.

Figure 101. If you want to flow the text from the bottom of a frame, click on the bottom box (□). This changes the cursor to the icon indicated in this figure.

You would use this option, for example, if there wasn't enough room in the column or page to fit the whole text frame. You could reflow the remaining text in a frame in the next column or the next page.

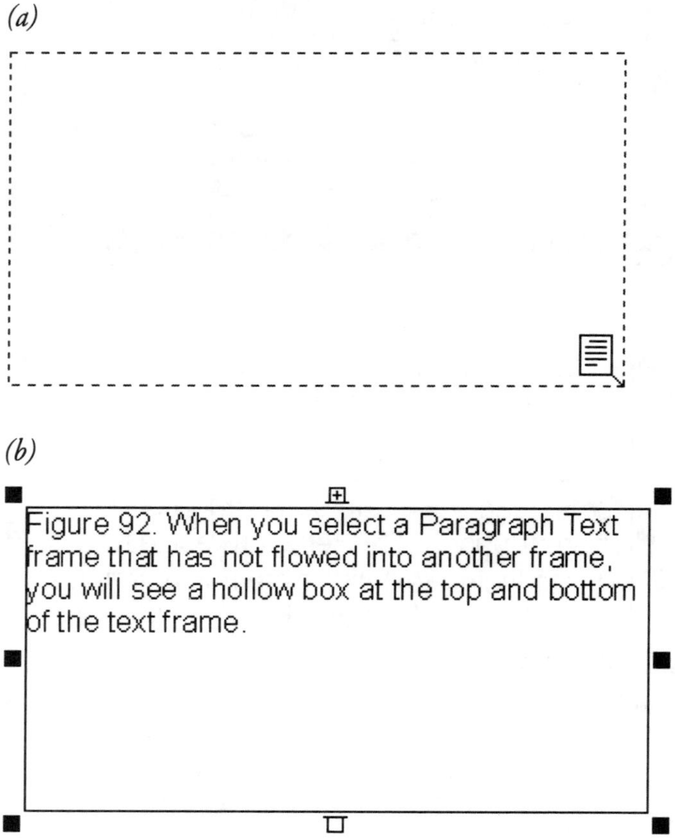

(a)

Figure 102. Immediately after clicking on the hollow box, draw a frame with the mouse the size you want the new text frame (a).

When you release the mouse, the text flows into this frame (b). When you select the frame with the Pick Tool, the hollow box at the top of the frame has a plus symbol in it (田). This shows that the text block is connected to the bottom of another text frame.

(b)

Figure 92. When you select a Paragraph Text frame that has not flowed into another frame, you will see a hollow box at the top and bottom of the text frame.

If you want to flow the text from the top of the frame, follow the steps just described, but click on the hollow box (□) at the top of the text frame.

PASTING TEXT

You can paste text directly onto the page from the Windows Clipboard; this text may have come from another Windows application. You can place this as either Artistic Text or Paragraph Text.

Before pasting text, make sure you have copied some text from a Windows application other than CorelDRAW. If you plan to place the text as Artistic Text, do not copy more than 250 characters. If you want to paste a large amount of text into CorelDRAW, you should place it as Paragraph Text, because Artistic Text is not as manageable.

Figure 103. To paste the text as Artistic Text, select the A Text Tool and click on the page where you want the text to appear (a).

(a)

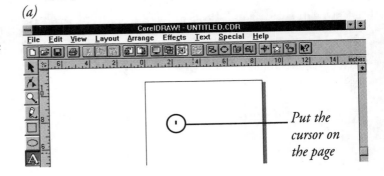

Put the cursor on the page

Now, choose *Paste* from the **Edit** menu (b).

(b)

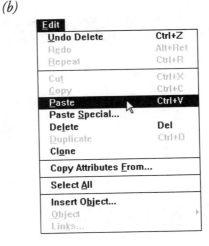

(c)

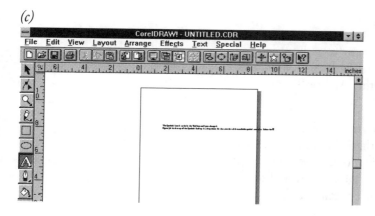

The text you copied now appears on the page as Artistic Text (c).

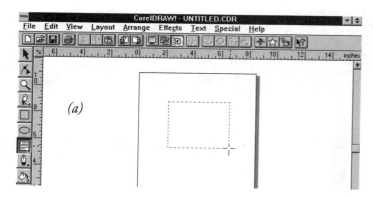

Figure 104. To paste the text as Paragraph Text, select the 🔲 Text Tool and draw a frame on the page where you want the text (a).

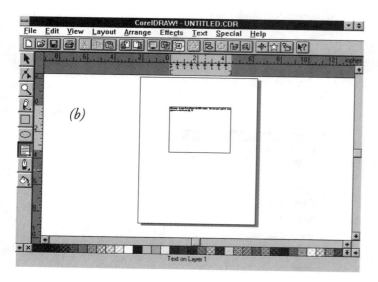

When you choose *Paste* from the **Edit** menu, the text you copied appears in the frame (b).

SYMBOLS

CorelDRAW comes with over 5,000 thematic symbols, covering a wide range of subjects. If you have installed the symbols, you can access them very easily, and at any stage.

Figure 105. You access symbols through the *Symbols* roll-up, which you can open through the **Special** menu or by clicking on the symbols ☆ icon on the ribbon bar.

Figure 106. At the top of the *Symbols* roll-up is a drop-down list that contains all the available symbol categories. Select the category you want to view.

Use the scroll bar and arrows to see all available categories.

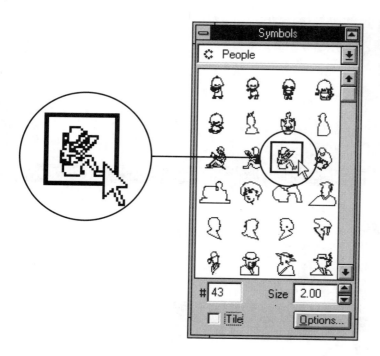

Figure 107. To place a symbol on the page, first hold the mouse down on the symbol to display a box around it.

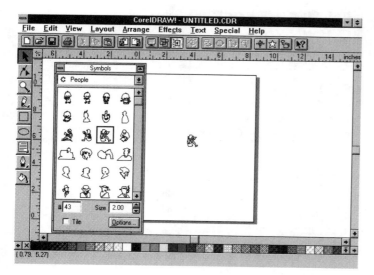

Figure 108. Then, drag the mouse out onto the page. A copy of the symbol moves with the mouse.

Figure 109. Release the mouse where you want the symbol to appear.

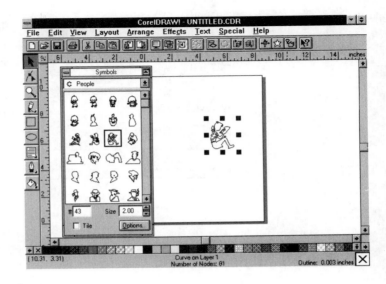

Figure 110. Click the arrows on the scroll bars to access all symbols available in each category.

If you know the number of the symbol, you can type the number into the # text box, and a box automatically appears around the corresponding symbol. You can then drag this symbol onto the page.

The *Size* option lets you set the size of the symbol on the page. The default size for a symbol is 2 inches.

Check the *Tile* option in the *Symbols* roll-up if you want to create a continuous tile pattern from a single symbol.

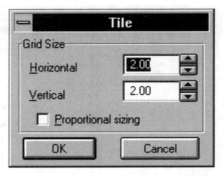

Figure 111. Click on the *Options* button at the bottom of the *Symbols* roll-up to open the *Tile* dialog box. The *Horizontal* and *Vertical* options let you set the size of the tiles.

If you check the *Proportional sizing* option, you need change only one value and CorelDRAW changes the other value to match.

To ensure that the symbol tiles do not overlap, make sure the *Horizontal* and *Vertical* values in the *Tile* dialog box are the same as or smaller than the actual tile size.

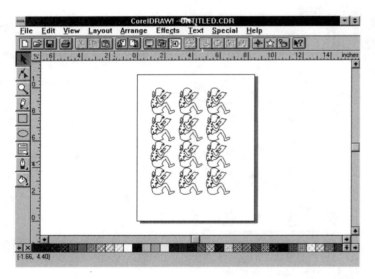

Figure 112. When you drag a symbol onto the page with the *Tile* option checked, a continuous tile pattern of the symbol appears.

OUTLINE AND FILL TOOLS 3

THE OUTLINE AND FILL TOOLS

When you have drawn an object or placed some text on the page, and want to color it, you use the Outline and Fill Tools. You also use the Outline Tool to change the thickness of an object's outline.

THE OUTLINE TOOL

Figure 1. Clicking on the Outline Tool (✒) in the Toolbox opens the *Outline Tool* fly-out. The options in this fly-out determine the outline color and thickness of an object that you have selected. You can also use these options to set the default for future objects or text.

THE OUTLINE PEN DIALOG BOX

Figure 2. To open the *Outline Pen* dialog box, select the first option in the top row of the *Outline Tool* fly-out (✒). After you have made any changes in this dialog box, click on the *OK* button to apply these changes to the selected line or object.

Before opening this dialog box, make sure you have the required object selected with the Pick Tool.

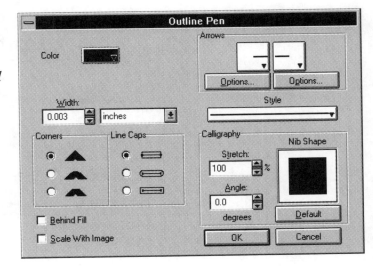

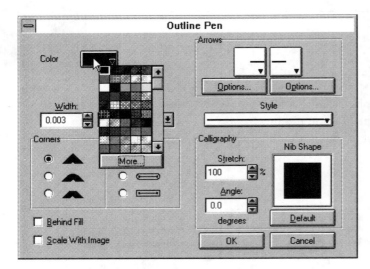

COLOR

Figure 3. The first option in the *Outline Pen* dialog box is the *Color* option. Clicking the mouse on the color swatch shows a Color palette where you can select a different color. This swatch displays the current outline color for the selected object.

Selecting the *More* button at the bottom of the Color palette activates the *Outline Color* dialog box. For more information on this dialog box, see **Outline Color** later in this chapter.

WIDTH

The *Width* option in the *Outline Pen* dialog box tells you the outline thickness for the currently selected object. Change this figure to alter the outline width.

CORNERS

Figure 4. You use the *Corners* options to modify the corners of an object. You can also use them at the intersection of two lines.

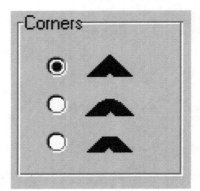

LINE CAPS

The three *Line Caps* options affect the end of a line. When you select the top option, the outline, no matter how thick, will not extend past the end of the line. Selecting the second option rounds off the end of a line; the third option extends the end of a line for a distance equal to half the line thickness.

BEHIND FILL

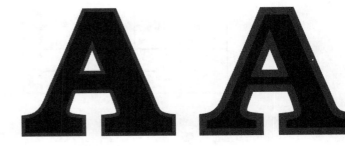

Figure 5. The *Behind Fill* check box lets you send the outline of a selected object behind the fill of the object. You will find this option useful when working with very thick outlines.

   In this example, the two text characters have the same outline, yet the outline of the text character on the left is behind the fill.

SCALE WITH IMAGE

The *Scale With Image* option scales the thickness of the outline when you resize an object. In other words, the outline thickens when you enlarge the object, and thins when you reduce the object.

ARROWS

Figure 6. The *Arrows* section of the *Outline Pen* dialog box lets you apply an arrowhead to either or both ends of a line. The left-hand arrow icon represents the start of a line, and the right-hand arrow icon represents the end of a line.

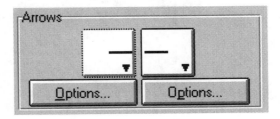

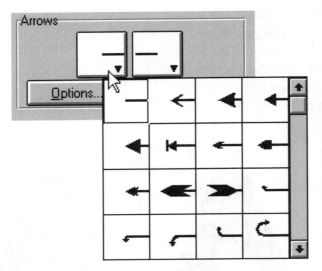

Figure 7. When you click the mouse on either arrow icon, you activate a pop-up palette containing different arrowheads.

You can use the scroll bar to the right of this pop-up palette to choose the arrowheads you can't see. Click on the arrowhead you want to select.

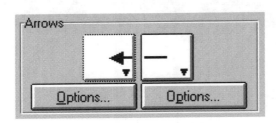

Figure 8. The arrowhead you select from the pop-up palette appears on the corresponding arrowhead button.

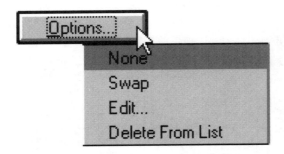

Figure 9. Selecting the *Options* button underneath each arrowhead button displays a pop-up list. The *None* command lets you remove the arrowhead from the corresponding button. Use the *Swap* command to swap the current left and right arrowheads.

Figure 10. Selecting the *Edit* option from the *Options* pop-up list (Figure 9) activates this *Arrowhead Editor* dialog box. Here you can resize, move, and change the direction of an arrowhead.

The *Delete From List* command in the *Options* pop-up list removes the currently selected arrowhead. You use this command to delete an arrowhead you have created.

For more information on creating arrowheads, see **Chapter 11, The Special Menu.**

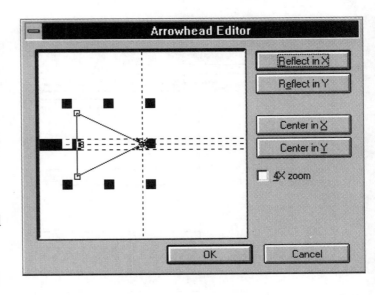

Figure 11. The thickness of a line determines the size of an arrowhead. You can view arrowheads in *editable preview* only, not in *wireframe* view.

You cannot copy or cut arrowheads to the Windows Clipboard.

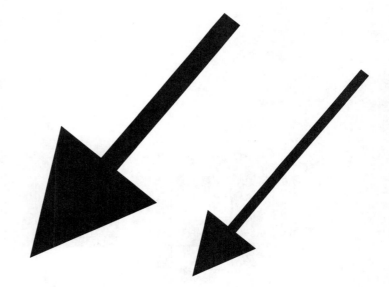

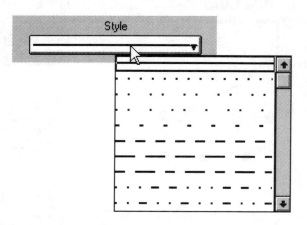

STYLE

Figure 12. The *Style* option in the *Outline Pen* dialog box lets you apply different dashed and dotted lines to a selected outline. Click on the *Style* button to open the associated pop-up menu.

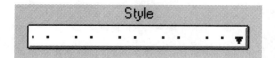

Figure 13. Select the dashed or dotted pattern you want. Clicking on *OK* in the *Outline Pen* dialog box applies the current style to the outline of the selected object.

CALLIGRAPHY

The options in this section of the *Outline Pen* dialog box let you apply a calligraphic outline to an object.

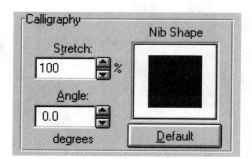

Figure 14. You can adjust the *Stretch* and *Angle* settings to create the calligraphic outline. The *Nib Shape* square changes to reflect the altered settings.

Figure 15. You can also hold the mouse button down with the cursor on the *Nib Shape* square and move it around until you get the right angle and stretch. The *Stretch* and *Angle* settings change accordingly when you alter the *Nib Shape* square.

Clicking on the *Default* button returns the *Nib Shape* square back to the normal settings of 100% *Stretch* and 0.0 *Angle*.

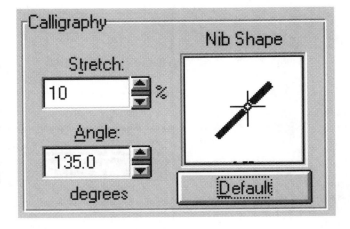

Figure 16. You can vary the *Width*, *Angle*, and *Stretch* options in the *Outline Pen* dialog box to create examples similar to this.

PEN ROLL-UP

Figure 17. To display the *Pen* roll-up, select the second option in the top row of the *Outline Tool* fly-out of Figure 1.

This window gives you a chance to change some of the pen options without having to open the *Outline Pen* dialog box discussed earlier.

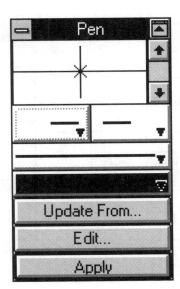

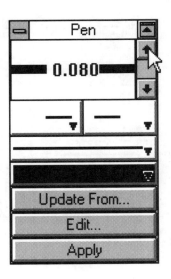

Figure 18. The first option in the *Pen* roll-up is a means of adjusting the thickness of a line or an object outline.

As you click on the up or down scroll arrow to alter the thickness, the new thickness of the line appears. Each click on the arrow changes the amount by 0.01 of an inch.

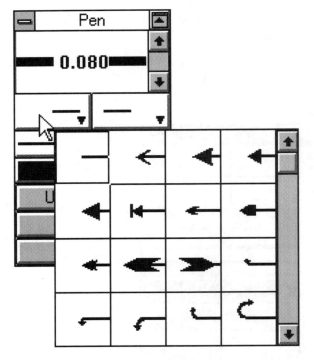

Figure 19. Below the thickness field is the arrowhead option. As with the arrowhead options in the *Outline Pen* dialog box, the left arrowhead button represents the left end of a line and the right is the right end.

Clicking on either icon displays the Arrowhead pop-up as shown. Choose the arrowhead you want from this list box.

Figure 20. The next option is the *Style* list. Click on the display field to view the options available for dashed or dotted lines.

This option is the same one discussed in Figures 12 and 13.

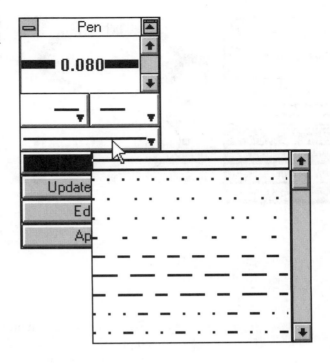

Figure 21. The next option is for outline color. Click on the *Color* button to get a Color palette, where you can choose a different outline color.

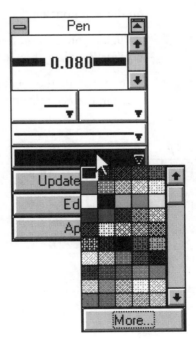

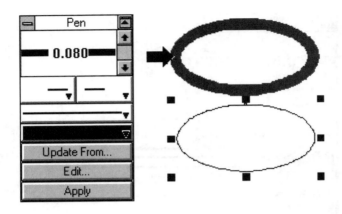

Figure 22. Clicking on the *Update From* button lets you copy an outline from one object to another.

First, select the object you want to copy the outline to (the bottom ellipse). Click on the *Update From* button and, using the arrow that appears, click on the object you want to copy the outline from (the top ellipse). You then must click on the *Apply* button to complete the process.

In this example, you are copying the thick outline of the top ellipse to the one below it.

When you update an outline from an object, the outline is temporarily stored in the *Pen* roll-up. You can reapply this outline to other objects by selecting them first and clicking on the *Apply* button.

Clicking on the *Edit* button in the *Pen* roll-up opens the *Outline Pen* dialog box for more editing.

You must use the *Apply* button to apply any changes you make in the *Pen* roll-up to the selected object.

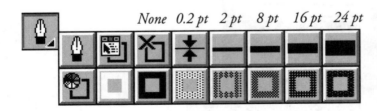

Figure 23. The remaining options in the top row of the *Outline Tool* fly-out determine the thickness of an outline. This figure shows the different preset thicknesses available.

OUTLINE COLOR

Figure 24. Choosing the first option in the bottom row of the *Outline Tool* fly-out opens the *Outline Color* dialog box. Pressing Shift+F12 also opens this dialog box.

Make sure you have selected the object you want to change before choosing this option.

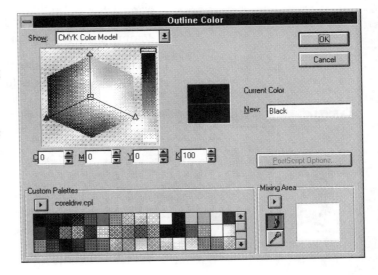

SHOW

Figure 25. Your first choice in the *Outline Color* dialog box is the method of coloring. Click on the *Show* drop-down list to view the color methods available.

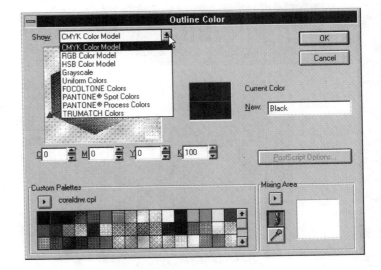

CMYK COLOR MODEL

The *CMYK Color Model* option (seen in the previous two figures) lets you create a color using a mixture of cyan, magenta, yellow, and black—which are known as "process colors."

Process colors use percentages of cyan, magenta, yellow, and black to make up a single color. If you are adding many colors to your drawing and are planning on printing it commercially, it is best to use process colors.

To create a color using the *CMYK Color Model*, change the values in the edit frames for each of the four colors available.

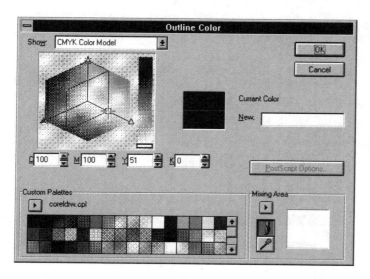

Figure 26. Alternatively, click and drag the boxes along the color axis in the visual selector window. Dragging along the axis changes the cyan, magenta, and yellow settings, while the bar to the right of the visual selector changes the black setting.

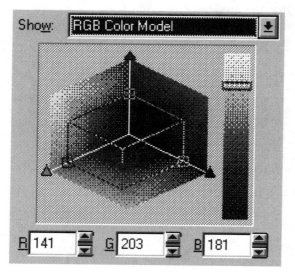

RGB COLOR MODEL

Figure 27. The *RGB Color Model* option uses percentages of red, green, and blue to create the color you want. Again you can use the visual selector box to create your color by dragging the markers along each color's axis. The vertical bar in this case increases or decreases the color's brightness.

HSB COLOR MODEL

Figure 28. You create colors in the *HSB Color Model* by varying hue, saturation, and brightness.

You can use the percentage boxes to create a color, or the color wheel to determine the hue and saturation. The long thin bar on the right determines the brightness.

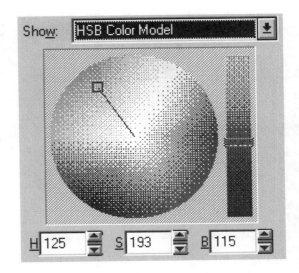

PANTONE SPOT COLORS

Figure 29. The *PANTONE Spot Colors* option lets you select a Pantone color. The Pantone library of colors is recognized by printers world wide.

You can use Pantone colors if you are using no more than four colors in your drawing. Click on the color you want from the palette. Use the scroll bar to see palette colors not showing.

You can click on the *Show Color Names* option if you want to see the *PANTONE Spot Colors* listed by name. The *Search for* text box lets you type in the number of the color (if you know it) to select it automatically.

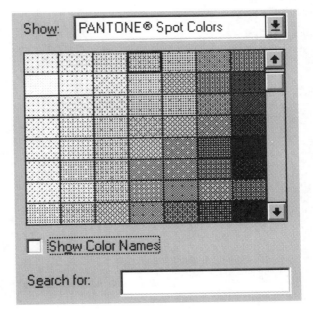

PANTONE PROCESS COLORS

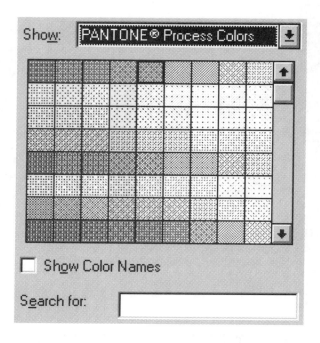

Figure 30. The *PANTONE Process Colors* option provides a library of Pantone colors that are made up of four colors: cyan, magenta, yellow, and black. Click on the color you want from the palette. Use the scroll bar to see colors that aren't showing.

Again you can click on the *Show Color Names* option to view the *PANTONE Process Colors* by name. Type the number of the color (if you know it) into the *Search for* text box to select it automatically.

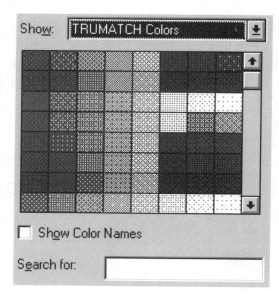

Figure 31. The *TRUMATCH Colors* option provides another library of process colors that are made up of four colors: cyan, magenta, yellow, and black. Click on the color you want from the palette. Use the scroll bar to see colors not currently displayed.

If you click on the *Show Color Names* option you'll see the *TRUMATCH Colors* by name. The *Search for* text box lets you type in the number of the color (if you know it) to select it automatically.

CUSTOM PALETTE

Figure 32. The *Custom Palettes* section of the dialog box (a) lets you select colors from one of the custom palettes that come with CorelDRAW, or one you may have created and saved yourself.

To select a color from the palette, click on the required color. The name of the color appears in the *New* text box (b). Use the scroll bar to the right of the palette to choose colors that aren't visible.

The default palette in CorelDRAW is the *coreldrw.cpl* palette.

(a)

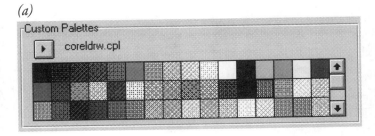

(b)

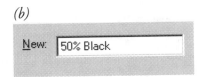

CUSTOM PALETTE MENU

Figure 33. Clicking on the *Custom Palettes* button brings up the **Custom Palette** pop-up menu.

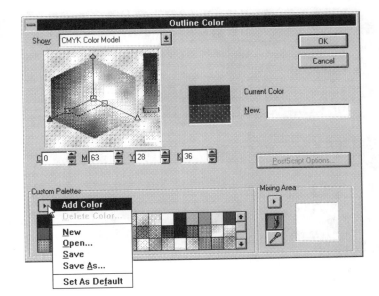

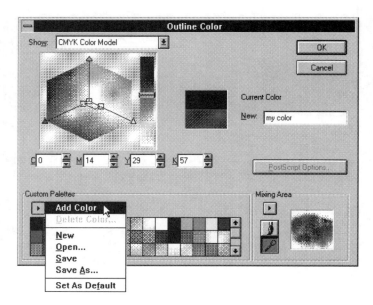

ADD COLOR

Figure 34. After creating a color from one of the three process color models (*CMYK, RGB,* or *HSB*), or by mixing a color in the *Mixing Area* (see later in this chapter for more information) type a name for the color in the *New* text box, and choose the *Add Color* command.

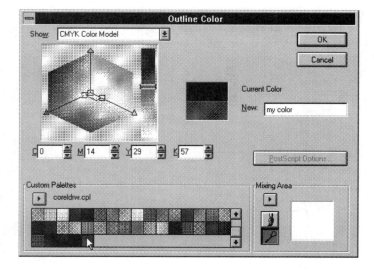

Figure 35. This command then adds the color to the end of the colors in the currently loaded custom palette.

DELETE COLOR

Figure 36. To remove a color from the currently loaded palette, select the color by clicking on it in the Custom palette and then choose *Delete Color* from the **Custom Palette** pop-up menu (a).

(a)

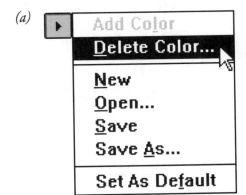

You are then asked to confirm your decision to delete the selected color (b). Click on *Yes* to delete the color, or *No* to cancel the procedure.

(b)

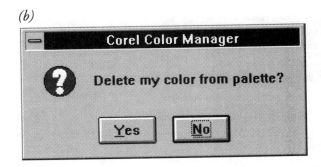

NEW

Figure 37. Selecting *New* from the **Custom Palette** pop-up menu opens an empty palette. The palette is automatically called *untitled.cpl*.

You can then add colors that you create and name from the three process color model options (*CMYK, RGB, HSB*) or through the *Mixing Area*.

OPEN

Figure 38. The *Open* command from the **Custom Palette** pop-up menu (a) lets you open a different Custom palette. This can be one of the palettes that comes with CorelDRAW or a palette you have created yourself.

(a)

(b)

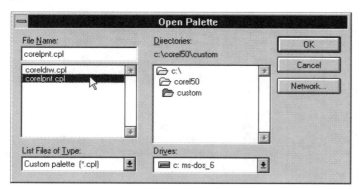

Double-click on the palette name from the list of files in the *Open Palette* dialog box (b).

(c)

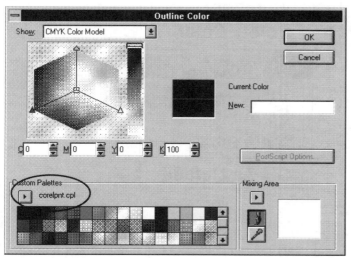

The palette you chose is now displayed in the *Outline Color* dialog box (c).

SAVE/SAVE AS

The *Save* command from the **Custom Palette** pop-up menu lets you save any changes you made to the currently loaded Custom palette; e.g. adding or deleting colors. As well as naming and saving a new palette, you can use the *Save As* command to save a palette under a different name, allowing you to make changes to this palette without affecting the original.

Figure 39. The *Save As* command from the **Custom Palette** pop-up menu opens the *Save Palette As* dialog box, where you can name the new palette. You might like to save it in the same directory as the Custom palettes that come with CorelDRAW. CorelDRAW automatically places a *.cpl* extension on the name you type in the *File Name* text box.

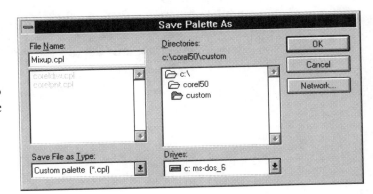

SET AS DEFAULT

Use the *Set As Default* command in the **Custom Palette** pop-up menu to save the current palette as the default palette. This palette will then display each time you open CorelDRAW.

CURRENT COLOR/NEW SWATCH

Figure 40. The outline color of your selected object displays in the *Current Color* swatch. When you select a new color from any of the methods in the *Outline Color* dialog box, this color appears in the *New* swatch. This lets you compare the current color with any new color you select, or name any new color you create.

MIXING AREA

The *Mixing Area* allows you to create the color you want by mixing colors as if with a paint brush. To do this you select the colors you want to mix and combine them in the paint area with the paint brush cursor.

Figure 41. To prepare a new mixing area, click on the *Mixing Area* button to activate the pop-up menu and choose *Clear*. This clears the area for a new mixing session.

Then, to mix your own color, select the eyedropper and choose a color from an available palette or the *Visual Selector* area. The eyedropper "picks-up" this color for your paintbrush (the color is displayed in the *New* area).

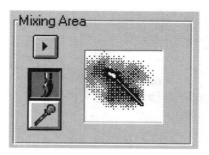

Figure 42. Now select the *Paintbrush* icon and paint in the *Mixing Area*.

Figure 43. You can repeat this process as many times as you want, picking up colors with the eyedropper and mixing them in the *Mixing Area*.

Figure 44. Once you have finished mixing your colors, you can choose the color you want from the mixing area with the eyedropper to display that color in the *New* area. You can then name and add it to a custom palette.

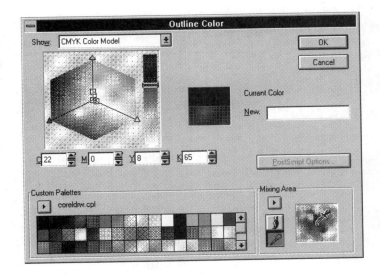

Figure 45. You can also extract a color from an image that you have saved by selecting the *Load* command (a) to load the image into the mixing area. Conversely, you can save your mixing area to use at a later date through the *Save* command (b).

(a)

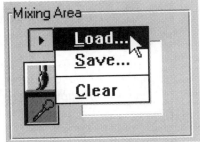

(b)

Click the PostScript Options button to open this dialog box.

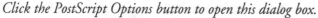

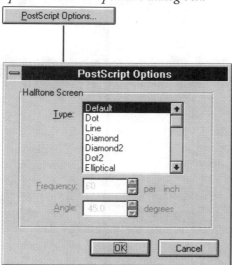

POSTSCRIPT OPTIONS DIALOG BOX

Figure 46. Click on the *PostScript Options* button in the *Outline Color* dialog box to activate the *PostScript Options* dialog box. You can access the *Halftone Screen* options in this dialog box only if you are using the *PANTONE Spot Colors* method.

The options available in the *Type* list provide you with a range of various shapes of halftone dots, lines, and ellipses. You cannot display them on screen; however they will appear when you print.

The *Frequency* option determines the number of times it displays the screen pattern per inch. The *Angle* option determines the angle at which it places the pattern. To access the *Frequency* and *Angle* options, you must select an option other than *Default* from the *Type* list.

Click on *OK* in the *PostScript Options* dialog box and the *Outline Color* dialog box to return to the drawing with the new color applied to the outline of the selected object(s).

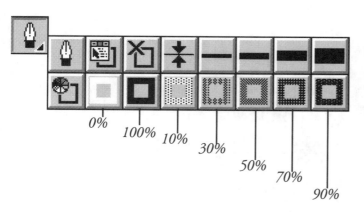

0% 100% 10% 30% 50% 70% 90%

Figure 47. The remaining options in the bottom row of the *Outline Tool* fly-out let you quickly apply a color to an outline, from white (no color) to full color (in percentages).

CONVERTING SPOT TO PROCESS

Figure 48. If you have a specific color you want to convert from *Spot* color to *Process*, follow these steps. First, select the Pantone spot color you want to change from the *PANTONE Spot Colors* palette.

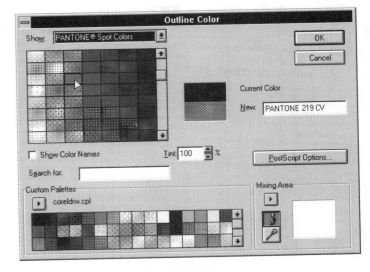

Figure 49. Next, choose the *CMYK Color Model* from the *Show* drop-down list (a), and you will see that CorelDRAW has converted the Pantone color to the closest possible mix of process colors (b).

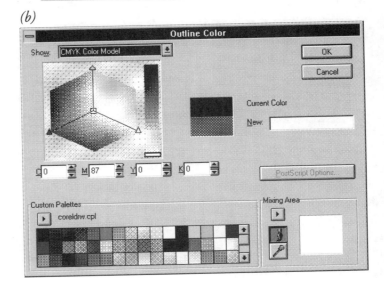

THE FILL TOOL

Figure 50. You use the Fill Tool to determine the fill of an object. Click on the Fill Tool (⚐) in the Toolbox to open the *Fill Tool* fly-out. You can apply a fill to any closed object.

Make sure you have selected the object you want changed before selecting options in the *Fill Tool* fly-out.

UNIFORM FILL

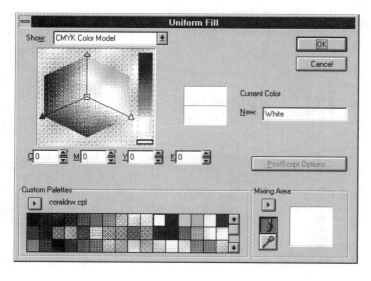

Figure 51. Selecting the first option from the top row of the *Fill Tool* fly-out (●) activates the *Uniform Fill* dialog box. You can also press Shift+F11 to activate this dialog box. The options in this dialog box function the same way as the *Outline Color* dialog box options, described previously.

The second option in the *Fill Tool* fly-out (▦) gives you the *Fill* roll-up. For more information on the options in this roll-up, see the **Fill roll-up** section later in this chapter.

FOUNTAIN FILLS

Figure 52. Clicking on the *Fountain Fill* icon (▦) in the *Fill Tool* fly-out opens the *Fountain Fill* dialog box. Fountain fills are made up of two colors which merge into one another.

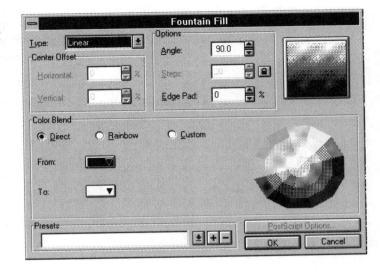

Figure 53. You select the two colors you are going to use in the fountain fill in the *Color Blend* section of the dialog box. When you click on the *From* color swatch, a Color palette appears.

The colors that appear in this palette are the colors that are in the currently loaded Custom palette. Click on the color you want as the *From* color in the fill. If you want to select a different color, or create your own, click on the *More* button at the bottom of the palette.

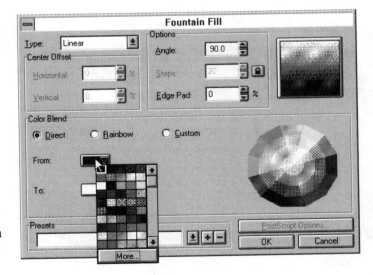

This opens another dialog box that is identical to the *Uniform Fill* dialog box and the *Outline Color* dialog box (explained earlier in this chapter).

Click on the *To* color swatch to select the color you want to blend to in the fountain fill. The *To* Color palette works the same way as the *From* palette.

If you plan to color-separate a CorelDRAW file, you can only use spot (Pantone) colors in fountain fills when the two colors in the one fill are a tint of the same color. If they aren't tints of one color, they are converted to the closest equivalent process colors when separated.

COLOR BLEND CONTROLS

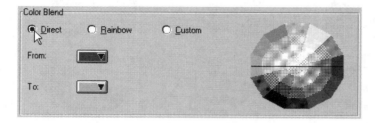

Figure 54. The options in the *Color Blend* section of the *Fountain Fill* dialog box give you access to blending options that determine how the two colors in the fountain fill blend together. The *Direct* option blends the two colors in the fountain fill in a straight line.

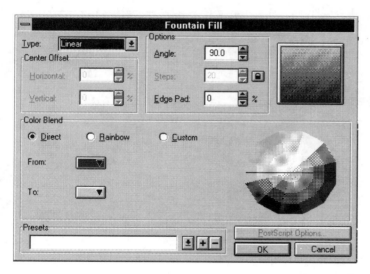

Figure 55. A line appears in the color wheel indicating the two colors you have selected in the fill.

In this example, the two colors in the fill are red and cyan, indicated by the line in the color wheel that stretches from red to cyan.

A sample color blend also appears in the sample square at the top of the dialog box.

Figure 56. The *Rainbow* option allows you to blend two colors through a spectrum of colors. You also have the choice with a rainbow fountain fill as to whether the color spectrum is clockwise (↻) or counterclockwise (↺). The line on the actual rainbow symbol changes to indicate the direction currently selected.

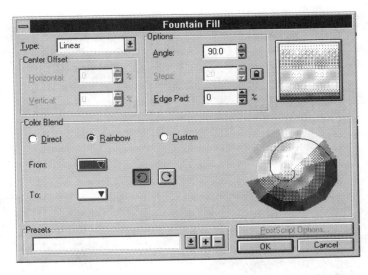

You can select the two colors for the Rainbow fill using the *From* and *To* palettes. In this example the colors are blending from red to white.

Figure 57. You can add colors to the fountain fill with the *Custom* option. You can add up to 99 colors to a fountain fill from the palette that appears when you select this radio button.

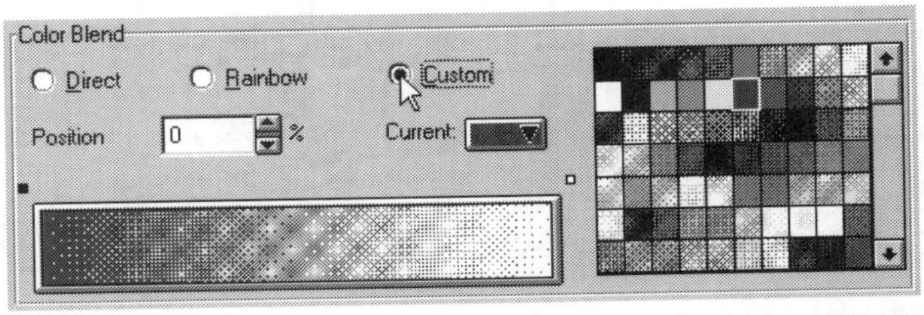

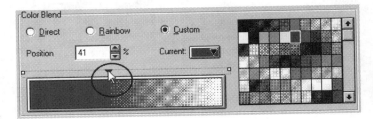

Figure 58. To add colors to the preview strip beside the palette, double-click between the small squares at either end of the preview strip. This adds a color location marker to the preview strip where you double-click. This color location marker remains selected until you add or select another one. A selected location marker is black, and an unselected one is white.

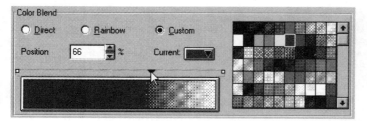

Figure 59. You can drag a color location marker along the preview strip. This changes the *Position* value and you will also notice a change in the preview strip.

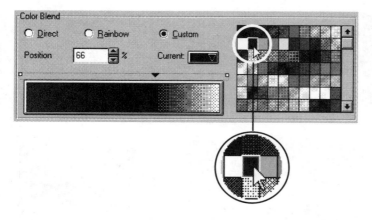

Figure 60. If you then click on a color from the Color palette, this adds the new color to the blend. This color will blend the two colors on either side of it—in this case the start and end colors.

Figure 61. You can keep adding more and more location markers and colors to the preview strip until you are happy with the fill.

Figure 62. You can quickly and easily delete a color location marker by double-clicking on it.

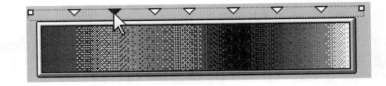

Figure 63. You have four choices in the *Type* section of the *Fountain Fill* dialog box.

The *Linear* option is the default setting for blending the two colors in the fountain fill in one direction (a).

The *Radial* option blends two colors along the radius of a circle (b), the *Conical* option blends the colors in a cone fashion (c), the *Square* option blends in squares (d).

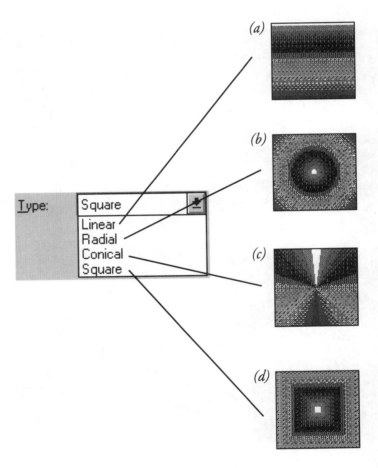

(a)

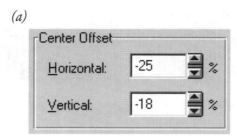

Figure 64. The *Center Offset* options within the *Fountain Fill* dialog box let you change the center of a fountain fill when you are using the *Radial, Conical,* or *Square Type* options.

(b)

You can alter the *Center Offset* values in the *Horizontal* and *Vertical* text boxes (a), or directly through the color display by holding down and dragging the mouse to reposition the center offset (b).

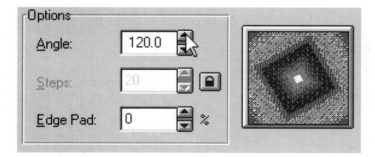

Figure 65. The *Options* features of the *Fountain Fill* dialog box do not work for all types of fountain fills.

Figure 66. The *Angle* option applies only to *Linear, Conical* and *Square* fountain fills. Here you can change the angle of the fountain fill.

When you change the *Angle* value, the preview square changes accordingly.

Figure 67. With *Linear* fills you can change the angle of the fill directly in the preview square with the mouse.

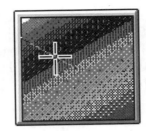

Figure 68. Click on the 🔒 icon to access the *Steps* option. Changing this value determines the amount of fountain fill steps that appear on screen and when you print the file.

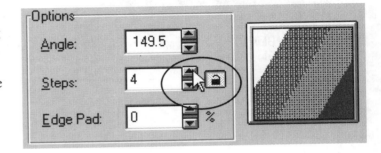

Figure 69. The *Edge Pad* option is available only for *Linear, Radial,* and *Square* fills. Choose this option to increase the amount of color at the start and end of the fill. A filled object acts as a window for the fountain fill, therefore the *Edge Pad* option is useful for asymmetrical options where part of the fill falls outside the object.

You cannot use a percentage higher than 45% in the *Edge Pad* option, and you can view your changes in the color display square. Compare the display square in this figure to the one above.

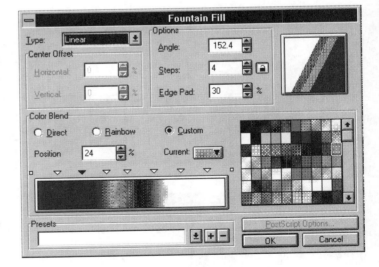

You can only access the *PostScript Options* button in the *Fountain Fill* dialog box if you are using Pantone spot colors. The options in this dialog box are discussed in the **Outline Color** section earlier in this chapter.

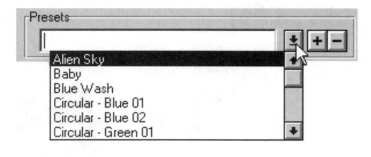

Figure 70. The *Presets* drop-down list contains some fountain fills that come with CorelDRAW. You can also save fountain fills that you have created yourself.

After creating the fill, type a name into the *Presets* text box and click on the plus (save) button. This then adds the fill to the *Presets* list. If there are any fills in the *Presets* list that you do not want, select them and click on the minus (delete) button.

Click on the *OK* button in the *Fountain Fill* dialog box to apply the fill to the selected object.

TWO-COLOR PATTERNS

Figure 71. You use the *Two-Color Pattern* icon (▓) in the *Fill Tool* fly-out (a) to activate the *Two-Color Pattern* dialog box (b).

(a)

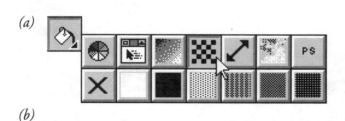

(b)

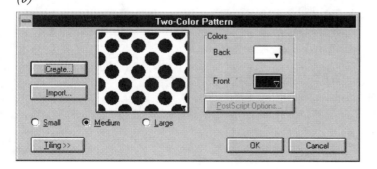

Figure 72. You can choose patterns directly by clicking on the large preview box, which opens a pop-up palette. Choose the pattern you want from the palette that appears, and click on *OK* in the menu bar of the palette of patterns. The *Cancel* option removes the palette.

Delete item in this palette's **File** menu removes a pattern from the palette, and *Import pattern* lets you import a file into the *Two-Color Pattern* dialog box.

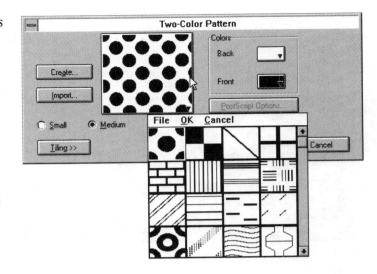

Figure 73. Clicking on the *Back* and *Front* color swatches lets you apply a foreground and background color to the pattern.

Clicking on the *More* button at the bottom of the Color palette opens a dialog box that works in the same way as the *Uniform Fill* dialog box.

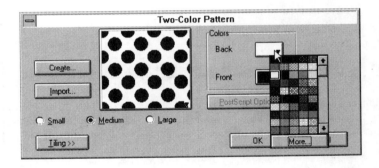

Figure 74. Clicking on the *Create* button in the *Two-Color Pattern* dialog box opens the *Two-Color Pattern Editor* dialog box. Here you create your own patterns, which you can then add to the bottom of the pop-up palette of patterns.

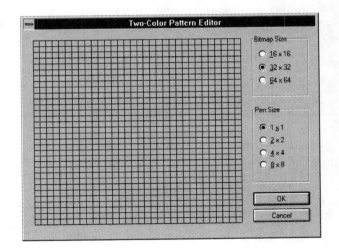

Clicking on the *Import* button, below the *Create* button in the *Two-Color Pattern* dialog box, gives you access to the *Import* dialog box. From here you can import a file to become a two-color pattern.

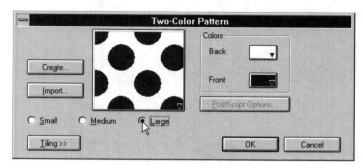

Figure 75. The *Small, Medium,* and *Large* options in the *Two-Color Pattern* dialog box let you change the tiling size of your pattern.

Clicking on the *PostScript Options* button opens the *PostScript Options* dialog box. The options available here were described in the **Outline Color** section. You can access the PostScript options only if you are working with Pantone spot colors.

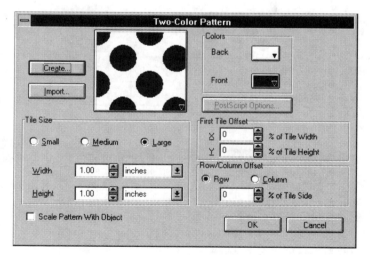

Figure 76. Selecting the *Tiling* button expands the *Two-Color Pattern* dialog box to include tile size and offset options. You can insert your own size for each tile for *Width* and *Height*. The tiles in the display square change size according to the changes you make in the *Tile Size* section.

By altering the *X* and *Y* options in the *First Tile Offset* section, you can alter the position of the first tile of a pattern. The first tile of a pattern is in the top left corner.

The *Row/Column Offset* options let you offset the orientation of the row or column.

FULL-COLOR PATTERNS

Figure 77. The *Full-Color Pattern* icon (▨) in the *Fill Tool* fly-out (a) opens the *Full-Color Pattern* dialog box (b).

(a)

(b)

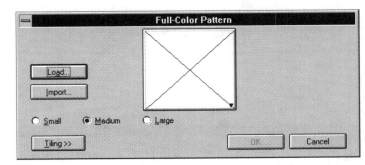

Figure 78. Click on the preview box to bring up the pop-up palette of patterns, from where you can select your own fill pattern.

This works in the same way as selecting a two-color pattern, although the **File** menu has one further option available: the *Save Current Fill* command. When you import a file into the *Full-Color Pattern* dialog box, you can save the fill so it appears in the full-color palette of patterns.

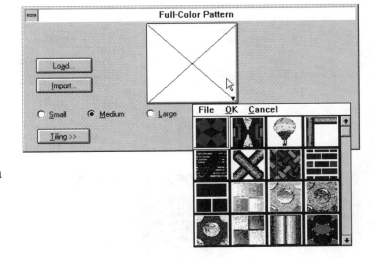

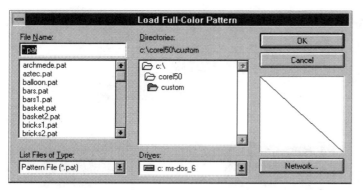

Figure 79. Clicking on the *Load* button in the *Full-Color Pattern* dialog box opens the *Load Full-Color Pattern* dialog box; from this box you can load a pattern file from anywhere on your machine. Full-color patterns have an extension of *.pat*.

For more information about creating your own full-color patterns, see the **Create Pattern** section in **Chapter 11, The Special Menu.**

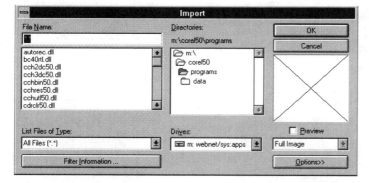

Figure 80. Selecting the *Import* button from the *Full-Color Pattern* dialog box opens the *Import* dialog box. You can import a file to become a full-color pattern here.

The *List Files of Type* drop-down list at the bottom of the dialog box contains a list of file formats that you can import.

For more information on importing, see **Chapter 4, The File Menu.**

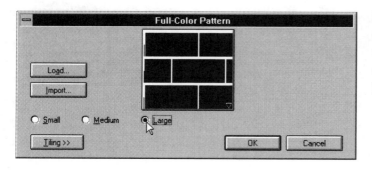

Figure 81. The *Small, Medium,* and *Large* options are three preset tile sizes. You can select any one of these for your full-color pattern.

Figure 82. As with the *Two-Color Pattern* dialog box, clicking on the *Tiling* button expands the *Full-Color Pattern* dialog box. The *Tile Size* options in the newly expanded dialog box give you control over the tile size, as discussed in the section on the *Two-Color Pattern* dialog box (Figure 76).

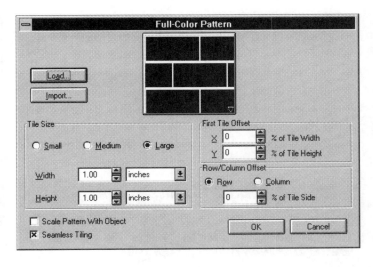

By altering the *X* and *Y* options in the *First Tile Offset* section, you can alter the position of the first tile of a pattern. The first tile of a pattern is in the top left corner.

The *Row/Column Offset* options allow you to offset the alignment of the row or column.

BITMAP TEXTURE FILLS

Figure 83. The *Texture* icon (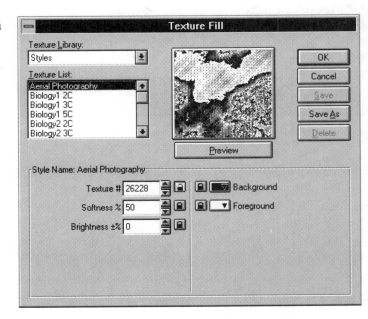) in the *Fill Tool* fly-out opens the *Texture Fill* dialog box. Texture fills look textured and you can change each fill to create literally millions of variations. They display on screen and can be printed on any laser printer.

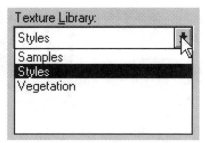

Figure 84. In the *Texture Fill* dialog box, choose a library from the *Texture Library* drop-down list.

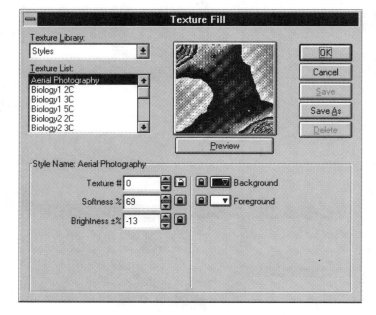

Figure 85. Then, from the *Texture List*, choose the texture name you want and the texture appears in the preview box.

You can modify texture styles yourself with the parameters at the bottom of the dialog box. You can have CorelDRAW randomly modify texture styles by unlocking any or all of the parameters at the bottom of the dialog box.

You unlock options by clicking on the 🔒 icon. Click on the *Preview* button to let CorelDRAW randomly alter the texture using the unlocked parameters.

Each texture fill has 32,768 variations. You can also change the *Texture #* from 0 to 32,767 to alter the texture.

Figure 86. Each texture style has a specific range of parameters that you can use to change the texture; change these parameters yourself to create different variations of a style. In this example we changed the *Texture #*, *Softness %*, and *Brightness ±%*, and clicked on the *Preview* button. Compare this to Figure 85.

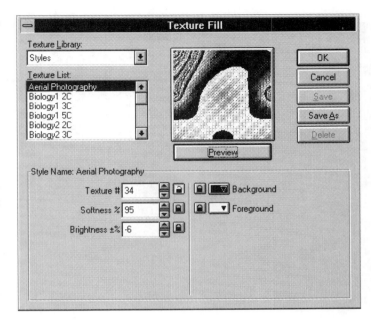

It is possible to save changes you have made to texture fills. There are two types of texture fills— "style" textures and "user" textures. Saving a style texture is different from saving a user texture.

You store style textures in the *Styles* library. You can make changes to any of the style textures, and these changes are assigned to the selected object, but you cannot save the new texture. Notice that when you have a texture selected from the *Styles* library, the *Save* button in the *Texture Fill* dialog box is dimmed.

Figure 87. You can however, use the *Save As* option to save a style texture under a different name. After changing the style texture, click on the *Save As* button. This opens the *Save Texture as* dialog box. Type the new name of the texture in the *Texture Name* text box. In the *Library Name* list, select any library name other than *Styles*, because texture fills you create (user textures) can't be saved in the *Styles* library.

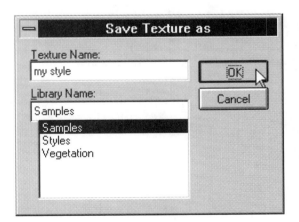

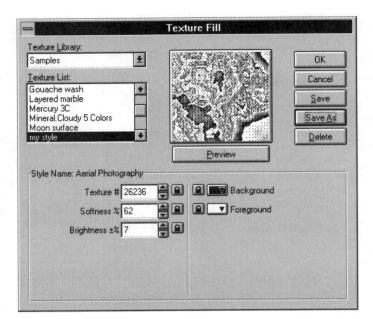

Figure 88. After clicking on *OK* in the *Save Texture as* dialog box, CorelDRAW adds the new texture to the style library that you have selected.

You can also create a new texture library by typing a new name in the *Library Name* text box in the *Save Texture as* dialog box.

User textures are derived from style textures. You can save changes to user textures, or you can use the *Save As* option with user textures so the original user texture remains unaffected.

Figure 89. Use the *Delete* option to delete user textures. After clicking on this button, confirm that you want to delete the texture fill.

POSTSCRIPT FILLS

Figure 90. Clicking on the *PS* option (▣) in the *Fill Tool* fly-out opens the *PostScript Texture* dialog box. You can fill the selected object with a variety of patterns from the list; however, you can see them only when you print to a PostScript printer.

Use the options below the list of available fills to modify the size and shades of the fills. Appendix A of the CorelDRAW manual provides a comprehensive listing of available PostScript fills.

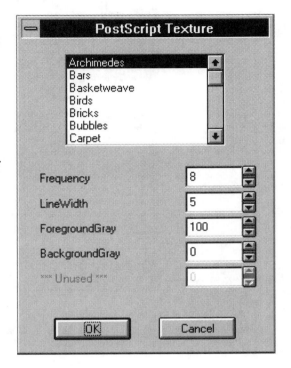

FILL ROLL-UP

Figure 91. Selecting the second option in the top row of the *Fill Tool* fly-out (▣) activates the *Fill* roll-up. All the fill options available in this roll-up are available in dialog boxes directly from the *Fill Tool* fly-out.

As with all roll-ups, you must click on the *Apply* button at the bottom of the roll-up to apply any changes to selected objects.

Fill Color ——

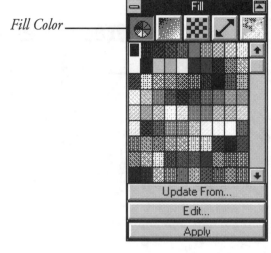

Figure 92. The first option in the *Fill* roll-up is the *Fill Color*. This lets you simply apply a fill color to your objects by selecting a color and clicking on *Apply*.

Fountain Fill ——

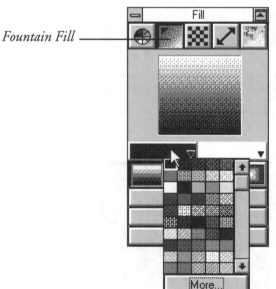

Figure 93. The next option in the *Fill* roll-up (■) is *Fountain Fill*. This lets you apply a fill ranging from one color to another. Clicking on either of the two color buttons below the fountain fill preview box opens a Color palette from where you can select a color.

The left color button is the start color and the right color button is the end color. Click on the *More* button at the bottom of the palette to expand the range of colors you can choose from.

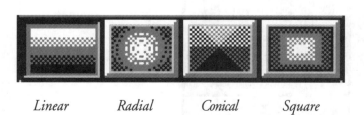

Linear   *Radial*   *Conical*   *Square*

Figure 94. The options below the two color buttons let you choose a *Linear, Radial, Conical,* or a *Square* fountain fill.

Figure 95. You can use the preview box to change the fill angle or center offset of the fountain fill, as you can with the preview box in the *Fountain Fill* dialog box described earlier.

After clicking on the *Fountain Fill* button, click on the *Edit* button in the *Fill* roll-up to access the *Fountain Fill* dialog box. This is this same dialog box that you open in the *Fill Tool* fly-out.

You can click on Edit to open the Fountain Fill dialog box.

Figure 96. The next icon in the *Fill* roll-up is the *Two-Color Pattern* fill button (▓) which activates the options for two color pattern fills. Clicking on the preview box pops-up a palette where you can select a pattern to fill an object with. Use the scroll bar to see more patterns.

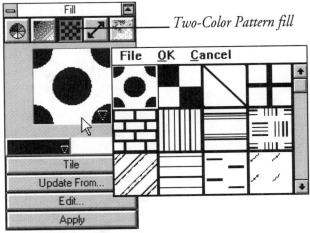

Two-Color Pattern fill

Figure 97. The pop-up palette for the two-color patterns has its own menu bar. Clicking on the *Cancel* option removes the pop-up palette and *OK* accepts the selected fill.

The options available in the **File** menu let you remove the currently selected pattern from the pop-up palette and import a new pattern into the pop-up palette.

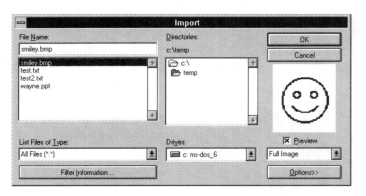

Figure 98. *Import Pattern* from the **File** menu in the pop-up palette opens the *Import* dialog box, where you can import a file to become a two-color pattern. Select a file format from the *List Files of Type* drop-down list.

For more information on importing, see **Chapter 4, The File Menu.**

Figure 99. Once you have selected your two-color pattern and it is in the preview box, you can use the two color buttons below to choose a foreground (left button) and a background (right button) color.

Click on the *More* button at the bottom of the palette to see all the color models and options.

Figure 100. Use the *Tile* button below the color buttons in the *Fill* roll-up to adjust tile size and orientation. Clicking on this button displays two squares over the top of your pattern, representing two adjacent tiles.

Before clicking on the *Tile* button, make sure you have selected the filled object with the Pick Tool.

Figure 101. Holding the mouse button down with the cursor on the left square and moving the mouse around adjusts the position of the tiles. Both squares move together.

Click on the *Apply* button to change the tile.

(a)

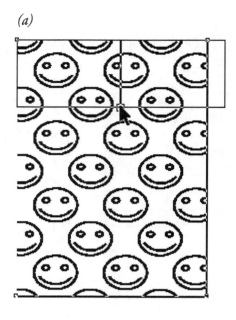

Figure 102. If you drag the node that's between the tiles (a), you change their size. After clicking on the *Apply* button, the size of the tiles changes, as in (b).

(b)

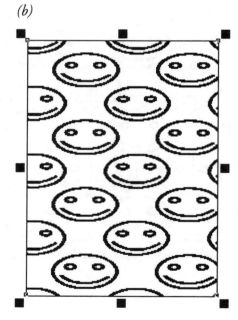

Figure 103. Moving the right square with the mouse changes the alignment of the two adjacent tiles (a). You can keep moving the right square down and under the left square to affect the horizontal alignment of the tiles (b).

Change the tiling by clicking on the *Apply* button. After you have selected the *Two-Color Pattern* fill button, you can also click on the *Edit* button to open the *Two-Color Pattern* dialog box.

You can make more precise adjustments in the *Two-Color Pattern* dialog box than you can with the mouse.

(a)

(b)

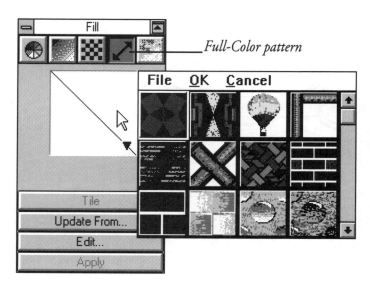

Full-Color pattern

Figure 104. The next button in the *Fill* roll-up is *Full-Color Pattern* (🖾). The patterns available in this palette are in full-color. The rest of the options in the roll-up work as they do for two-color patterns, except that you don't select a foreground and a background color for full-color patterns.

You open the *Full-Color Pattern* dialog box with the *Edit* button in the *Fill* roll-up. You can also open this dialog box from the *Fill Tool* fly-out.

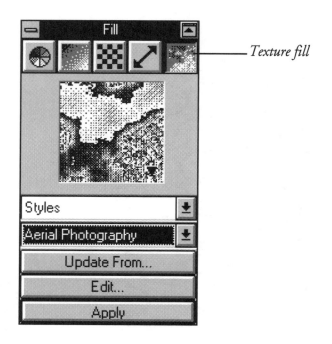

Texture fill

Figure 105. The last button in the *Fill* roll-up is *Texture Fill*. From here you can select a *Texture Library* and a texture from the two drop-down lists. Click on the *Edit* button to open the *Texture Fill* dialog box.

Figure 106. The *Update From* button lets you copy a fill from one object on the screen to another.

Select the object you want to copy the fill to and click on the *Update From* button. With the arrow that appears, click on the object that you want to copy the fill from.

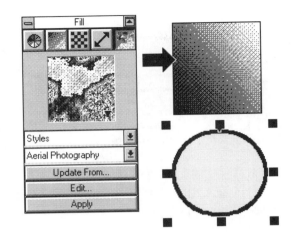

Figure 107. Next, click on the *Apply* button, and the object you originally selected with the Pick Tool (b) is given the same fill as the object you selected with the arrow (a).

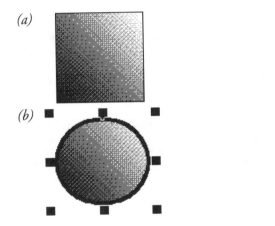

(a)

(b)

NO FILL

Figure 108. The first option in the bottom row of the *Fill Tool* fly-out (⊠) applies a fill of *None* to a selected object(s).

The remaining options in the bottom row of the *Fill Tool* fly-out allow you to apply a color quickly, as a fill, from 0% (white) to 100% (in preset percentages).

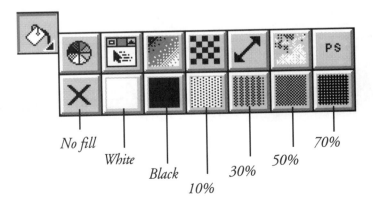

No fill

White

Black

10%

30%

50%

70%

SETTING UP OUTLINE AND FILL DEFAULTS

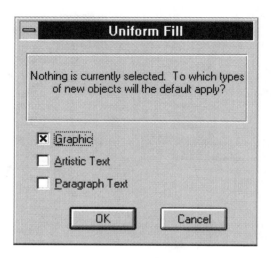

Figure 109. To set up a default for an outline or fill, choose the option you want with nothing selected on the page. This action displays a dialog box similar to this; make your selection and click on *OK*.

The new color or outline you choose is now the default setting for whichever options you selected.

THE FILL INDICATOR

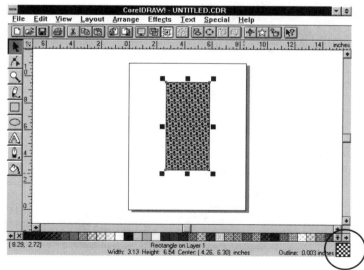

Figure 110. The *Fill Indicator* is displayed in the right corner of the status bar. This displays the outline and fill of any object selected with the Pick Tool.

Use this as your reference point to check the fill and outline details of any object. The *Fill Indicator* is active in both *editable preview* and *wireframe* views.

THE FILE MENU 4

THE FILE MENU COMMANDS

The commands contained in the **File** menu are common to most applications that run under Windows. These commands generally relate to a whole CorelDRAW file, whereas most of the other commands in the CorelDRAW menus relate only to certain objects on your page.

Figure 1. This figure displays the File menu and its commands.

File	
New	Ctrl+N
New From Template...	
Open...	Ctrl+O
Save	Ctrl+S
Save As...	
Import...	
Export...	
Mosaic Roll-Up	Alt+F1
Print...	Ctrl+P
Print Merge...	
Print Setup...	
Color Manager...	
Exit	Alt+F4
1 C:\COREL50\DRAW\TEMP.CDR	

NEW

Figure 2. Selecting the *New* command creates a new CorelDRAW file, and closes the CorelDRAW file currently open. If you haven't saved the current file, you are asked if you would like to now (see **Save** and **Save As** later in this chapter).

You can also click on the *New* icon on the ribbon bar to open a new file.

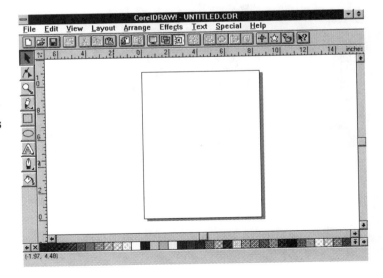

NEW FROM TEMPLATE

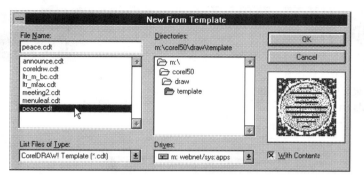

Figure 3. The *New From Template* command from the **File** menu opens the *New From Template* dialog box. If you have made any changes to the current file you have the opportunity to save these changes. In this dialog box you can select a template to open. A template contains a collection of styles and graphics that you can use as a basis for a CorelDRAW document.

Find the template file you want using the *Directories* and *Drives* drop-down lists and double-click on the template from the file list. CorelDRAW comes with a directory of template files, which have a *.cdt* extension.

Figure 4. When you double-click on a template file from the *New From Template* dialog box, it appears as though you have opened a CorelDRAW file. However, the title bar shows that this is a new file; you have, in effect, opened a copy of a CorelDRAW template ready to format in any way you like.

You can open a template as an untitled file and then make changes you want. The template files supplied with CorelDRAW are varied and you should be able to find a template to suit you.

For more information on creating, managing, and saving templates, see **Styles roll-up** in **Chapter 7, The Layout Menu**.

OPEN

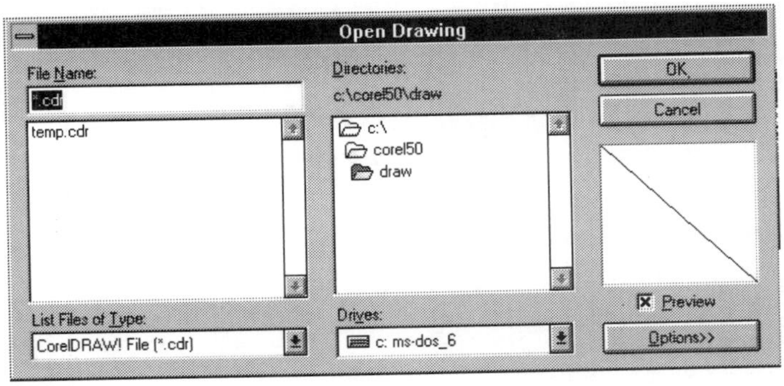

Figure 5. Selecting the *Open* command brings up the *Open Drawing* dialog box. If you have not saved the changes to the current file, CorelDRAW asks if you would like to now (see **Save** and **Save As**).

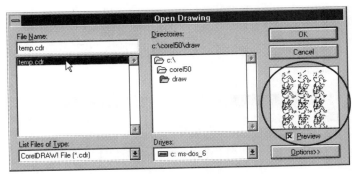

If the current directory includes any CorelDRAW (*.cdr*) files, the *Open Drawing* dialog box lists these files in a box below the *File Name* text box.

You can also bring up the *Open Drawing* dialog box by clicking on the *Open* icon on the ribbon bar.

Figure 6. Clicking on a *cdr* file from this list usually displays the file's image header in the preview box. The image header is a bitmapped version of the file. You can set the resolution of this image when you save a file.

Figure 7. The *List Files of Type* drop-down list, at the bottom left of the *Open Drawing* dialog box, has three options. The default option is the *cdr* format. You can also open full-color pattern files by selecting the *Pattern File (*.pat)* option; these files display in the *Full-Color Pattern* dialog box available from the *Fill Tool* fly-out.

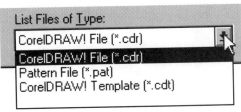

For more information on full-color patterns, see **Chapter 3, Outline and Fill Tools**.

The third option is *CorelDRAW Template (*.cdt)*, so you can open a template file. For more information on creating, managing, and saving templates, see **Styles roll-up** in **Chapter 7, The Layout Menu**.

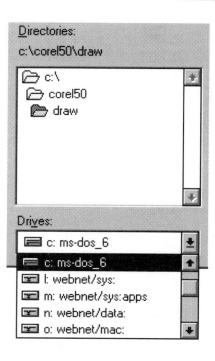

Figure 8. The *Directories* list box in the *Open Drawing* dialog box shows you all the directories and subdirectories on the current directory or drive.

Double-clicking on the drive letter (in this case c:) takes you back to the root directory. To open a specific directory, double-click on the directory name from this list.

The *Drives* list at the bottom of this figure gives you access to the computer's drives.

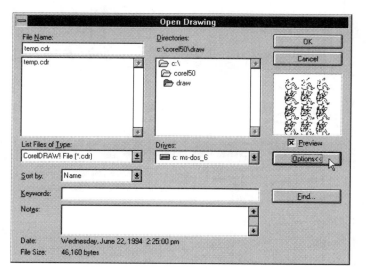

Figure 9. When you click on the *Options* button at the bottom right of the *Open Drawing* dialog box, it expands to provide more options.

Figure 10. The first option in the newly enlarged *Open Drawing* dialog box is *Sort by*. Your choices here are whether you list the files alphabetically (*Name*) or in chronological order (*Date*).

To display an image header for a selected *cdr* file in the preview box, click on the *Preview* check box.

Figure 11. The *Keywords* text box (also available in the *Save Drawing* dialog box) displays a selected file's keywords, which were added when the file was saved. The *Notes* text box displays any notes that were saved with a selected file. You can add keywords or notes to any file you select and save them as a part of the file. Keywords must be separated by a comma (,) or a plus (+) sign.

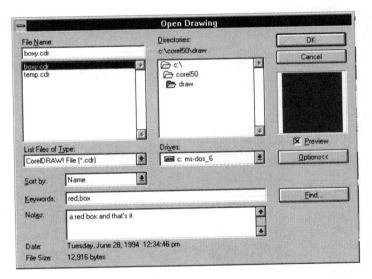

Figure 12. Clicking on the *Find* button opens the *Keyword Search* dialog box where you search the current (or all) directories for files with the same keywords. Separating keywords with a comma lists all files with any of these keywords. Separating keywords with a + displays only the files including both words.

After inserting the keyword(s), click on the *Search* button to display all the relevant files.

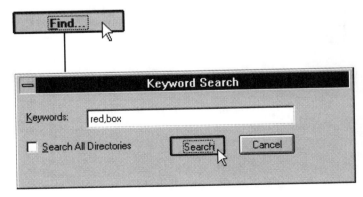

(a)

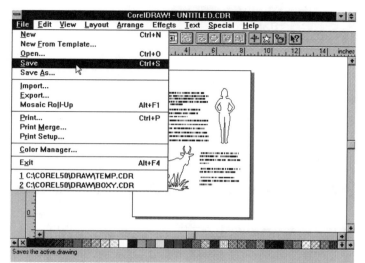

SAVE

Figure 13. If you are currently in an untitled CorelDRAW file, selecting the *Save* command (a) opens the *Save Drawing* dialog box (b). Here you name the file and decide where you are going to save it. The names of the *cdr* files in the current directory appear in gray.

Type the name of the file in the *File Name* text box. CorelDRAW adds a *.cdr* extension automatically to CorelDRAW files when you save them.

(b)

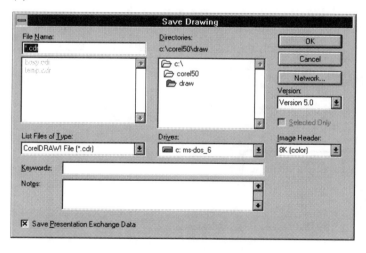

Figure 14. Use the *Directories* list box and *Drives* drop-down list to determine where you save the file.

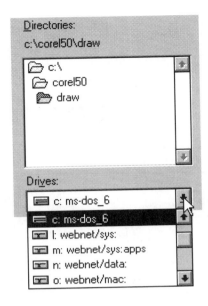

Figure 15. If you need to save the file in a previous format, click on the *Version* drop-down list.

The *Selected Only* option lets you save a selection instead of a whole file.

Figure 16. The *List Files of Type* option lets you save the file as a normal *CorelDRAW File*, as a *Pattern File*, or as a *CorelDRAW Template*. If you save the file as a *Pattern File,* you can then access this file through the *Full-Color*

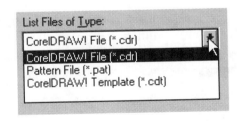

Pattern dialog box available from the *Fill Tool* fly-out, or from the *Open Drawing* dialog box.

If you save the file as a template, you can open the file through the *New From Template* command in the **File** menu, the *Styles* roll-up from the **Layout** menu, and the *Open Drawing* dialog box.

Figure 17. With the *Image Header* option in the *Save Drawing* dialog box, you can set the quality of the image in the preview box in the *Open Drawing* dialog box. The size of the saved file increases as the *Image Header* option does.

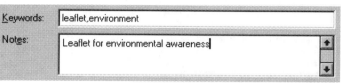

Figure 18. The *Keywords* text box in the *Save Drawing* dialog box is to insert words that relate to the file. In the *Open Drawing* dialog box, you can use keywords to find and highlight files with the same keywords (see Figure 11). You must separate keywords with a comma (,) or a + sign.

You use the *Notes* text box to put in any information you want saved with the file.

Choosing the *Save* command, after you have named a file, saves the changes made to the file since you last used the command, but does not open the *Save Drawing* dialog box.

The *Save* icon on the ribbon bar works in the same way as the *Save* command.

SAVE AS

The *Save As* command opens the *Save Drawing* dialog box (Figure 13b). If you have already saved the file, you can then make a copy of it by giving it a new name, or saving it into a different directory. If you haven't saved the file, using the *Save As* command is the same as using the *Save* command.

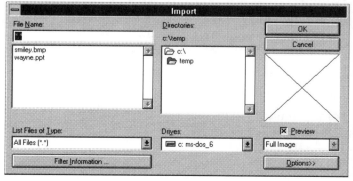

IMPORT

Figure 19. The *Import* command from the **File** menu brings up the *Import* dialog box. Use the *Directories* list box and *Drives* drop-down list to find the directory containing the files you want to import. You can also bring up the *Import* dialog box by clicking on the *Import* icon on the ribbon bar.

Figure 20. The options in the *List Files of Type* drop-down list show you which files you can import, including *cdr* (native Corel-DRAW format).

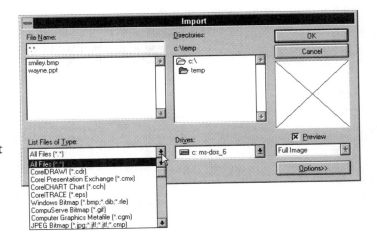

When you have selected the file type you want from the *List Files of Type* drop-down list, the file list displays all files in the current directory in the selected format. To import a file into CorelDRAW, select it from the list of files, and click on the *OK* button.

Figure 21. Clicking on the *Options* button in this dialog box expands the dialog box to include helpful information about the selected file, and allows you to sort the files by name or date.

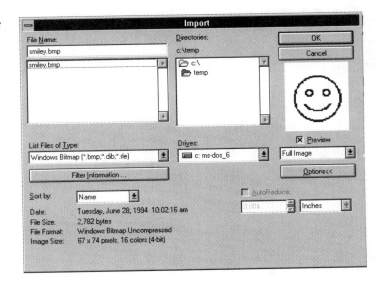

Figure 22. When importing a vector file, the *AutoReduce* check box allows you to reduce the edit nodes in your graphic.

This functions in the same way as the *AutoReduce* function in the *Node Edit* roll-up. The spin box lets you set the maximum deviation allowable when removing nodes from a curve. The resulting curve is more accurate the smaller the value you enter.

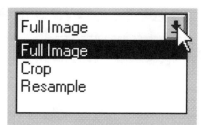

Figure 23. When importing bitmap files you can choose to import the whole image, crop the image, or resample the image from the *Import* dialog box.

Selecting *Full Image* imports the entire bitmap into your CorelDRAW file. However, when you select *Crop* or *Resample*, a further dialog box opens when you click on *OK*.

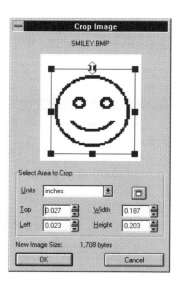

Figure 24. The *Crop Image* dialog box reduces the size of the file by cropping the image before you import it. Drag the handles to resize the image or use the spin boxes available for precise measurements.

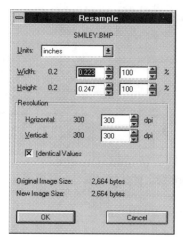

Figure 25. The *Resample* dialog box allows you to change your image's size, or change the resolution of your file.

EXPORT

Figure 26. Selecting the *Export* command from the **File** menu opens the *Export* dialog box. Here you can save a file in various formats, allowing you to import it into other programs that don't read the *cdr* format. You must have drawn an object before you can select the *Export* command.

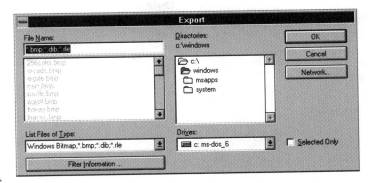

You can also bring up the *Export* dialog box by clicking on the *Export* icon on the ribbon bar.

Figure 27. In the *Export* dialog box, select the format of your choice from the *List Files of Type* drop-down list. Change the drive and directory if the current drive and directory is not where you want to save the exported file.

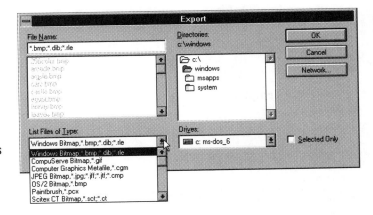

The *Selected Only* option exports only the section of your drawing that you selected with the Pick Tool.

Figure 28. Certain file formats that you can export open a second export dialog box. For instance the *EPS* option (a) opens the *Export EPS* dialog box (b).

(a)

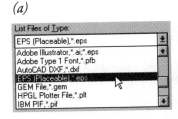

(b)

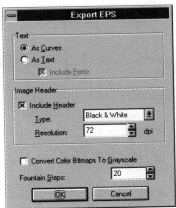

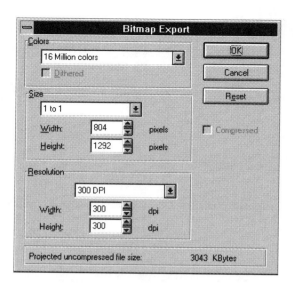

(a)

Figure 29. Exporting to any of the *Bitmap* formats opens this dialog box.

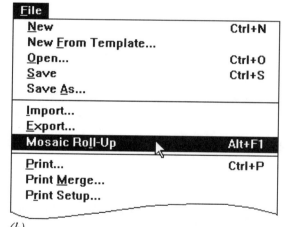

(b)

Figure 30. The next command in the **File** menu is the *Mosaic Roll-Up* command (a). This command opens the *Mosaic* roll-up (b), allowing you to use the Corel-MOSAIC features for viewing files. For more information on CorelMOSAIC, see your CorelDRAW user manual.

You can also bring up the *Mosaic* roll-up by clicking on the *Mosaic Roll-Up* icon on the ribbon bar.

PRINT

Figure 31. Selecting the *Print* command from the **File** menu opens the *Print* dialog box. The dialog box in this example displays the options for a PostScript printer. If you do not have a PostScript printer, some of the options discussed will not be available.

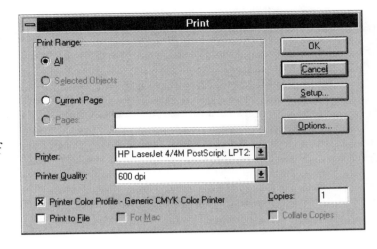

Figure 32. The *Printer* drop-down list allows you to select your required printer. Choose the printer that you plan to output the CorelDRAW file from.

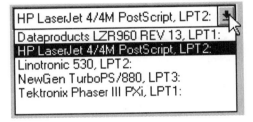

Figure 33. Clicking on the Control box for this dialog box and selecting *Printer Information* (a) opens the *Printer Information* dialog box. This dialog box describes the current printer's capabilities (b).

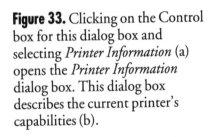

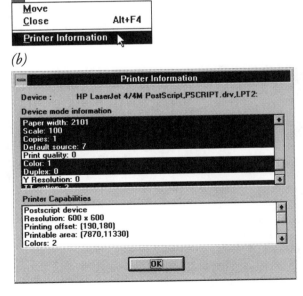

Figure 34. The *Print Range* section of the dialog box allows you to determine what range of your document you print.

The *All* option prints your entire file, *Selected Object* prints only the objects you currently have selected with the Pick Tool, *Current Page* prints only the current page, and the *Pages* radio button allows you to specify the pages or page range you want to print.

Figure 35. The *Printer Quality* drop-down list allows you to specify the output quality of your printed file for the selected device driver. However, it is important to remember that the resolution quality can only be set to the maximum setting allowable for the printer you are printing to. In other words, the print quality is only ever as good as the printer's resolution capabilities.

Figure 36. The *Copies* option in the *Print* dialog box lets you specify the number of copies of your file that you want to print.

Figure 37. The *Printer Color Profile* check box forces the printer to use the current *System Profile*. You specify this through the *System Color Profile* dialog box, which you access by selecting the *Color Manager* command in the **File** menu (see later in this chapter).

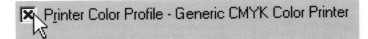

Figure 38. Check the *Print to File* option in the *Print* dialog box, and click on *OK* to open the *Print To File* dialog box. Here you decide where you wish to save the print file. You must also give the print file a title, which you type into the *File Name* text box.

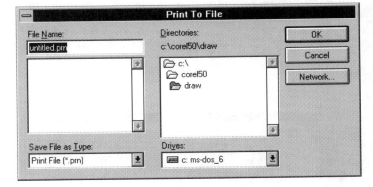

CorelDRAW uses the standard industry extension of *.prn* for print files. Before creating the print file, there may be other options in the *Print* dialog box you may want to select.

You create print files if you plan to send the file to a service bureau or want to print the file from a computer that does not have CorelDRAW. Before you create a print file, you should select the printer you plan to output the print file from.

When you select the *Print to File* option, you can select the *For Mac* check box. Selecting this option allows you to create a print file that will print from an Apple Macintosh printer. You create the print file in exactly the same way.

OPTIONS

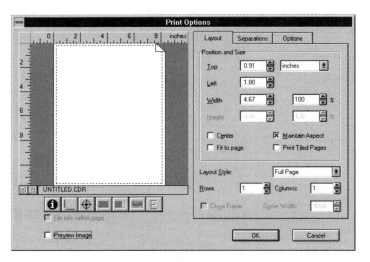

Figure 39. Clicking on the *Options* button in the *Print* dialog box opens the *Print Options* dialog box.

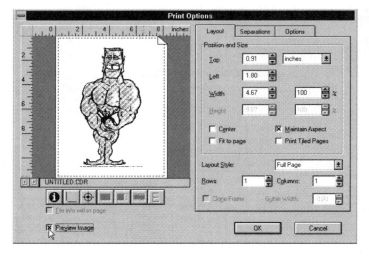

Figure 40. The *Preview Image* check box here allows you to display your graphic in the display page as shown.

You can move through a multi-page document by using the page forward and back icons at the bottom left of the preview area.

Figure 41. By default, the *Layout* tab is selected in the *Print Options* dialog box. This tab allows you to change the size, position, and layout style of your file.

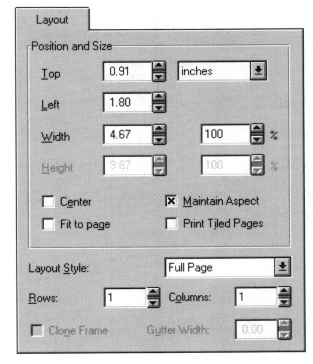

The *Position and Size* section of this tab gives you the option to set the size the drawing prints at, regardless of the size of the actual drawing. Click on the *Fit to page* option to fit everything in the drawing automatically to the page size. This affects the printed output only, not the actual drawing.

Choosing the *Center* option moves the drawing to the center of the page. The *Center* option is the default for the *Fit to page* option.

Use the *Print Tiled Pages* option to print files that are larger than the printer's page size. You can print different sections of the file on separate pages, and then paste them together to create posters or banners.

If you deselect the *Fit to page* and the *Center* options, you can use the *Top* and *Left* options to change the position of the image in the display window. The *Left* option represents the top left corner of the graphic, while the *Top* value represents the top of the graphic.

The *Maintain Aspect* check box ensures that the height and width of the image remain in their correct proportions. If you deselect this check box you can adjust the *Height* and *Width* settings independently of each other.

You can change the unit of measurement for all the options in this dialog box through the measurement drop-down list which displays inches by default.

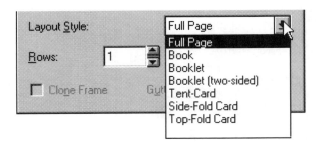

Figure 42. You can set the layout style for your file through the drop-down list of available page layout types.

Figure 43. You can also set the number of rows and columns of the chosen layout through the available spin boxes.

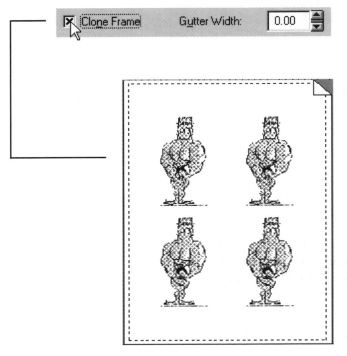

Figure 44. The *Clone Frame* check box allows you to fill the sheet with a series of copies of each page.

You can use the *Gutter Width* settings to determine the distance, or "gutter" of space, between frames.

Figure 45. Click on the *Separations* tab to access the options for printing color separations for your file.

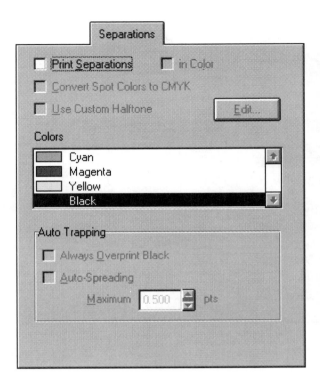

Check the *Print Separations* box to print your file as color separations. When you print the file as separations, you get a separate printed page for each color specified. If you used the four process colors (cyan, magenta, yellow, and black) in your document, you will get a maximum of four printouts, one for each of the four process colors. If you chose only two of the process colors, you will get two printouts.

If your document is made up of spot colors, you get a separate printout for every Pantone color you selected. You determine the maximum number of separations by the number of Pantone colors you use. You can print color separations to film or to paper. When you want to output color separations to film, you can create a print file and send this file to a bureau that outputs the file to film.

After checking the *Print Separations* option, click on the *In Color* option if you are printing separations to a color printer. This option allows you to print each separation using its true color rather than printing in shades of gray.

If you have spot (Pantone) colors in your drawing, you can select the *Convert Spot Colors to CMYK* option. With this option, CorelDRAW temporarily converts the spot colors to the closest equivalent process colors. This is sometimes necessary if you have a large number of spot colors, yet you only want a maximum of four color separations. This affects the printout only, not the colors in the drawing.

(a)

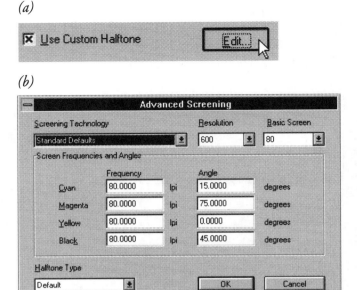

(b)

Figure 46. Choose the *Use Custom Halftone* option (a) and click on the edit button to change the angle and frequency settings in the *Advanced Screening* dialog box (b).

You can usually leave these settings at their default, unless the commercial printer or bureau tells you to change a setting.

The *Screen Frequencies and Angles* options determine the color angle and frequency for each separation. CorelDRAW may change these settings automatically depending on the output device you have selected.

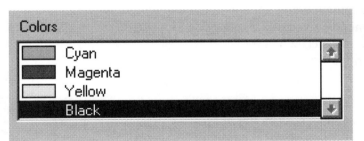

Figure 47. The *Colors* section of the *Separations* dialog box lists all the colors used in your drawing. Select the colors you want to print as separations from this list.

Figure 48. The first option in the *Auto Trapping* section in the *Separations* tab is the *Always Overprint Black* option. Checking this option ensures that any object with a greater than 95% black fill will overprint when it overlaps another color. Normally, when different colors overlap, the area underneath is knocked out.

Choose the *Always Overprint Black* option to ensure these knockouts do not occur with colored objects below black objects. This is known as trapping. CorelDRAW achieves *Auto Trapping* by applying an outline to the object the same color as its fill. When you select the *Auto-Spreading* option, CorelDRAW spreads the foreground color into the background to all objects in the drawing that have no outline and have a uniform fill. You can determine the amount of trapping by changing the *Maximum* value after checking the *Auto-Spreading* option. The amount of trapping applied is also determined by the object's color.

The main reason for overprinting is to avoid gaps that sometimes occur when printing from separations. If you overprint colors other than black, the two colors will mix and you may get a result you don't want.

Trapping objects and printing color separations is a complex process. You should talk to your bureau or commercial printer when creating color separations to find out exactly what options to choose.

Figure 49. Select the *Options* tab to display all of the *Options* settings for the *Print Options* dialog box.

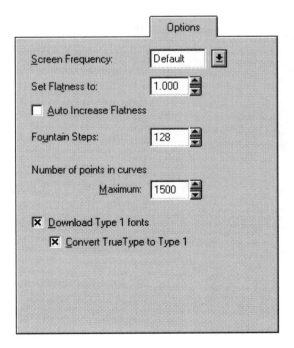

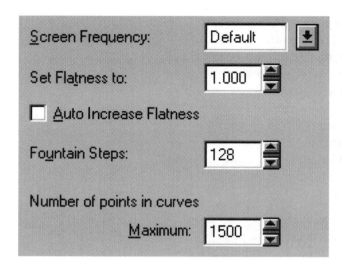

Figure 50. The *Screen Frequency* refers to the number of lines per inch for printing and is set to a default value and should be left alone. Check with your bureau before changing this value.

You can use the *Set Flatness to* feature to decrease the complexity of a drawing, which in turn speeds up printing time. This option simplifies complex images when printing.

When you increase the number in the *Set Flatness to* box, it reduces the smoothness of your curves, as CorelDRAW decreases the number of segments in a curve. This affects the printed image only.

If you have trouble printing a graphic, use the *Auto Increase Flatness* option and CorelDRAW will increase the flatness value by increments of two each time you print. If this value ever exceeds the *Set Flatness to* value by ten, the printer will not print your graphic.

You use the *Fountain Steps* option to determine the number of stripes a PostScript printer uses to create a fountain fill. The smaller the value, the quicker the printing time, but the transition between the two colors is not as smooth. If you increase the value, the fill becomes smoother, but the printing time increases. When you output the file to a Linotronic typesetter, the *128* default setting is recommended for 1270 dpi, and *200* for 2540 dpi. If you alter the *Steps* value in the *Fountain Fill* dialog box (see **Chapter 3, Outline and Fill Tools**), the *Fountain Steps* value in this options dialog box is ignored.

You can also use the *Number of points in curves* option to set a maximum curve complexity for printing. This option sets the maximum number of control points per curve and can be used instead of the flatness settings to help control printing complex images.

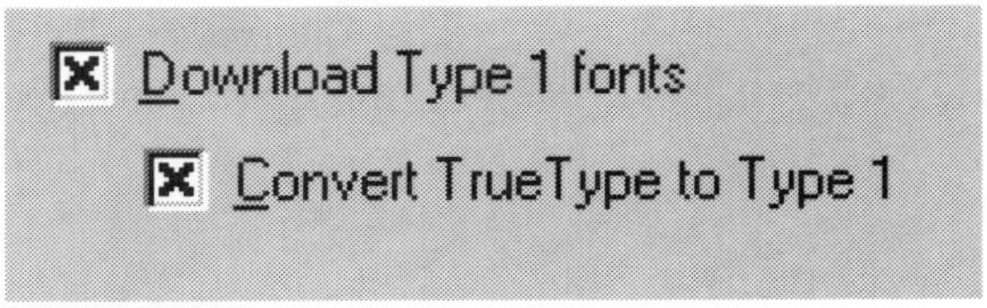

Figure 51. Select *Download Type 1 fonts* to download the Type 1 fonts to the output device. This can be useful when you have a lot of text that uses only a few fonts as printing will be much faster because each font is downloaded first and then referenced by text that uses it.

☒ Download Type 1 fonts

☒ Convert TrueType to Type 1

Choosing this option selects *Convert True Type to Type 1* by default to make sure that any True Type fonts are converted to Type 1 to be downloaded to the output device.

If you disable the *Download Type 1 fonts* option, fonts are printed as graphics (curves or bitmaps) which can be quicker if your file contains a large number of different fonts that would take a long time to download.

JOB MANAGEMENT TOOLS

Figure 52. The remaining tools in the *Print Options* dialog box are the job management tools below the preview window.

Choosing the *File Information* button prints the filename, date, time, and tile number on the page. When you are printing separations, it also includes the separation information. The program displays this information outside the crop marks, so if you are printing a page the same size as the printer paper, you would check the *Within Page* option to ensure the information appears on the page when printing proofs only.

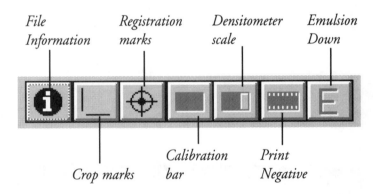

File Information   Registration marks   Densitometer scale   Emulsion Down

Crop marks   Calibration bar   Print Negative

Choosing the *Crop Marks* tool prints crop marks to indicate the page size. This works if you are printing a page smaller than the printer's paper size. They are used as the final trim size for the printed document.

The *Registration Marks* tool is available only if you are printing separations. Registration marks are lines that appear on each separation which the printer uses to align film separations.

The *Calibration Bar* tool tells CorelDRAW to add a strip of colors and grayscales to the printout for calibrating purposes.

The *Densitometer Scale* tool is available only when you are printing color separations. It adds a scale to each separation that shows the intensity of the CMYK inks for each separation.

Choosing the *Print Negative* tool prints your image as a negative. This is sometimes necessary if you are printing to film, and the commercial printer needs negative film.

The *Emulsion Down* tool also relates to the printing of film. The emulsion of film is the light-sensitive coating and is usually printed facing up. In some cases your commercial printer may require the emulsion down. If this is the case, check this option.

PRINTER SETUP

Once you have made all the changes you want in the *Print Options* dialog box, click on *OK* to return to the *Print* dialog box. Now click on the *Setup* button to make the final settings for your print job.

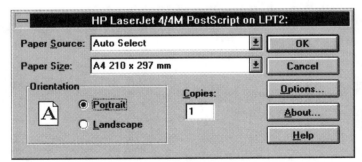

Figure 53. CorelDRAW then opens this *Setup* dialog box. Here you set up the *Paper Size* you are printing to and the *Orientation* (*Portrait* or *Landscape*). Your *Orientation* option should match the orientation on the page you are printing.

Once you have set up your *Print Setup* dialog box as you need, click on the *OK* button to return to the *Print* dialog box and start the printing process. Click on the *Print* icon on the ribbon bar to print with the current print settings, bypassing the *Print* dialog box.

PRINT MERGE

Use the *Print Merge* option in the **File** menu to combine a word processing document with a CorelDRAW file. This feature is useful for things such as mailing lists, where you keep the image constant, and change the name and address for each printout.

CorelDRAW inserts the merged text in the appropriate places in the document and sends this to the printer; this prints multiple copies of the file with newly merged text in each one.

PRINT SETUP

Figure 54. Select *Print Setup* to open the *Print Setup* dialog box. Choose a printer from the drop-down list of printer names, and then a resolution for your print job from the available resolutions for the printer that you select.

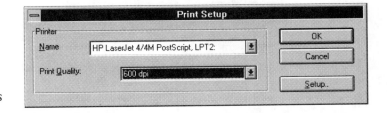

Selecting the *Setup* button opens the dialog box shown in Figure 53, where you can alter the print setup for the currently selected printer.

COLOR MANAGER

Figure 55. Select the *Color Manager* command from the **File** menu to build a system profile of your publishing system, including information about your monitor, printer, and scanner (if necessary) so that you can acquire, view, and reproduce colors more accurately.

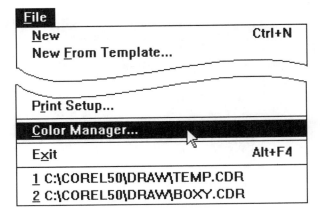

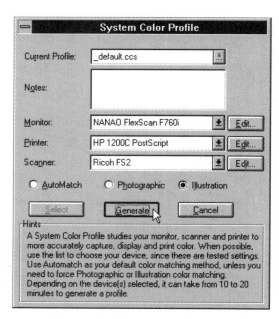

Figure 56. This opens the *System Color Profile* dialog box. Now simply select your monitor, printer, and scanner from the drop-down lists of available types and add any notes that you need to help you manage your system. Once you have done this, click on the *Generate* button.

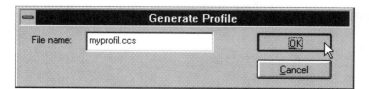

Figure 57. This opens the *Generate Profile* dialog box. Now simply name your profile and click *OK*. You can also select the *Automatch* option (see Figure 56) to ensure automatic color matching.

EXIT

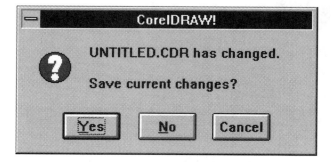

Figure 58. Select the *Exit* command from the **File** menu when you have finished working with CorelDRAW. If you have made any changes since last saving the current file, you are given the choice of whether or not to save these changes.

Figure 59. The last four CorelDRAW files you opened and saved appear at the bottom of the **File** menu. You can select a filename from the **File** menu to open the file.

File	
New	Ctrl+N
New From Template...	
Open...	Ctrl+O
Save	Ctrl+S
Save As...	
Import...	
Export...	
Mosaic Roll-Up	Alt+F1
Print...	Ctrl+P
Print Merge...	
Print Setup...	
Color Manager...	
Exit	Alt+F4
1 C:\COREL50\STARS.CDR	
2 C:\COREL50\YAPPY.CDR	
3 C:\COREL50\DRAW\TEMP.CDR	
4 C:\COREL50\DRAW\BOXY.CDR	

THE EDIT MENU 5

THE EDIT MENU COMMANDS

You use the commands in the **Edit** menu for basic editing options. Some of these commands, such as *Undo, Cut, Copy, Paste, Delete,* and *Select All* are common to most Windows applications. You also use this menu for managing linked or embedded files.

Figure 1. This figure displays the Edit menu and its commands.

Edit	
Undo Move	Ctrl+Z
Redo	Alt+Ret
Repeat Move	Ctrl+R
Cu**t**	Ctrl+X
Copy	Ctrl+C
Paste	Ctrl+V
Paste **S**pecial...	
De**l**ete	Del
Duplicate	Ctrl+D
Cl**o**ne	
Copy Attributes From...	
Select **A**ll	
Insert O**b**ject...	
Object	▶
Links...	

UNDO

The *Undo* command lets you reverse the last action you made in CorelDRAW. For instance, you can return a graphic to the state it was in before you performed the last process on it.

The number of previous actions you can undo is determined by the *Undo Levels* value you set in the *Preferences* dialog box (for more information, see the **Preferences** section in **Chapter 11, The Special Menu**). You cannot undo a change of view, any command in the **File** menu, or any selection process.

REDO

You can access the *Redo* command only after you have used the *Undo* command. It reinstates whatever you changed with the *Undo* command.

REPEAT

You use this command to repeat the very last process performed on an object. The repeated process is carried out on the currently selected object. In the example of Figure 2, we used the *Repeat* command after rotating an object.

(a)

(b)

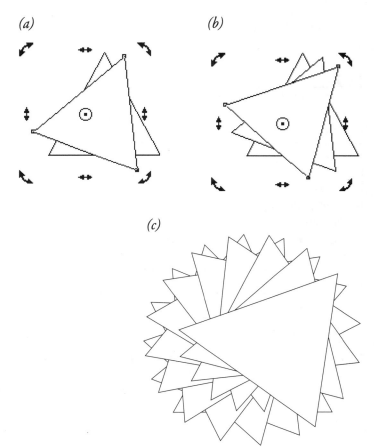

(c)

Figure 2. You can rotate and duplicate an object using the Pick Tool (a). (Press the + key on the numeric keypad, or the right mouse button, to duplicate the object while rotating it.)

When you select the *Repeat* command after rotating and duplicating the object, you repeat the rotation and duplication (b).

If you keep selecting the *Repeat* command before doing anything else, you can continue this process (c).

CUT

Use the *Cut* command to delete any selected object or objects from the page. *Cut* also transfers a copy of the deleted object to the Windows Clipboard. It remains there only until you use the *Cut* or *Copy* command again.

You can also click on the *Cut* icon on the ribbon bar.

COPY

Choosing the *Copy* command copies any selected object or objects to the Windows Clipboard, leaving the original object behind. The copy remains in the Clipboard only until you use the *Cut* or *Copy* command again.

You can also click on the *Copy* icon on the ribbon bar.

PASTE

The *Paste* command lets you reinsert the last object or objects that you cut or copied.

Alternatively, you can click on the *Paste* icon on the ribbon bar.

PASTE SPECIAL

You use the *Paste Special* command for linking documents. Linking connects a source document with CorelDRAW (the destination document). Any changes you make in the source document appear automatically in the destination document.

Figure 3. Before copying the information you intend to paste into CorelDRAW, make sure you have saved the source document (in this case *Paintbrush*). Then, select the information you want, and choose *Copy* from the **Edit** menu. You can now either close the source document or switch to CorelDRAW.

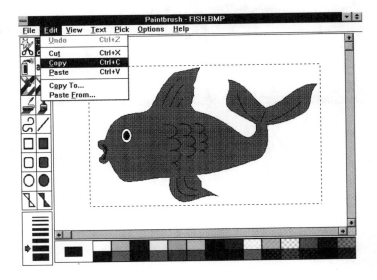

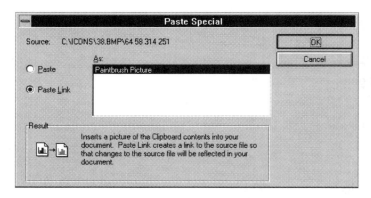

Figure 4. In CorelDRAW, select *Paste Special* from the **Edit** menu to open the *Paste Special* dialog box. Select the appropriate option from the list (in this case select the *Paintbrush Picture* option) and click on the *Paste Link* option.

Choosing the *Paste* option will also insert the copied information into CorelDRAW; however, this option does not create a link between the two programs.

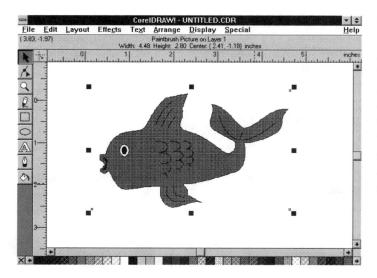

Figure 5. When you click on *OK*, the information you copied from *Paintbrush* is now in CorelDRAW. Any changes you now make in the source document are automatically updated in the CorelDRAW file, unless you change the *Update* option in the *Links* dialog box. See the **Links** section later in this chapter for more information.

DELETE

To remove a selected object from the screen, select the *Delete* command. If you delete an object by mistake, you can reverse this command by using the *Undo* command immediately after using *Delete*.

DUPLICATE

When you use the *Duplicate* command, it places a copy of the selected object on the screen. You can alter where CorelDRAW displays the duplicate with the *Preferences* command in the **Special** menu (see **Chapter 11, The Special Menu**).

Figure 6. Select the object you want to duplicate, and choose *Duplicate* from the **Edit** menu. After selecting this command, CorelDRAW places the duplicate on top of the original object according to the *Place Duplicates and Clones* option in the *Preferences* dialog box.

In this example, we moved the bottom object down and to the left slightly, and gave it a black fill. We then gave the object on top a white fill. We did this to create a drop shadow effect.

You can also duplicate an object if you click on the right mouse button while in the process of moving, resizing, rotating, or skewing an object. Or, if you press the + key on the numeric keypad, a duplicate of the selected object appears directly on top of the original object.

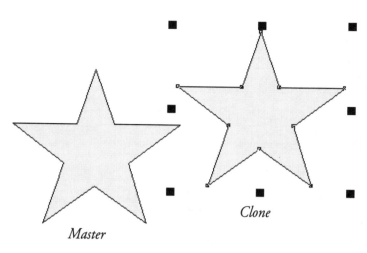

Master

Clone

CLONE

Figure 7. The *Clone* command from the **Edit** menu is similar to the *Duplicate* command, in that selecting it makes a copy of the selected object. The *Clone* command, however, takes this one step further by applying most changes you make to the original object (the master object) to the clone object as well.

After selecting this command, CorelDRAW places the clone on top of the original object, governed by the *Place Duplicates and Clones* option in the *Preferences* dialog box.

Figure 8. If you then rotate the master object for example, the cloned object also rotates.

If you change a certain attribute of the cloned object, however, this attribute is no longer affected by the changes made to the master object. For example, if you rotate the clone, it will then be unaffected when you rotate the master object.

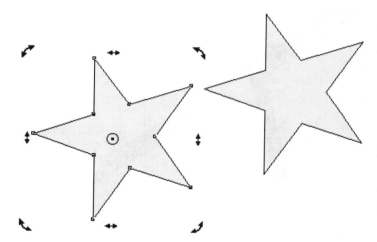

Figure 9. To determine which object is the master and which object is the clone, put the mouse cursor over the object and hold the right mouse button down. When the **Object** menu appears, you will see either the *Select Master* or the *Select Clones* command at the bottom. The master object will have the *Select Clones* command and the clone, *Select Master*.

In this example, we held the right mouse button down on the master object. For more information on the **Object** menu, see **Chapter 12, The Object Menu**.

You cannot clone an already existing clone. You can, however, duplicate a clone, and the changes made to the master object will also apply to the duplicate of the clone.

If you apply an envelope or change the perspective of the master object, this will also affect the clone. However, the other special effects commands in the **Effects** menu will not affect the clone.

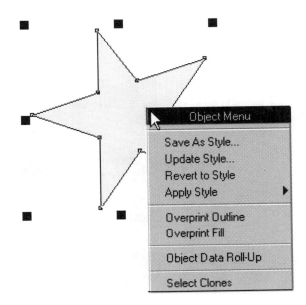

(a)

COPY ATTRIBUTES FROM

Figure 10. The *Copy Attributes From* command allows you to copy the *Outline Pen, Outline Color, Fill,* and *Text Attributes* from one object to another quickly. Select the object to which you want to copy the attribute (in this case (a), the top line of text), and choose the *Copy Attributes From* command.

(b)

> **Copy Attributes**
>
> ☒ Outline **P**en
> ☒ Outline **C**olor
> ☒ **F**ill
> ☒ **T**ext Attributes
>
> [OK] [Cancel]
>
> After pressing OK, choose the object to copy from.

Select the options you want in the *Copy Attributes* dialog box, and click on *OK* (b).

Then with the arrow, click on the object from which you want to copy the attribute (in this case (c), the bottom line of text).

The top text string now has the same attributes as the bottom text string (d).

(c)

(d)

SELECT ALL

Figure 11. The *Select All* command selects every object on your screen and automatically activates the Pick Tool, if you have not already selected it.

The status line in this example indicates that this command has selected all three objects on the page.

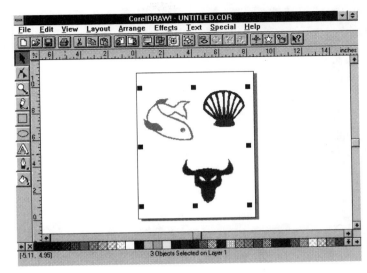

INSERT OBJECT

The *Insert Object* command takes advantage of the OLE capabilities of CorelDRAW running under Windows 3.1. OLE stands for *Object Linking and Embedding*, which enables you to transfer information from one application to another. In the case of *Insert Object* in CorelDRAW, this embeds an object from another application (source document) into CorelDRAW (destination document). For information on linking, see **Paste Special** earlier in this chapter.

Figure 12. Selecting *Insert Object* opens the *Insert Object* dialog box. From the list in this dialog box, you choose the application in which you want to create the source document. The programs you have installed determine the list of available applications. This dialog box displays only applications with OLE capabilities. In this example, we selected the *Paintbrush Picture* option and clicked on *OK*.

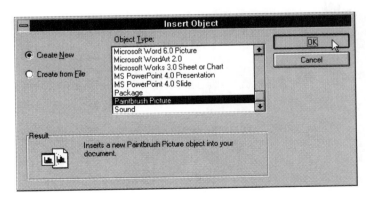

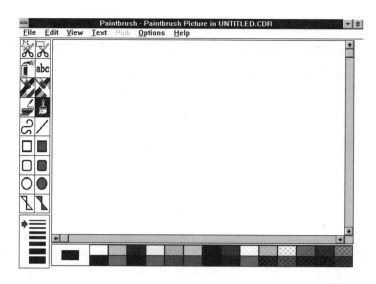

Figure 13. Clicking on *OK* in the *Insert Object* dialog box opens the *Paintbrush* application.

You can work with the *Paintbrush* window as it appears, or you can maximize it as we did in this example. The title bar of *Paintbrush* displays the title of your CorelDRAW file.

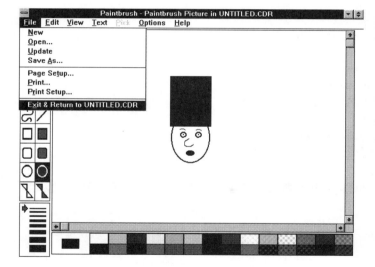

Figure 14. Once you have created the source document, you then embed the object into the CorelDRAW file. The way you do this differs depending on the application you are using. In *Paintbrush,* for example, you can use either the *Update* or the *Exit & Return to...* command from the **File** menu.

Using the *Update* command inserts the object into Corel-DRAW, while keeping *Paintbrush* open.

You can then continue to make changes to the *Paintbrush* document, updating the object in CorelDRAW when necessary by choosing *Update* again. We are selecting *Exit & Return to...* in this example.

Figure 15. Using the *Exit & Return to...* command brings up this warning. Click on the *Yes* button to embed the object into your CorelDRAW file.

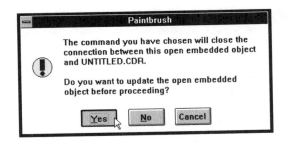

Figure 16. Once you have placed the object in CorelDRAW, you can move it around with the Pick Tool, just as you would do any CorelDRAW object.

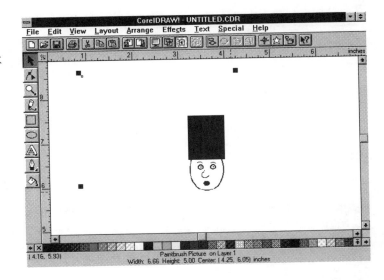

Figure 17. Because you have embedded the object, you can select it and choose *Edit Paintbrush Picture Object* from the **Edit** menu to open the original application to make any changes. Again, you can use the *Update* or *Exit* command in Paintbrush to update the destination file.

Alternatively, double-click on the embedded object to open the source program.

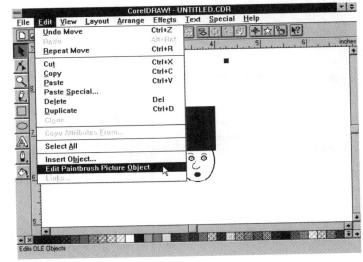

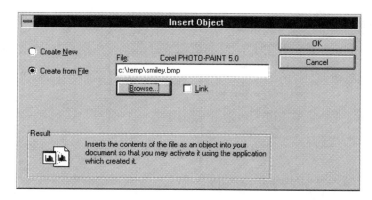

Figure 18. The *Create from File* option lets you insert an existing file as an embedded object. Type the path and name of the file into the *File* text box after you click on the *Create from File* option.

Alternatively, click on the *Browse* button to open a dialog box similar to the *Open* dialog box where you can choose the file you want. Then click on *OK* to embed the file into the current CorelDRAW drawing.

If you check the *Link* option, the file you select is linked to the CorelDRAW file. For more information on linking, see the **Paste Special** section earlier in this chapter.

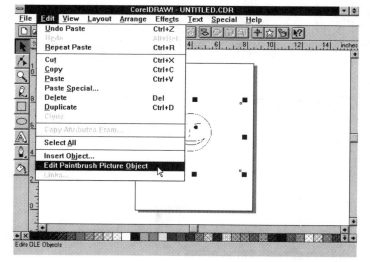

OBJECT

Figure 19. You can access the *Object* command only when you have selected a linked or embedded item on the CorelDRAW screen. The command changes according to the type of item you select.

Choosing this command opens the program that you created the selected object in. You can now edit this object in its original program and update the changes in the CorelDRAW file.

For more information, see the **Paste Special** and **Insert Object** sections earlier in this chapter.

LINKS

Figure 20. When you select the *Links* command, the *Links* dialog box appears. You can access this dialog box only when you have linked items in the current CorelDRAW file. This dialog box lists all the items that you have linked to the CorelDRAW file.

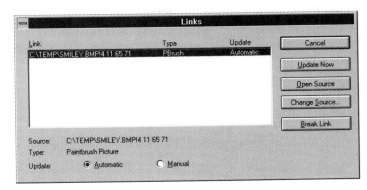

The information in this dialog box contains the source path, the source type (what program it was created in) and whether CorelDRAW updates the file automatically or manually.

Checking the *Automatic* option in the *Update* section ensures that CorelDRAW automatically updates any changes you make to a linked file in the source program. With the *Manual* option selected, you must click on the *Update Now* button in the *Links* dialog box to update any changes to source files. You must first select the link from the list in this dialog box before you can update it.

Choosing the *Open Source* button in the *Links* dialog box opens the source program and file that you have selected from the *Links* list.

Choosing the *Break Link* option removes the link between the source file selected in the *Link* list and CorelDRAW.

Figure 21. Click on the *Change Source* button in the *Links* dialog box to open the *Change Source* dialog box. From the list in this box, select a file to become the new source file. CorelDRAW then receives the OLE information from the new file.

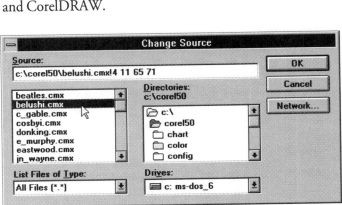

THE VIEW MENU 6

THE VIEW MENU COMMANDS

The commands in the **View** menu do not have a direct effect on any objects on your page. Rather they make changes to the screen and its components.

Figure 1. This figure shows the View menu and its commands.

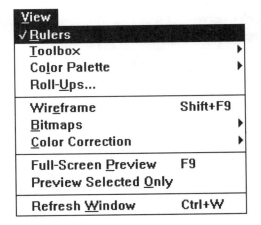

SHOWING RULERS

Figure 2. The *Rulers* command from the **View** menu displays or hides the horizontal and vertical rulers on the screen.

In this example we have disabled the rulers.

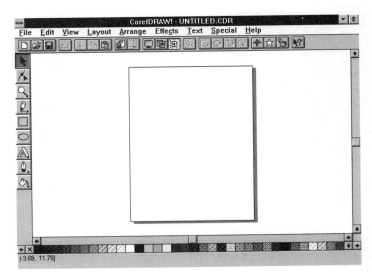

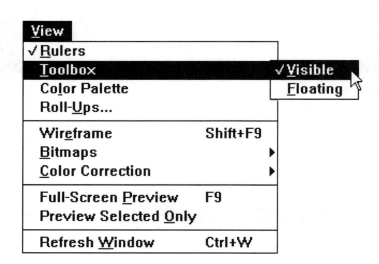

FLOATING TOOLBOX

Figure 3. Selecting the *Toolbox* command in the **View** menu activates this submenu. You can select the *Visible* command here as a toggle switch to either show or hide the Toolbox.

Figure 4. Selecting the *Floating* command (see Figure 3) switches the Toolbox from its normal position at the extreme left side of the screen to a floating tool palette.

As an alternative to selecting the *Floating* command, you can hold down the Shift key and drag the Toolbox to where you want it.

Figure 5. You can move the floating Toolbox around the screen by dragging its title bar. Release the mouse button when the Toolbox is where you want it to be.

   You can also resize the Toolbox by dragging its sides to the size you want.

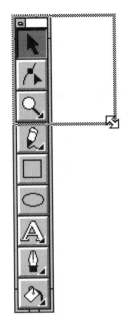

Figure 6. To return the Toolbox to its original spot, choose the *Floating* command again (see Figure 3), or activate the Toolbox's **Control** menu (▣) and deselect the *Floating* option, as in this example.

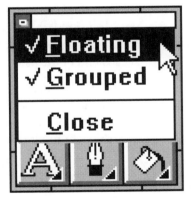

Figure 7. You can also select the *Grouped* command from the Toolbox's **Control** menu (see Figure 6) to ungroup or group the tools in the Toolbox. When you ungroup the Toolbox tools, all of the subsets of tools in the Toolbox are visible.

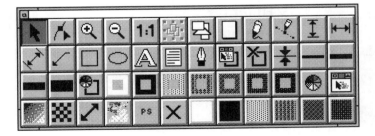

COLOR PALETTE

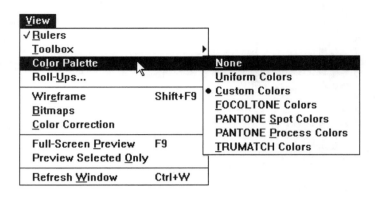

Figure 8. This command activates a submenu with seven options. The *None* option removes the Color palette from the bottom of the screen. The *Uniform Colors* option displays a RGB color palette and the *Custom Colors* option displays the current Custom palette you have loaded. The next four options let you use Focoltone, Pantone spot or process colors, or Trumatch Process colors. (See **Chapter 3, Outline and Fill Tools**, for more information on Color palettes.)

The Color palette lets you apply a different fill or outline color to a selected object quickly and easily. Click on the color you want with the left mouse button to apply a fill to the selected object. To change the outline color, click on the color you want with the right mouse button. Use the arrows at each end of the palette to scroll to colors you can't see.

The (✗) button at the very left of the palette lets you remove the fill and outline of a selected object. Clicking on it with the left mouse button removes the fill, and clicking on it with the right mouse button removes the outline.

DISPLAYING ROLL-UPS

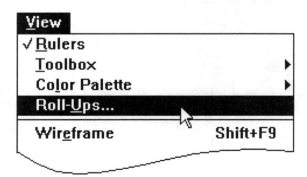

Figure 9. The *Roll-Ups* command in the **View** menu opens the *Roll-Ups* dialog box where you can select the roll-ups you want to display on your screen.

Figure 10. Select the roll-up you want to display from the *Roll-Ups* list. To display the selected roll-up on your screen, check the *Visible* box. By default the *Arranged* check box is selected to automatically arrange your roll-ups on your screen.

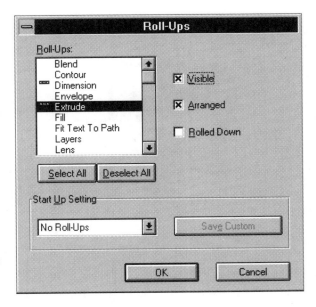

You can also click in the *Rolled Down* check box if you want your roll-ups to display rolled-down on your screen.

The *Select All* and *Deselect All* buttons select or deselect all of the roll-ups in the list so that you can apply the commands to them all at once.

Figure 11. The *Start Up Setting* drop-down list allows you to determine which roll-ups you want to display every time you start CorelDRAW.

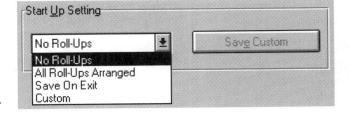

When you click on *OK*, the roll-ups you selected appear on your screen, either arranged or not, depending on the choices you made in the *Roll-Ups* dialog box.

(a)

(b)

WIREFRAME

Figure 12. The *Wireframe* command switches you back and forth between *editable preview* (a), and *wireframe* view (b). You may find it easier and faster to work in *wireframe* view, and then move back to *editable preview,* to preview the drawing.

Use the Shift+F9 keys to move between the two views quickly.

You can also move to and from *wireframe* view using the *Wireframe* icon on the ribbon bar.

BITMAPS

Figure 13. Selecting the *Bitmaps* command in the **View** menu activates this submenu. The *Visible* command allows you to show or hide any bitmaps when you are in the *wireframe* view only; when you deselect the *Visible* command, bitmaps appear as empty rectangles. A bitmap that you have hidden on the *wireframe* screen still displays in *editable preview,* or when previewing a drawing.

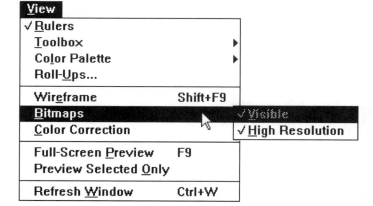

The *High Resolution* command is only available in *editable preview* and allows you to view your bitmaps in high resolution.

COLOR CORRECTION

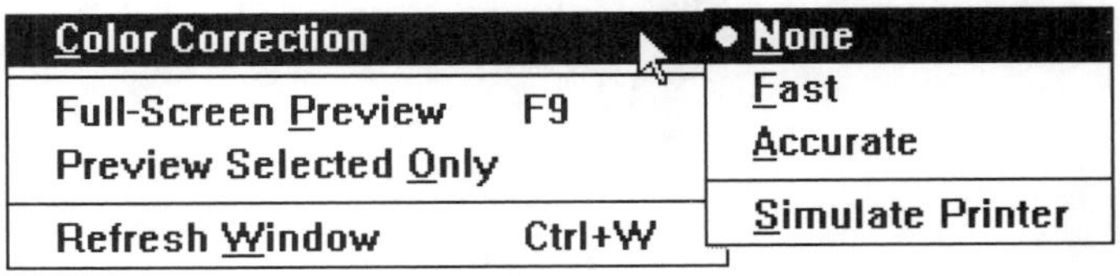

Figure 14. The *Color Correction* command allows you to determine how you want your preview colors to display. The options in this submenu only affect the way your colors appear on your screen, not how they will print out. The *Color Correction* options are simply a way of determining how accurately you display colors on screen compared to the final printout colors.

To use this command you first need to establish a *System Profile* (see **Color Manager** in **Chapter 4, The File Menu**) in which you tell CorelDRAW details of the various aspects of your system. CorelDRAW can then use these details to predict how colors will print out.

Select the *None* command from the *Color Correction* submenu for CorelDRAW to use no color correction, resulting in the fastest screen redraws. The *Fast* command uses a limited amount of color correction while at the same time allowing a fast screen draw. The *Accurate* command takes a longer time for colors to display, but the end result is a more accurate approximation of the real color. The *Simulate Printer* command slows the screen refresh rate as it approximates your colors to how they will print out on the printer you specified in your *System Profile*.

FULL-SCREEN PREVIEW

Figure 15. The *Full-Screen Preview* command previews your page without any page boundaries, Toolbox, status line, or menu bar. The F9 key moves you quickly back and forth between the preview and your artwork. You can also deactivate the preview screen by pressing any key on the keyboard.

You can also move to the preview screen by clicking on the *Full-Screen Preview* icon on the ribbon bar.

PREVIEW SELECTED ONLY

The *Preview Selected Only* command acts as a toggle switch that operates with the *Full-Screen Preview* command. When you select *Preview Selected Only*, the full preview screen only displays objects that you have selected.

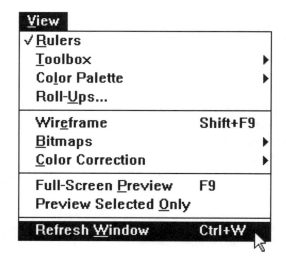

REFRESH WINDOW

Figure 16. If you have interrupted a screen redraw, you can redraw the objects on it by selecting the *Refresh Window* command. This also cleans up any remnants of previous CorelDRAW editing that may remain on the screen.

Alternatively, clicking on either scroll button (▣) redraws the screen. This works in either *editable preview* or *wireframe* view.

THE LAYOUT MENU 7

THE LAYOUT MENU COMMANDS

The commands in the **Layout** menu generally relate to the whole document. These commands include page, layer, style, grid, and guideline options.

Figure 1. This figure displays the **Layout** menu and its commands.

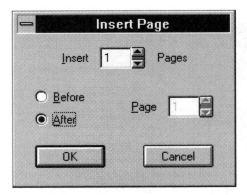

Layout
Insert Page...
Delete Page...
Go To Page...
Page Setup...
Layers Roll-Up   Ctrl+F3
Styles Roll-Up   Ctrl+F5
Grid & Scale Setup...
Guidelines Setup...
Snap To Grid   Ctrl+Y
√ Snap To Guidelines
Snap To Objects

INSERT PAGE

Figure 2. The first command in the **Layout** menu is the *Insert Page* command. This opens the *Insert Page* dialog box.

Change the number in the *Insert # Pages* option to the amount you want to include in your CorelDRAW file. You can have up to 999 pages.

Insert Page

Insert [1] Pages

○ Before
◉ After
Page [1]

OK   Cancel

You then specify where the page or pages insert in your document. Click on the *Before* or *After* option and then choose the page before or after which you want to insert the pages. Click on *OK* to insert the new pages.

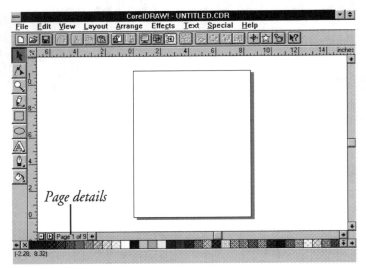

Page details

Figure 3. After you insert some pages, depending on where and how many you inserted, you will see a page add icon (⊞), or a page forward icon (▶), and a page back icon (◀). You will also see the total number of pages and the number of the current page, as shown in this figure.

A page add icon (⊞) appears when you are on the last or first page of the document. Clicking on it brings up the *Insert Page* dialog box so you can add more pages.

The page forward (▶) and page back (◀) icons move you from one page to the next. If you have more than five pages in your document, clicking on one of these icons with the right mouse button moves you five pages at a time. If you click on the page back icon with the Ctrl key held down, you will move to the first page of the document. Using the page forward icon and the Ctrl key produces the opposite effect.

DELETE PAGE

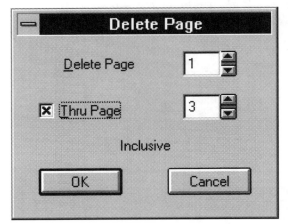

Figure 4. If you need to delete a page, choose the *Delete Page* command from the **Layout** menu to open the *Delete Page* dialog box. Here you can choose the page number which you want to delete. If you click on the *Thru Page* option, you can delete a number of pages ranging from the number you have in the top edit box through to the number you have in the one below.

GO TO PAGE

Figure 5. The *Go To Page* command in the **Layout** menu opens the *Go To Page* dialog box which allows you to move directly to a page number that you specify. Key in the number of the page you want, and click on *OK*. CorelDRAW then moves you to that page.

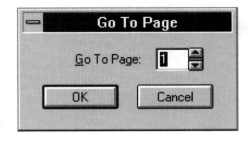

Figure 6. You can also open the *Go To Page* dialog box by clicking once on the page number indicator.

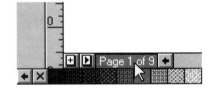

PAGE SETUP

Figure 7. Selecting the *Page Setup* command in the **Layout** menu opens the *Page Setup* dialog box. By default, the *Size* tab is selected. The first option in this tab is the paper size drop-down list which determines the size of the page you are working on.

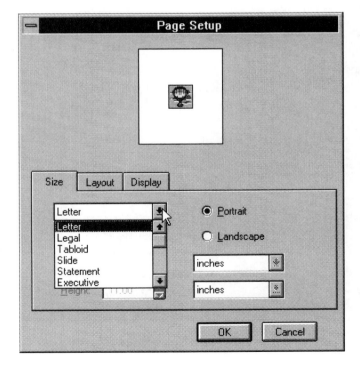

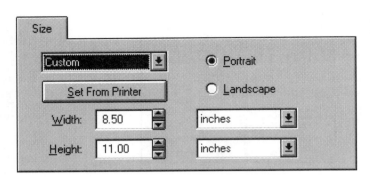

Figure 8. You can choose one of the preset page size options from the drop-down list, or you can select the *Custom* option from the bottom of this list. This then activates the *Width* and *Height* edit boxes where you can set your own page size.

If you click on the *Set From Printer* button, CorelDRAW automatically assigns the paper size and orientation to match the current paper size you've set for printing.

You also have the option of choosing either *Portrait* (vertical) or *Landscape* (horizontal) layouts.

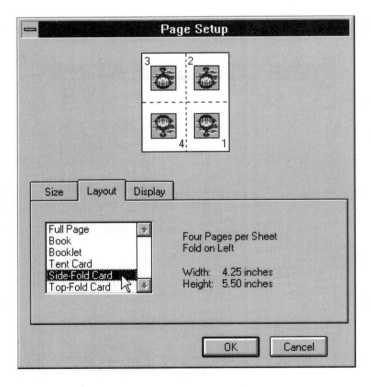

Figure 9. Selecting the *Layout* tab activates the *Layout* options for the *Page Setup* dialog box. The list box here contains a number of preset page layouts you can select. The *Full Page* option is the normal, default setting. If you choose one of the other options, CorelDRAW arranges the pages so they are in the correct order for publication, even though each page appears separately in CorelDRAW.

For instance, selecting the *Side-Fold Card* option displays the print layout CorelDRAW uses to prepare your document to be made into a card. In this case, page one is the bottom right of the card, page two inverted is the top right, three inverted is the top left and four the bottom left. You can then fold this layout to make your card.

Figure 10. In the *Display* tab of the *Page Setup* dialog box, you can choose to display facing pages (i.e. side by side if you have multiple pages in the document). If you do select the *Facing Pages* option, you can choose whether the pages start to face each other on an odd or an even page.

For instance, if you choose the *Facing Pages* and *Left First* options, pages 1 and 2 of your document would display together, where choosing *Right First* would leave page one on its own and display pages 2 and 3 together.

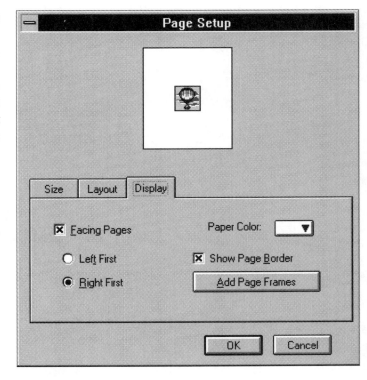

Figure 11. The *Paper Color* palette lets you apply a color to the page when you are working in *editable preview* or viewing the preview screen. This only affects the page on screen; it doesn't print with this color.

Click on the *More* button at the bottom of the palette to access all the color methods. Select white from this palette to return the page to normal.

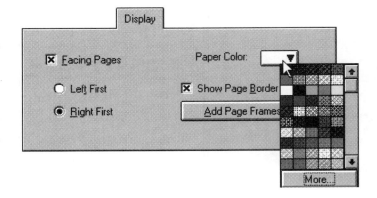

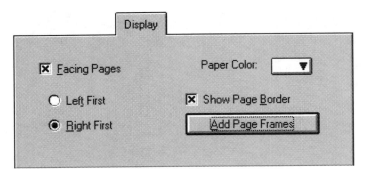

Figure 12. If you deselect the *Show Page Border* option on the *Display* tab of the *Page Setup* dialog box, the page border on the screen disappears.

Clicking on the *Add Page Frame* options on the *Display* tab puts a rectangle on the page that is the same size as the current page. You can fill, outline, or resize this rectangle as you would any other rectangle. Double-clicking on the Rectangle Tool also adds a rectangle to the page.

Click on the *OK* button in the *Page Setup* dialog box to return to the drawing with any changes you have made. Changing any of the *Page Setup* options affects all pages in the document.

LAYERS ROLL-UP

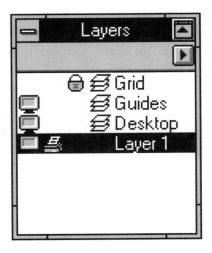

Figure 13. Selecting the *Layers Roll-Up* command from the **Layout** menu brings up the *Layers* roll-up. CorelDRAW lets you create as many layers in a document as you need. You can place objects on different layers. The advantages of layers are discussed in this section.

The *Layers* roll-up contains four layers that appear in each new file. When you begin drawing objects in a new file, CorelDRAW places them on *Layer 1*. Selecting a layer from the list in the roll-up switches to that layer.

GRID LAYER

You cannot draw or place objects on the *Grid* layer. It contains only the grid, which you access through the **Layout** menu. Having a separate layer for the grid lets you disable the grid quickly and easily.

GUIDES LAYER

Any guidelines you place on the page are automatically placed on the *Guides* layer. Objects on all layers will snap to the guidelines if you select *Snap To Guidelines* from the **Layout** menu. You can put objects on the *Guides* layer; these are known as guide objects and are dashed like guidelines. Any objects on the *Guides* layer act as normal guides and objects snap to them.

DESKTOP LAYER

Figure 14. Objects are automatically placed on the *Desktop* layer if you drag them off the page onto the pasteboard area.

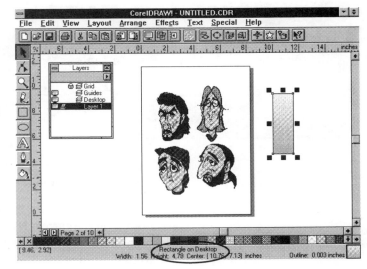

When you are working with multiple page documents, you can see the *Desktop* layer (objects not on the page) on any page you are viewing. This lets you drag objects from the *Desktop* layer onto any page in the document without having to copy and paste them through the Windows Clipboard.

The status line in this example indicates that the selected object off the page is on the *Desktop* layer.

LAYERS FLY-OUT MENU

Figure 15. Clicking on the ▶ icon in the *Layers* roll-up opens the *Layers* fly-out menu.

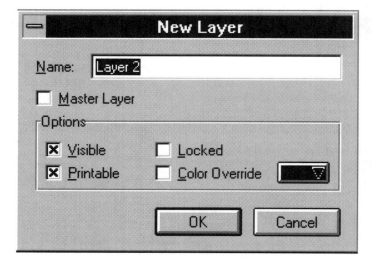

Figure 16. Selecting *New* from the *Layers* fly-out menu brings up the *New Layer* dialog box. This box automatically displays a name for the *Layer* you are about to create.

CorelDRAW assumes you are going to name the layers in order (e.g. the next layer after *Layer 1* will be *Layer 2*). You can keep this name or create your own, with a maximum of 32 characters. After clicking on *OK,* the *Layers* roll-up displays the new layer name in its list.

For more information on the *Master Layer* option, see **Master Layer** later in this chapter.

Deselecting the *Visible* option lets you temporarily hide the objects on the current layer. This does not affect the printing of these objects. Hiding layers also lets you speed up screen redrawing time.

Selecting the *Locked* option from the *New Layer* dialog box locks the objects on the current layer. You can't select or edit the objects on the locked layer. You can add and edit objects on a locked layer, but as soon as you deselect the object, you can't select it again.

The *Printable* option lets you print only the layers that you have checked this option for. If you don't want to print a layer, deselect this option.

Color Override gives you the option of assigning an outline color to all objects in the layer. This doesn't affect the true fill and outline of the objects, it simply lets you see through them if you are working on the objects underneath. Select the color from the Color palette that appears when you click on the color swatch.

CorelDRAW assigns this color to the objects only when you place a check mark in the *Color Override* option.

The *Locked* option in the *Grid* layer is constantly on; you can't deselect it. The *Color Override* option is a default in the *Guides* and *Grid* layers; you can't deactivate it.

Figure 17. Selecting *Edit* from the *Layers* fly-out menu opens the *Edit Layers* dialog box, which has the same options as the *New Layer* dialog box. Only this time you can select each layer and alter its properties as you need. The name of the active layer appears in the text box at the top of the dialog box.

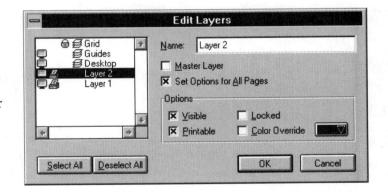

Figure 18. The *Edit Layers* dialog box for the *Guides* and *Grid* layers also includes a *Setup* button. Clicking on this button opens the *Guidelines* or *Grid Setup* dialog box—depending on which layer is active.

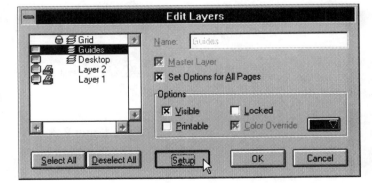

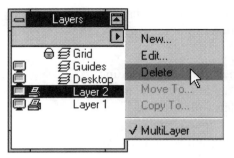

Figure 19. Selecting *Delete* from the *Layers* fly-out menu removes the active layer and all the objects on it. The layer directly below the layer that you delete then becomes the active layer.

Figure 20. The *Move To* command from the *Layers* fly-out menu lets you move selected objects to another layer. Select *Move To* to display the () arrow. With this arrow, click on the layer in the list where you want to move the selected objects.

The *Copy To* command from the *Layers* fly-out menu works in the same way as the *Move To* command, except it places a copy of the selected object on the selected layer. The original object remains on its original layer.

The *MultiLayer* command is active when it has a checkmark next to it in the *Layers* fly-out menu. When the *MultiLayer* command is active, you can select any object on any layer. If you deselect this option, you can select only the objects on the current layer. You can't select objects on locked layers, even with the *MultiLayer* option selected.

Figure 21. Changing the order of the layers in the roll-up list also changes the order of the layers in the drawing.

Using the mouse, you can drag a layer name into a new position in the *Layers* roll-up. This changes the order of the layers in the drawing. In this example we have moved *Layer 1* to the top of the list.

Figure 22. This may cause some objects to cover other objects that previously covered them. The stacking order commands in the *Order* submenu of the **Arrange** menu (*To Front, To Back, Forward One, Back One,* and *Reverse Order*) change the order of the selected objects within a layer only. Choosing *To Back,* for example, moves a selected object behind all other objects in that layer, but it will still be on top of any objects in lower layers.

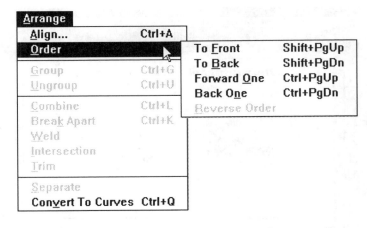

You can select objects from different layers simultaneously. You can also group and combine them. When you group or combine objects from different layers, the objects move to the current layer.

When combining objects, CorelDRAW assigns the fill and color of the last object selected (or the most recently selected object if marquee selecting). The status line always tells you which layer a selected object is on.

MASTER LAYER

Figure 23. To create a master layer, select the *Edit* command from the *Layers* fly-out menu to open the *Edit Layers* dialog box. You can then select the layer you want as a master layer from the list of layers and check the *Master Layer* option in this dialog box. This makes all of the objects in the current layer appear on every page of your document.

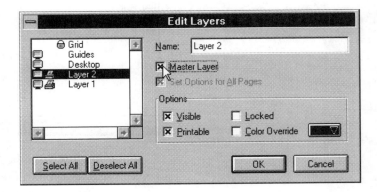

In this example we applied the *Master Layer* option to *Layer 2*. All our *Layer 2* options will now appear on every page.

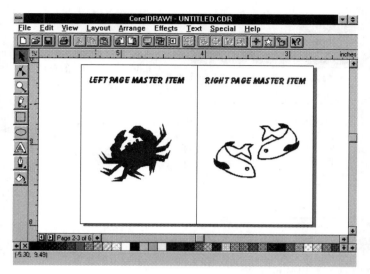

Figure 24. If you have facing pages, all left page items will appear on the left pages in the document, while all right page items will appear on the right pages in the document.

If you do not want a *Master Layer* item to appear on a certain page, deselect *Set Options for All Pages* on that page.

If you delete or move a *Master Layer* item on any page, this affects all corresponding *Master Layer* items on other pages.

STYLES ROLL-UP

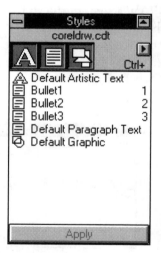

Figure 25. The *Styles Roll-Up* command in the **Layout** menu brings up the *Styles* roll-up. This roll-up lets you apply styles to items on the page. Styles are a group of saved attributes that you can use to format Artistic Text, Paragraph Text, and graphics quickly and easily.

If you have experience with a word processing or a page layout program, you will be familiar with styles.

When you first open the *Styles* roll-up (and you have no objects selected) you will see a number of styles already listed. The styles listed in this figure are the default template styles. If you have another template file loaded, the styles will be different. These styles include the default settings for Artistic Text, Paragraph Text and graphics, as well as three extra Paragraph Text styles.

Figure 26. The three icons at the top of the *Styles* roll-up let you show/hide some or all of the style types, including Artistic Text styles (Ⓐ), Paragraph Text styles (▤), and graphics styles (▨). In this example, we clicked on all three buttons to deactivate them, and thus hide all the styles.

STYLES FLY-OUT MENU

Figure 27. Clicking on the ▶ icon in the *Styles* roll-up brings up the *Styles* fly-out menu.

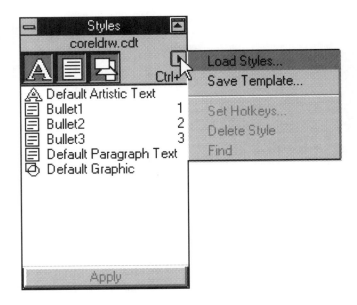

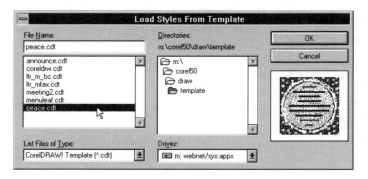

Figure 28. The *Load Styles* command in the *Styles* fly-out menu opens the *Load Styles From Template* dialog box.

In the ***corel50\draw\template*** directory you will see a list of files with a *.cdt* extension. These are the template files that come with CorelDRAW, and they all contain different styles.

You can load new styles into your *Styles* roll-up by selecting a new template from the list in this dialog box and clicking on *OK*. A template is a special kind of document that you save to include all your style details.

For more information on templates, see the **New From Template** section in **Chapter 4, The File Menu**.

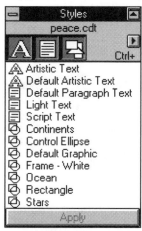

Figure 29. After selecting a template from the *Load Styles From Template* dialog box and clicking on *OK*, the styles in the *Styles* roll-up change to include the styles contained in the selected template.

CREATING AND SAVING A STYLE TEMPLATE

You can create and save your own template of styles and then open this template to create documents later or load the styles from this template into any CorelDRAW document.

After creating all the necessary styles, you can save them in a template file. This does not affect naming or saving the current CorelDRAW file.

For more information on creating styles, see **Chapter 12, The Object Menu**.

Figure 30. To save a template, choose *Save Template* from the *Styles* fly-out menu in the *Styles* roll-up. This opens the *Save Template* dialog box. This dialog box works like the *Save Drawing* dialog box, in that you must name the file and choose where you want to save it.

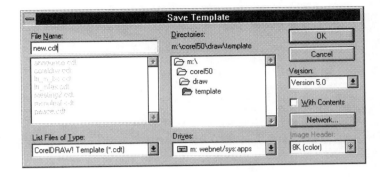

CorelDRAW automatically applies a *.cdt* extension to the file name.

The *With Contents* option saves the file with any objects you have on the page when you save the template. You can choose the *Image Header* option if you save the template with any objects on the page; you can then view the template file in the preview box of the *Load Styles From Template* dialog box (Figure 28).

Figure 31. You can also save a template through the *Save Drawing* dialog box. Choose the *CorelDRAW Template (*.cdt)* option from the *List Files of Type* drop-down list. However, when you save a template this way, the name of the file takes on the name of the template.

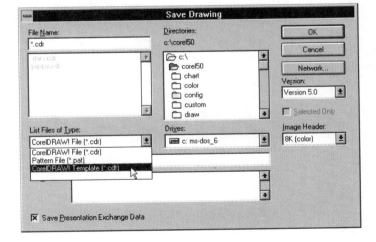

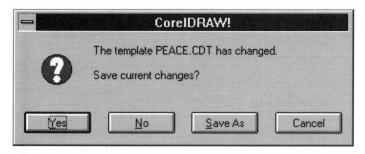

Figure 32. If you make changes to the current template (like adding or deleting a style), you are warned whenever you go to load new styles or exit CorelDRAW.

If you click on the *Save As* option on the screen prompt in this figure, you activate the *Save Template* dialog box, where you can save the amended template file under a new name. The changes you made to the template will then not affect the original template file.

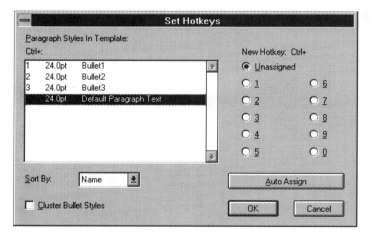

Figure 33. You can choose the *Set Hotkeys* option in the *Styles* fly-out menu (Figure 27) only if you have one of the Paragraph Text styles selected in the *Styles* roll-up. Choosing this option opens the *Set Hotkeys* dialog box.

Here you can assign keystrokes to your Paragraph Text styles. You can then apply these styles to selected Paragraph Text quickly and easily by pressing a key combination.

The Paragraph Text styles of the current template appear in the list in this dialog box. Listed under the *Ctrl+* heading are the current hotkeys assigned to a style. The number here is the key you press in conjunction with the Ctrl key to apply the style.

Figure 34. To assign a hotkey to any of the styles not already assigned, select the style from the list and click on a number (one that is not already used in a key combination). In this example, we selected the *Default Paragraph Text* style and clicked on the number *4*. This number then appears next to the style in this dialog box.

If you choose a number that is already assigned to a style, this key combination is then removed from the original style and is assigned to the new style.

You can change the keystroke for a style by choosing the style from the list in this dialog box and clicking on a different number.

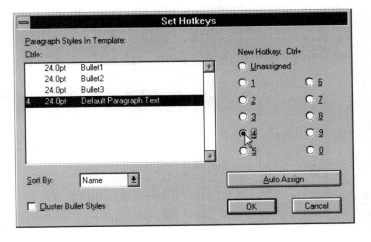

Figure 35. If you do not want a style to have a key combination assigned to it, select the style from the list in the *Set Hotkeys* dialog box and click on the *Unassigned* option.

You can use the *Auto Assign* button in the *Set Hotkeys* dialog box to have CorelDRAW automatically assign keystrokes to any listed Paragraph Text styles that are unassigned.

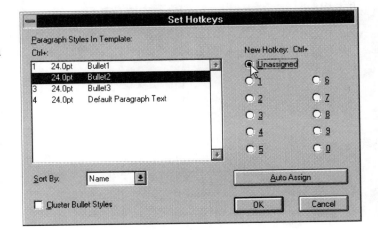

Figure 36. The *Sort By* drop-down list in the *Set Hotkeys* dialog box gives you two options for listing the styles in this dialog box. You can list them either by *Name* (alphabetically) or by *Font Size* (from largest to smallest).

The *Cluster Bullet Styles* check box lets you group all the styles in the *Set Hotkeys* dialog box that include bullets. For more information on bullets, see **Chapter 10, The Text Menu**.

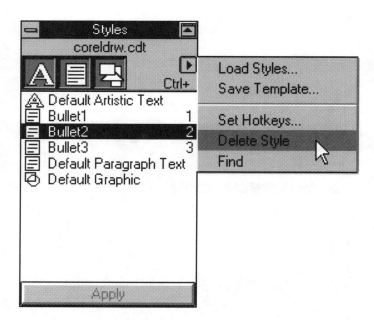

Figure 37. The *Delete Style* option in the *Styles* fly-out menu lets you delete the style currently selected in the *Styles* roll-up. You cannot delete a default style.

The *Find* command automatically selects the first object (text or graphic) in your drawing that is using the style currently highlighted in the *Styles* roll-up. This command then changes to *Find Next*, letting you find the next object with this style.

APPLYING STYLES

Figure 38. To apply a style to an object (text or graphic), first select the object with the Pick Tool, choose the required style from the *Styles* roll-up and click on the *Apply* button (a). The result in this example is shown in (b).

If you are applying styles to Paragraph Text, you can use Hotkeys to apply the style. See Figures 33 through 36 earlier in this chapter for more information.

(a)

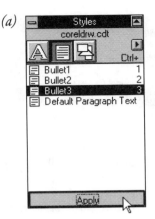

(b)

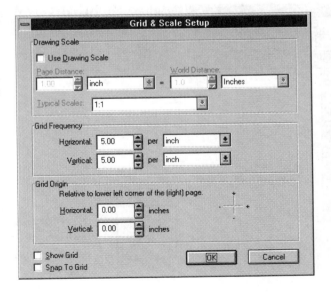

GRID & SCALE SETUP

Figure 39. The *Grid & Scale Setup* command in the **Layout** menu opens the *Grid & Scale Setup* dialog box, which you can also open by double-clicking anywhere on the vertical or horizontal ruler.

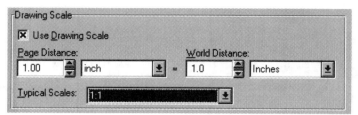

Figure 40. Check the *Use Drawing Scale* option when you want to set a particular scale in your drawing with one unit of measurement equaling another unit of measurement in the rulers.

The options in the first drop-down list in this section of the dialog box let you set the page unit of measurement in relation to the *World Distance* unit of measurement in the second drop-down list.

The *Typical Scales* drop-down list allows you to quickly apply a typical drawing scale to your settings.

The *Grid Frequency* settings in the *Grid & Scale Setup* dialog box determine the spacing of the grid. For example, if you have 1 per inch for both the *Horizontal* and *Vertical* settings, your grid will consist of 1 inch squares.

Changing the *Grid Origin* settings determines where the zero point of the rulers is on your page. The default *Grid Origin* is the bottom left of the current page. If, for example, you are working in inches, and you change the *Horizontal* and *Vertical Grid Origin* settings to 5 and 5, the zero point moves up and across the page 5 inches.

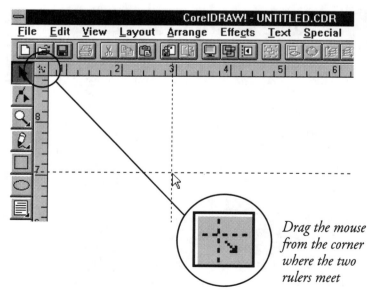

Figure 41. You can also change the zero point of the rulers with the mouse. To do this, drag the icon in the corner where the two rulers meet down and across. Wherever you release the mouse button is the new zero point.

Drag the mouse from the corner where the two rulers meet

Figure 42. The *Show Grid* option, at the bottom left of the *Grid & Scale Setup* dialog box (Figure 39), gives you the option of displaying the grid on the screen. Checking this option covers the screen in dots representing the grid.

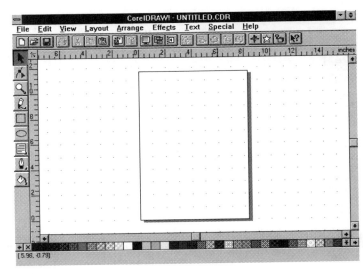

The *Snap To Grid* option at the bottom left of the *Grid & Scale Setup* dialog box is the same as the *Snap To Grid* command at the bottom of the **Layout** menu (discussed later in this chapter).

GUIDELINES SETUP

Figure 43. The *Guidelines Setup* command in the **Layout** menu brings up the *Guidelines Setup* dialog box. The options available here let you place horizontal and vertical guidelines on the page. The *View* section of this dialog box allows you to set the guideline type; *Horizontal* or *Vertical*. You can then determine where this horizontal or vertical guideline goes on the page by entering a value for it in the text box available. The guideline will appear at that point on the corresponding ruler. The setting is in relation to the zero point of the rulers.

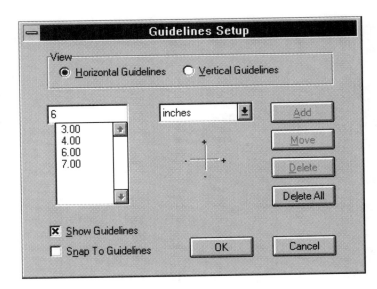

Click on the *Add* button once to add this guideline to the guidelines list and to your page. You can continue adding guidelines to your page in this way for the vertical or horizontal guide list.

The *Delete* option removes the selected guideline from the list and your page.

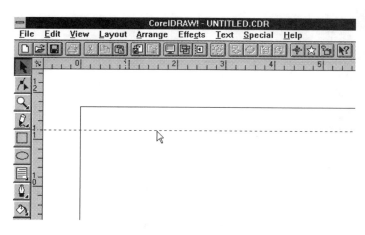

Figure 44. You can also add guidelines to your page by holding the mouse button down when the cursor is on the vertical or horizontal ruler and dragging out onto the page. Release the mouse button where you want the guideline.

You can move guidelines by dragging them to a new position. Dragging a guideline back into the ruler removes it from the page. Double-clicking on a guideline brings up the *Guidelines Setup* dialog box in Figure 43. Selecting the *Snap To Guidelines* option from this dialog box is the same as the command of the same name in the **Layout** menu (discussed later in this chapter) and the *Show Guidelines* check box allows you to determine if the guidelines appear on your screen.

SNAP TO GRID

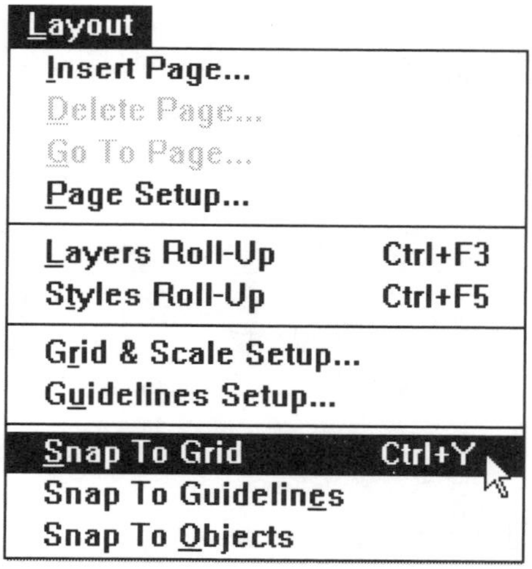

Figure 45. The *Snap To Grid* command in the **Layout** menu forces the mouse to stay on the grid you specified in the *Grid & Scale Setup* dialog box when you are creating, moving, and resizing objects (see **Grid & Scale Setup** earlier in this chapter). There are some exceptions to this rule: selecting objects; drawing curves with the Pencil Tool and autotracing; rotating and skewing objects; manipulating ellipses with the Shape Tool; and using the Zoom Tool.

The status line always shows if the *Snap To Grid* option is on. Activating or deactivating this command is the same as selecting or deselecting the same option in the *Grid & Scale Setup* dialog box (Figure 39).

SNAP TO GUIDELINES

If you have placed any guidelines on your page (see **Guidelines Setup** above), any objects you move or draw near a guideline snap to it when you select the *Snap To Guidelines* command from the **Layout** menu. The *Snap To Guidelines* command takes precedence over the *Snap To Grid* command. You can also set the *Snap To Guidelines* command by clicking on the *Snap To Guidelines* icon on the ribbon bar.

SNAP TO OBJECTS

Figure 46. CorelDRAW provides every object with a certain number of snap points. Each one of these snap points has a restricted gravity range similar to the gravity range of a guideline. The type of object determines the position of these snap points. In this example, we have indicated the snap points of objects with a ⊕.

The *Snap To Objects* command lets you snap an object you are moving to another object that is anchored. The snap point of the object you are moving is where you selected it. If you selected the object within the gravity range of one of its snap points, it uses this snap point for the two objects.

When you move an object within the gravity range of one of the snap points on the anchored object, they will snap together like magnets.

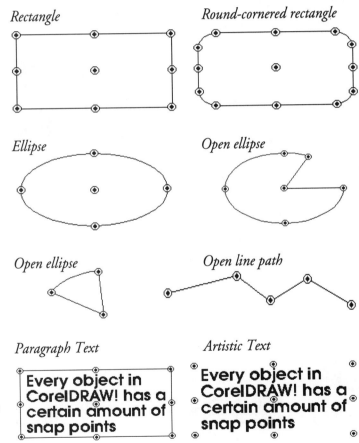

Rectangle

Round-cornered rectangle

Ellipse

Open ellipse

Open ellipse

Open line path

Paragraph Text

Every object in CorelDRAW! has a certain amount of snap points

Artistic Text

Every object in CorelDRAW! has a certain amount of snap points

Bitmap

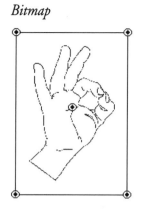

Rotated bitmap

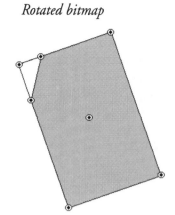

You can add snap points to an object simply by adding a node where you want to put the snap point. In the case of rectangles, ellipses, and text, you must convert them to curves before you can add a node.

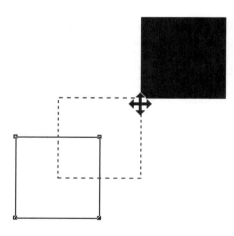

Figure 47. In this example we are moving the white rectangle, with the mouse in the top right corner of the rectangle. (This means that the top right snap point of the white rectangle is the active snap point.) As we move it closer to the black rectangle, it snaps to the bottom left snap point of the black rectangle.

THE ARRANGE MENU 8

THE ARRANGE MENU COMMANDS

The commands in the **Arrange** menu affect the arrangement and position of objects in your current file, and determine whether the objects are independent or connected to other objects.

Figure 1. This figure displays the **Arrange** menu and its commands.

Arrange	
Align...	Ctrl+A
Order	▶
Group	Ctrl+G
Ungroup	Ctrl+U
Combine	Ctrl+L
Brea**k** Apart	Ctrl+K
Weld	
Intersection	
Trim	
Separate	
Con**v**ert To Curves	Ctrl+Q

ALIGN

Figure 2. The *Align* command in the **Arrange** menu opens the *Align* dialog box, which lets you horizontally and vertically align objects. No matter what alignment options you choose, the last object you selected does not move—all other selected objects align around it. If you marquee select, the first object you created is the object around which all others align.

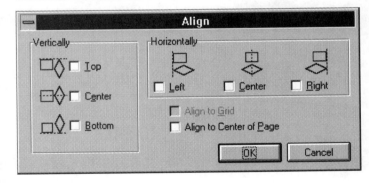

The *Align to Grid* option lets you align objects to the grid, while *Align to Center of Page* aligns objects to the center of the page. Selecting *Align to Center of Page* center aligns the objects in relation to each other and then moves them to the center of the page. If you don't want the objects to center align in relation to each other before moving them to the center of the page you must group the objects first.

You can also bring up the *Align* dialog box by clicking on the *Align* icon on the ribbon bar.

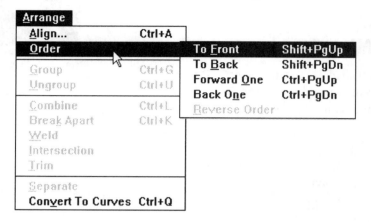

ORDER

Figure 3. The *Order* submenu of the **Arrange** menu contains these commands: *To Front, To Back, Forward One, Back One,* and *Reverse Order.* You use these commands on selected objects to change their drawing position.

TO FRONT

Figure 4. By default, the last object you draw or place on the page sits on top of all other objects.

If you want an object in front of all others on its layer, select it with the Pick Tool, then choose the *To Front* command or click on the *To Front* icon on the ribbon bar.

In this example, we selected the circle (a) and chose *To Front* (b).

(a)   *(b)*

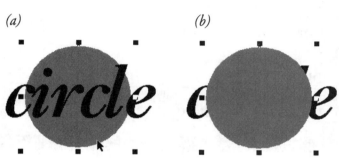

TO BACK

To Back is the opposite of the *To Front* command. If you wish to send to the back any object that is on top of all other objects on its layer, select it with the Pick Tool, then choose *To Back* or click on the *To Back* icon on the ribbon bar.

FORWARD ONE/BACK ONE

Selecting *Forward One* moves the current object forward one place in its layer. Similarly, selecting *Back One* moves the selected object back one place in its layer.

REVERSE ORDER

Figure 5. Using the *Reverse Order* command reverses the places of two or more objects in the layer, either from front to back (a) or back to front (b).

(a)   *(b)*

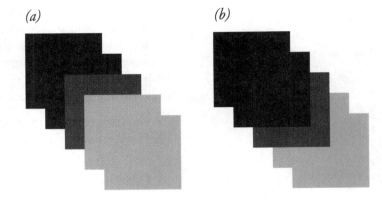

GROUP

Figure 6. The *Group* command in the **Arrange** menu lets you combine objects so that you can then treat them as a single object. You can color and manipulate the grouped objects as you would a single object. This makes applying attributes to more than one object at a time easier.

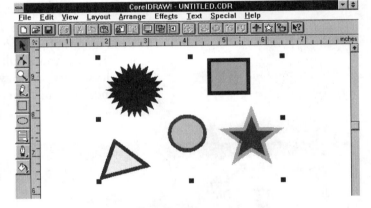

To group objects, select them all with the Pick Tool and choose the *Group* command. When you select any object from a group, CorelDRAW selects the rest of the objects in the group automatically. You cannot use the Shape Tool on a grouped object, but you can use the Pick Tool to resize and move it.

You can apply most features to a grouped object, except for the following: *Combine, Break Apart, Edit Text, Fit Text To Path, Straighten Text, Align To Baseline,* and *Extrude.*

Note: You can group grouped objects with other objects or other groups. You can have up to 10 levels of grouping within a group.

UNGROUP

Selecting *Ungroup* separates a group of objects, returning each object to its independent status, so that you can manipulate them as single objects. If you have levels of grouping, the *Ungroup* command separates what the last *Group* command combined. You must ungroup each set of objects you grouped or each level of grouping, individually.

The *Group* icon on the ribbon bar allows you to switch between grouping and ungrouping objects.

COMBINE

The *Combine* command in the **Layout** menu is a different type of grouping, which you can use for a number of effects and reasons. When you combine two or more objects, wherever they overlap will be a gap or window that you can see through. You can use this to create a mask effect, where you can see one object through parts of another. CorelDRAW automatically converts text, ellipses, and rectangles to curves when you group them with the *Combine* command. You can't edit them as you could before you combined them.

Figure 7. To create this image, we selected the text and the rectangle and combined them. This created a transparent area where the text and the rectangle overlapped. We then placed the image of the unicorn at the back. Because we placed the unicorn on the page last, we needed to use the *To Back* command.

BREAK APART

You apply the *Break Apart* command to objects that you have combined.

WELD

The *Weld* command lets you join or "weld" objects that overlap so they become the one object. It differs from the *Combine* command in that it removes all the overlapping object parts.

Figure 8. Choose the overlapping objects with the Pick Tool before choosing the *Weld* command. Here we are working in *wireframe* view so you can see what happens when you use this command.

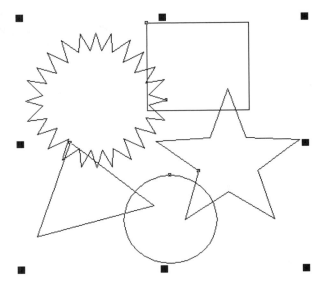

Figure 9. After you choose the *Weld* command, the objects become one continuous object.

When you weld objects, they take on the fill and outline of the last object you selected before you welded them. If you marquee select the objects, they take on the fill and outline of the object at the bottom.

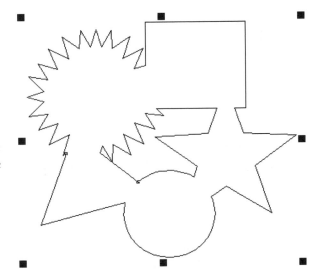

You can also weld single objects that have lines that cross. This breaks the object into several subpaths.

You can weld as many objects as you like at one time. If the objects are on different layers, you must have the *MultiLayer* option checked in the *Layers* fly-out menu (see Figure 20 in **Chapter 7, The Layout Menu**). If the objects are on different layers, select them one by one (with the Shift key held down) to move them to the layer that contains the object you selected last.

If you marquee select the objects, they will all move to the layer containing the object you created first when you weld them. For more information on *Layers*, see **Chapter 7, The Layout Menu**.

INTERSECTION

Figure 10. You use the *Intersection* command in the **Arrange** menu to create a new, additional, object out of the intersection of existing objects. Select the overlapping objects with the Pick Tool (a) and then choose the *Intersection* command from the **Layout** menu. CorelDRAW then creates a new object from the intersection of the original objects (b).

The new object takes the fill and outline attributes of the last object you selected, or the bottom object of a marquee selection. If you have the *MultiLayer* option selected in the *Layers* roll-up you can intersect objects on different layers.

You cannot apply the *Intersection* command to grouped objects.

(a)

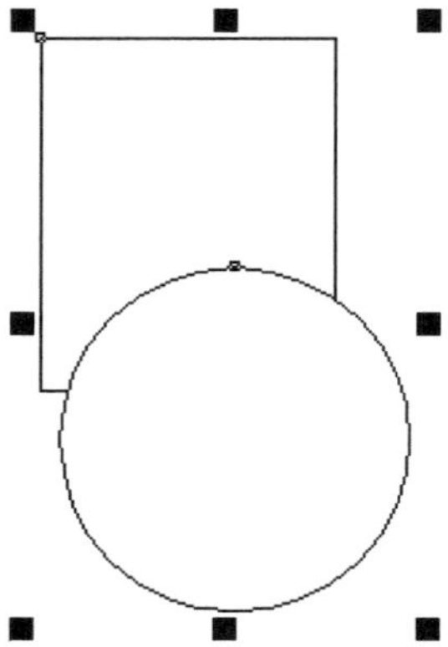

(b)

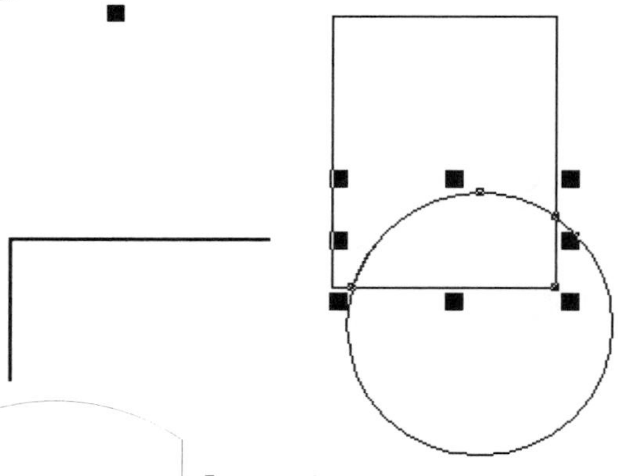

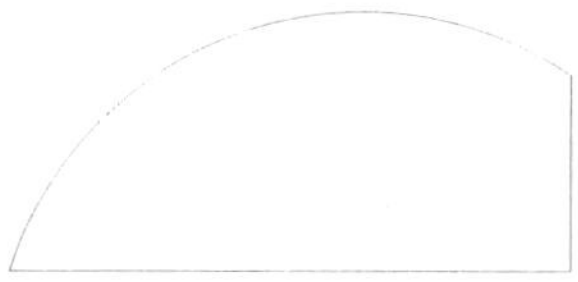

Intersecting the objects in (a) produces a third object as shown here.

TRIM

Figure 11. You use the *Trim* command in the **Arrange** menu to remove (or trim) an area common to overlapping objects. Select the overlapping objects with the Pick Tool (a) and choose the *Trim* command. This trims the last object you selected, or the bottom object of a marquee selection (b). The trimmed object keeps its outline and fill settings.

You cannot apply the *Trim* command to grouped objects. You can trim objects on different layers by making all layers active.

(a)

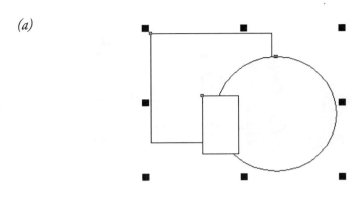

(b)

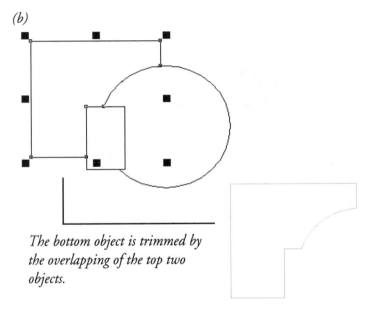

The bottom object is trimmed by the overlapping of the top two objects.

SEPARATE

You use the *Separate* command from the **Arrange** menu on objects that CorelDRAW dynamically links. It dynamically links, for example, the objects that make up the steps of a blend group to the start and end objects of a blend. Dynamic linking also applies between the original object and the objects that form an extrusion.

CONVERT TO CURVES

Figure 12. You apply *Convert To Curves* from the **Layout** menu to text, ellipses, or rectangles, so you can manipulate them with the Shape Tool, as you would any freehand line. In this example, we applied the command to a text string. You can now change the shape of any text character with the Shape Tool.

We converted to curves and then broke apart the letter "A." You cannot see the middle section of the letter, as it also has a black fill. Combining the two objects solves this problem.

Figure 13. Whenever you *Break Apart* text that you have converted to curves, you should remember that some characters, such as an "A," are made up of two objects. You must combine both objects that make up the letter so that it displays correctly.

THE EFFECTS MENU 9

THE EFFECTS MENU COMMANDS

The commands in the **Effects** menu directly relate to the manipulation and applying of special effects to objects.

Figure 1. This figure displays the **Effects** menu with its commands.

Effects	
Transform Roll-Up	
Clear Transformations	
Add Perspective	
Envelope Roll-Up	Ctrl+F7
Blend Roll-Up	Ctrl+B
Extrude Roll-Up	Ctrl+E
Contour Roll-Up	Ctrl+F9
PowerLine Roll-Up	Ctrl+F8
Lens Roll-Up	Alt+F3
PowerClip	▶
Clear Effect	
Copy	▶
Clone	▶

TRANSFORM ROLL-UP

Figure 2. Choosing the *Transform Roll-Up* command from the **Effects** menu opens the *Transform* roll-up. Here you can change the position, size, shape, rotation angle, and scale of any objects on your screen using precise values.

You can also open this roll-up in the same mode it was in the last time you used it by clicking on the *Transform Roll-Up* icon (⊞) on the ribbon bar.

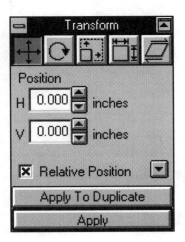

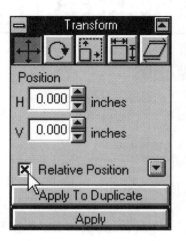

MOVE

Figure 3. The first button in the *Transform* roll-up allows you to enter specific values to move your selected objects. You can either move the selected object relative to the page or to its own position through the *Relative Position* check box. Checking this box means that you will move the object in units relative to its current position, where leaving this box unchecked moves your object to a specific location on your page.

Enter values in the *H*orizontal and *V*ertical spin boxes and click on *Apply* to move your object. To make a copy of the original object and move it, click on the *Apply To Duplicate* button.

(a)

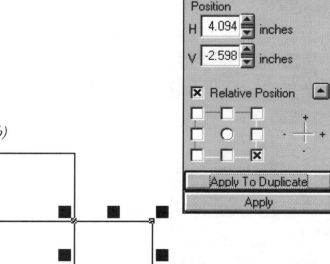

Figure 4. Clicking on the down-arrow button at the bottom of the roll-up extends it to include the object anchor points.

Select an anchor point which the measurements you enter in the *H*orizontal and *V*ertical boxes will be relative to. For instance, if you select the top left corner as an anchor point, any values you enter move your object relative to this point.

(b)

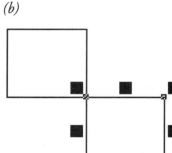

Using anchor points with the *Relative Position* option checked allows you to quickly align objects using the *Apply To Duplicate* button. For instance, figure (b) shows the effect of clicking the bottom right anchor point and clicking the *Apply To Duplicate* button.

ROTATE

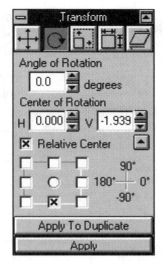

Figure 5. The second button in the *Transform* roll-up allows you to rotate objects using exact values. Enter the amount you want to rotate your objects by in the *Angle of Rotation* spin box. You must then determine the center of rotation for your object (i.e. the point that the object will rotate around).

You can choose a center of rotation quickly and easily by selecting one of the anchor points.

Alternatively, you can enter values in the *Center of Rotation* spin boxes.

If you have *Relative Center* checked, these values move the center of rotation in relation to the current center of rotation for your object. If *Relative Center* is deselected, the values for the *Horizontal* and *Vertical Center of Rotation* are absolute coordinates for your page.

To rotate the original object, click on *Apply*, or click on *Apply To Duplicate* to create and rotate a duplicate of the selected object.

SCALE AND MIRROR

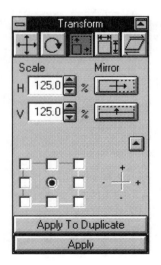

Figure 6. The third button in the *Transform* roll-up allows you to scale and mirror any objects that you have selected, using precise values.

Enter the percentage you want to scale the object by in the *Horizontal* and *Vertical* boxes. Then choose an anchor point for the object to scale from (e.g. the center anchor point scales from the center of the object outwards).

To mirror your object horizontally, click on the top mirror button (Figure 6), and click on the bottom mirror button to mirror your object vertically.

Select *Apply* to scale or mirror your object, or *Apply To Duplicate* to create a duplicate and scale or mirror it.

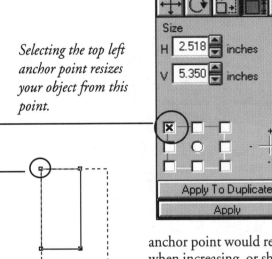

Selecting the top left anchor point resizes your object from this point.

RESIZE

Figure 7. The fourth button in the *Transform* roll-up allows you to size selected objects in exact dimensions.

Enter values in the *H*orizontal and *V*ertical boxes in the *Size* section and then choose an anchor point where you want your object to size from. For instance, choosing the center anchor point resizes your object from the center of the object, whereas choosing the top left anchor point would resize the object to the right and down when increasing, or shrink the object up and left when decreasing its size.

Once again select *Apply* to resize your object, or *Apply To Duplicate* to create a copy of your object to resize.

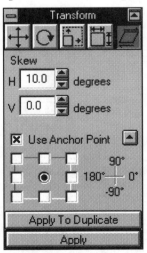

SKEW

Figure 8. The last button in the *Transform* roll-up allows you to skew a selected object using precise values.

Enter the degrees you wish to skew your object by in the *H*orizontal and *V*ertical boxes. Negative values skew clockwise and positive values skew counter-clockwise. You can then also choose an anchor point to determine where your object skews from.

CLEAR TRANSFORMATIONS

Use the *Clear Transformations* command in the **Effects** menu
to return selected objects to their original state.
Transformations are stretching, mirroring, resizing, rotating,
moving the object's center of rotation, and skewing.

If the objects are part of a group, choosing the *Clear
Transformations* command clears only the transformations
you applied to the group, not to any transformation you
made to the individual objects before grouping them.

ADD PERSPECTIVE

Figure 9. You use the *Add
Perspective* command in
conjunction with the Shape Tool
to change the depth of an object.
Applying the *Add Perspective*
command to a selected object
displays a perspective frame
around the object.

The Shape Tool is automatically
selected when you apply a
perspective to an object.

Effects	
<u>T</u>ransform Roll-Up	
<u>C</u>lear Transformations	
<u>A</u>dd Perspective	
<u>E</u>nvelope Roll-Up	Ctrl+F7
<u>B</u>lend Roll-Up	Ctrl+B
E<u>x</u>trude Roll-Up	Ctrl+E
Co<u>n</u>tour Roll-Up	Ctrl+F9
<u>P</u>owerLine Roll-Up	Ctrl+F8
<u>L</u>ens Roll-Up	Alt+F3
Po<u>w</u>erClip	▶
Clear Perspective	
Cop<u>y</u>	▶
Cl<u>o</u>ne	▶

Figure 10. Use the Shape Tool to
move one of the four corner
nodes to alter the perspective of
the object.

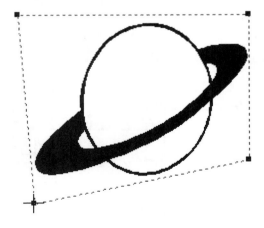

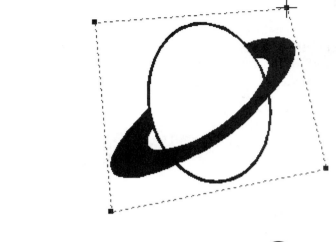

Figure 11. Continue moving the perspective box until you are satisfied with the results. Watch the status line to see the position of the vanishing points.

Shortening two sides of the object lets you create a two-point perspective. Using the Ctrl and Shift keys while dragging a handle forces the opposite handle to move an equal distance in the opposite direction.

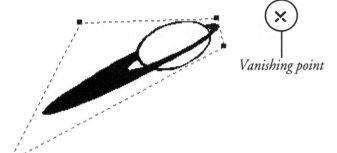

Vanishing point

Figure 12. The × symbol that sometimes appears when you are altering an object's perspective shows the vanishing point. Move this symbol to alter the object's vanishing point.

ENVELOPE ROLL-UP

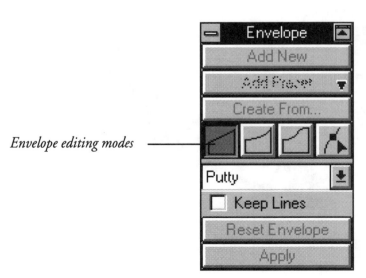

Envelope editing modes

Figure 13. Selecting the *Envelope Roll-Up* command from the **Effects** menu opens the *Envelope* roll-up. You use the options in the *Envelope* roll-up in conjunction with the Shape Tool to change the shape of an object.

ENVELOPE EDITING MODES

Figure 14. There are four envelope editing modes (see Figure 13) corresponding to the four edit options in the *Envelope* roll-up. The editing modes are: (a) *Straight Line*, (b) *Single Arc*, (c) *Two Curves*, and (d) *Unconstrained*.

The first three envelope editing modes let you move one handle at a time horizontally or vertically.

The *Unconstrained* mode gives you more flexibility when you alter the shape of an object. This option has two control points attached to each handle so you can alter it further. It also lets you select more than one handle at a time by holding the Shift key down and clicking on the handles. Alternatively, you can marquee select the required handles.

The active mode in the roll-up affects all objects on the page that you have applied envelopes to. Note that you can switch modes at any time.

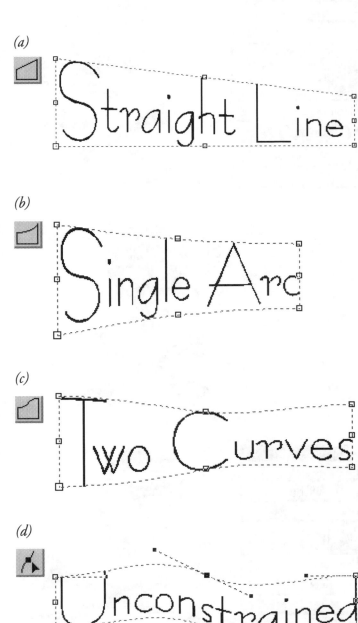

(a)

(b)

(c)

(d)

Figure 15. You can apply an envelope to any selected object (except bitmaps). Clicking on the *Add New* option at the top of the *Envelope* roll-up adds an envelope frame around the object. This frame has eight handles around it so you can change the shape of the object with the Shape Tool.

Figure 16. Once you have added a new envelope frame to the object, CorelDRAW automatically selects the Shape Tool. Hold the Shape Tool on any one of the handles around the envelope frame and drag it to a new position.

Figure 17. Once you have changed the position of one, some, or all of the handles, click on the *Apply* button at the bottom of the *Envelope* roll-up to apply the envelope changes to the object.

Figure 18. The *Add Preset* pop-up palette contains a range of envelope frames that you can apply to an object. Use the scroll bar to the right of this list to gain access to the preset options not in view; click on one of the preset options to attach that envelope frame to your object.

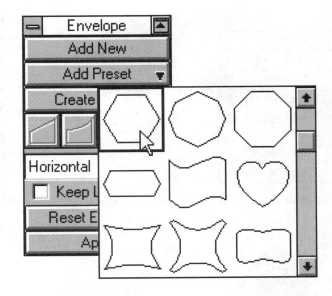

Figure 19. When you have selected a preset envelope, click on the *Apply* button to apply the envelope to the object. You can edit a preset envelope frame with the Shape Tool as you can any envelope frame, although not all envelope editing modes are available with all the preset envelope frames.

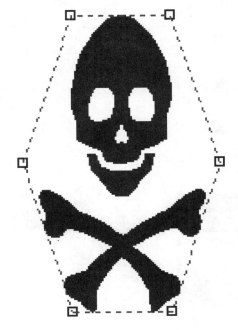

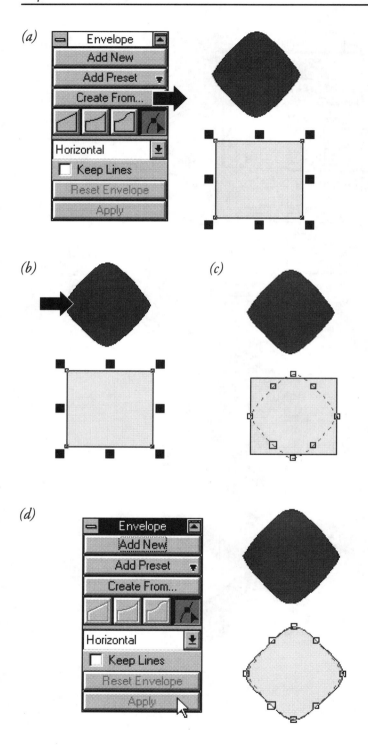

(a)

(b)

(c)

(d)

Figure 20. You use the *Create From* option in the *Envelope* roll-up to copy the shape of one enveloped object to that of another. The object you are creating the envelope from must be a single curved object. With the Pick Tool, select the object that you want to copy the envelope to (in this case the square) and click on the *Create From* button. This displays the arrow (a).

Now click on the object which you want to copy the envelope from (b). CorelDRAW then applies an envelope frame to the object you selected with the Pick Tool (c). Click on the *Apply* button to complete the procedure (d).

If you click on an inappropriate object with the arrow or you miss the object, you are alerted and then given the option of trying again.

Figure 21. The drop-down list in the *Envelope* roll-up, displayed in this figure, contains the Mapping Modes. These options have a direct effect on how the object fits to the envelope frame.

Selecting the *Keep Lines* option below this drop-down list in the *Envelope* roll-up ensures that straight lines in the object are not converted to curves when you apply an envelope to them.

The *Reset Envelope* option in the *Envelope* roll-up returns the envelope frame to what it was before you applied the envelope.

Figure 22. If you apply an envelope to Paragraph Text, the text is not enveloped but the Paragraph Text frame is. The text will flow inside the shape of the text frame so you can create interesting text wraps. In this example, we added a preset envelope frame to a block of Paragraph Text.

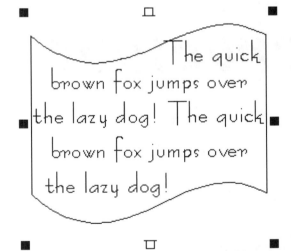

CTRL AND SHIFT KEYS

Holding the Ctrl and Shift keys down while using the envelope option lets you create mirrored and identical sides of the enveloped object. You can use these keys only with the first three envelope modes.

(a)

(b)

(c)

Figure 23. Using the Ctrl key while enveloping forces the handle opposite the one you are manipulating to move in the same direction (a).

Using the Shift key while enveloping forces the handle opposite the one you are manipulating to move in the opposite direction (b).

Holding the Ctrl and Shift keys down together when enveloping forces all other handles to move in opposite directions (c).

Figure 24. You can add a new envelope to an object that you have already enveloped. To do this, make sure the object is selected and click on the *Add New* button in the *Envelope* roll-up.

BLEND ROLL-UP

Figure 25. Clicking on the *Blend Roll-Up* command opens the *Blend* roll-up. The options in this window let you blend two objects into the one blend group.

Along the top of the *Blend* roll-up there are three icons. CorelDRAW selects the top icon (⌐) by default when you first open this roll-up.

The drop-down list below this has two options. The *Steps* option lets you set the number of blend steps there are between the two objects. The *Spacing* option lets you set the amount of space there is between each step in the blend.

These two options are mutually dependent—changing one affects the other. You can use the *Spacing* option only when you have blended two objects along a path.

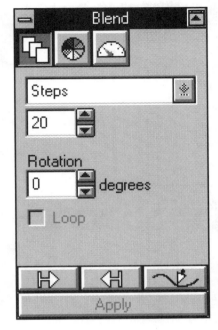

BLENDING OBJECTS

Figure 26. In this example we have blended two objects in 10 steps.

To achieve this simple blend, make sure your *Blend* roll-up is open. Then, with the Pick Tool, select the two objects you want to blend. In this example we created and selected an ellipse and a rectangle as our blend objects. Change the *Steps* value to *10* and click on the *Apply* button.

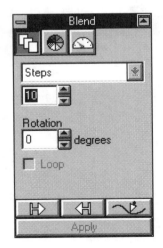
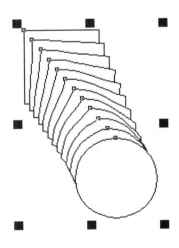

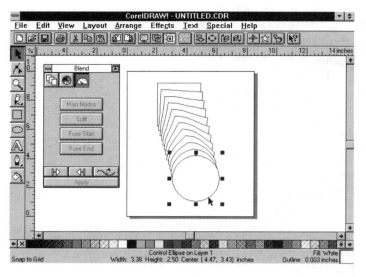

Figure 27. Once you have blended two objects together, they are all part of the one blend group. You can, however, select the start or end objects of the blend individually. You do this by deselecting the entire blend group and clicking on either the start or end object (the original objects you blended). These objects are known as the Control objects and the status line tells you when you have selected a Control object.

If you click on one of the objects that make up the blend, you select the entire blend group.

Figure 28. You can move either the start or the end object (a) and have the blend update immediately (b).

You can also resize, rotate, skew, change the perspective, add an envelope, and edit the start or end objects as you would normally edit them; most changes are updated automatically in the blend.

(a)

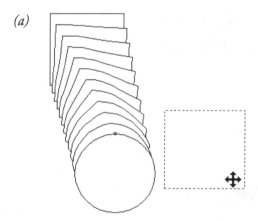

(b)

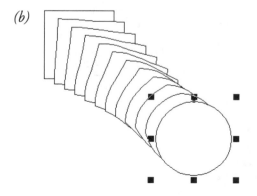

Figure 29. You can change the color of either the start or the end object (or both), with the changes updating automatically.

Figure 30. You can use the *Rotation* option in the *Blend* roll-up to rotate the blend steps. In this example, we have shown two objects blended together in 10 steps with 360 degrees rotation.

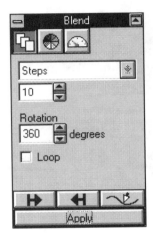

Figure 31. Check the *Loop* option to rotate the blend steps around a point that is halfway between the start and end objects of the blend.

You can access the *Loop* option only when the *Rotation* value is greater than zero.

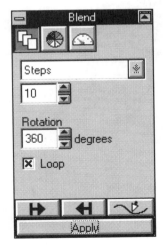
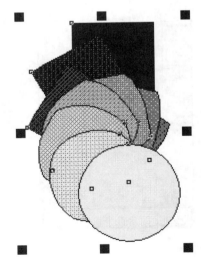

CHANGING BLEND COLORS

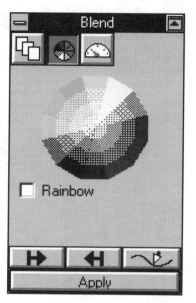

Figure 32. Clicking on the ⊛ icon displays the *HSB* color wheel. The options here change the color of the blend steps.

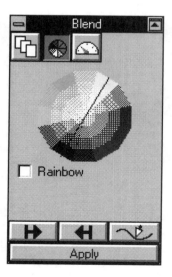

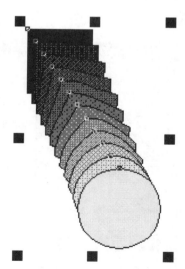

Figure 33. Initially, there is no check mark in the *Rainbow* option. This means that when you select the blend group, a straight line appears on the color wheel, lying between the two colors of the start and end objects. This line determines the color of the blend steps.

Figure 34. If you change the color of one of the Control objects, the color changes in the blend steps automatically to accommodate the change.

In this example, we selected the start object (the rectangle) and changed its color by clicking on a different color from the color palette. The line in the color wheel changes to indicate the new color used when we reselected the whole blend group.

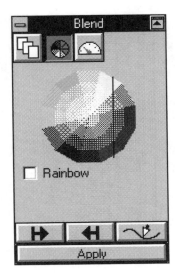
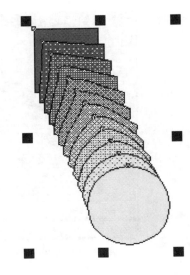

Figure 35. When you check the *Rainbow* option, the straight line on the color wheel in the previous figure moves to the perimeter of the wheel. If you now click on the *Apply* button, the blend steps change color. Compare this figure to the previous one.

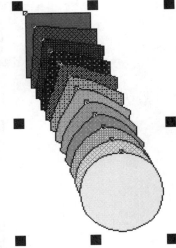

Counterclockwise    *Clockwise*

Figure 36. The two options immediately below the *Rainbow* check box determine the direction this line takes around the color wheel; they represent clockwise and counterclockwise. The line around the perimeter of the color wheel changes direction (which changes the color blend) when you select the two different options.

   If your blend group has no fill but only colored outlines, the *Rainbow* option applies to the object's outline.

MAP NODES/SPLIT/FUSE

Figure 37. Clicking on the ⌂ icon in the *Blend* roll-up gives you access to the options in this figure. You can access these options only under certain circumstances.

   The *Map Nodes* option blends two objects according to the nodes you select. You can do this when blending the objects for the first time, or after you have blended them already.

Figure 38. Click on the *Map Nodes* button after selecting the two objects you want to blend. An arrow icon appears and highlights one of the object's nodes. With this arrow, click on the node you want as the blend point (a).

With the second arrow that then appears, click on one of the other object's nodes (b).

Lastly, click on the *Apply* button to blend the objects. You have now blended the two objects according to the nodes you selected (c).

Figure 39. Clicking on the *Split* option splits the blend group at the object you click on with the arrow (✔) (a).

The blend group is now split into two, with the object you clicked on becoming the start object of one blend and the end object of the other blend that makes up this formation. This object is now also a Control object. In this example, we changed the formation of the blend by moving the new Control object (b).

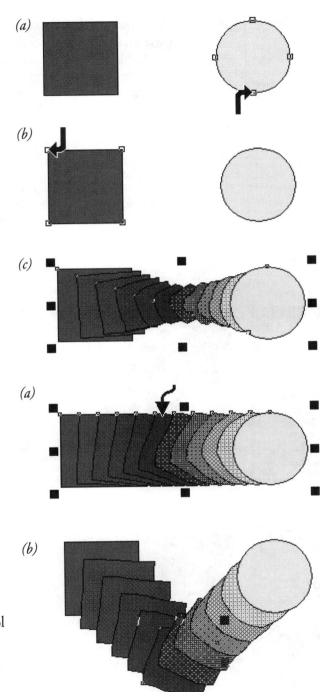

(a)

(b)

(c)

You can select the start and end objects in a blend group individually. If you click on any of the objects that make up the blend steps, you select the entire blend group including the start and end objects. If you have split a blend group into two blend groups, you must hold down the Ctrl key to select one blend group individually, otherwise you select both blend groups. When you select an entire blend group, you change the (➡◀◀) icons in the *Blend* Roll-up to black, otherwise they are white (see Figure 27).

You can use *Separate* in the **Arrange** menu to separate the blend steps from the start and end objects. You can then use *Ungroup* in the **Arrange** menu to separate the steps that make up the blend, so you can select them individually.

(a)

(b)

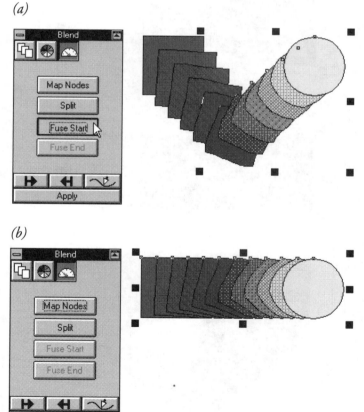

Figure 40. The *Fuse Start* and *Fuse End* options recombine split blends. Hold the Ctrl key down and select one of the split blend groups; either the *Fuse Start* or *Fuse End* button becomes active (depending on which blend group you selected). Click the appropriate fuse button (a) and the original start and end objects are fused, rejoining the two split blend groups (b).

If your Control object is the start or end object for more than one blend group, hold the Ctrl key down and select the blend group you want to fuse. Then click on the *Fuse Start/Fuse End* button, and with the special pointer that appears, click on an intermediate object at least one object away from the Control object you are using in the fuse.

START AND END OBJECTS OF A BLEND

Figure 41. Choosing *Show Start* from the ➡ menu in the bottom section of the *Blend* roll-up (a) highlights the start object in a selected blend (b). This is useful if you have a complex drawing and cannot find the start of the blend.

Selecting *Show End* from the ◀ menu finds the end of the blend group.

After finding the start or end of a blend group, you can drag it to a new position. When you release the mouse button, the entire blend group adjusts accordingly.

(a)

The *New Start* and *New End* commands from these menus let you change the start and end objects of a blend respectively (see Figure 42).

(b)

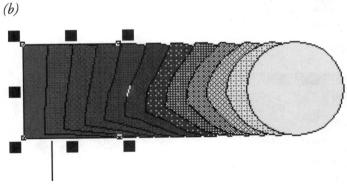

The start object in this blend group is currently selected

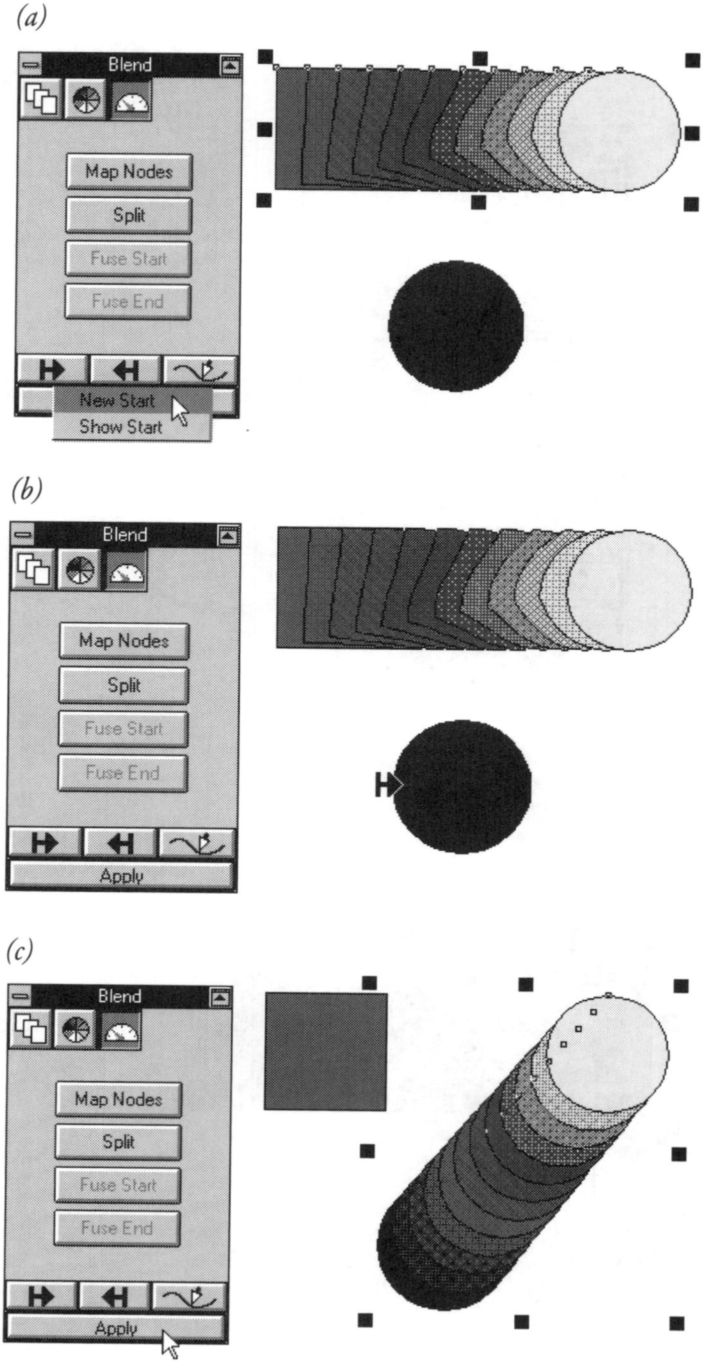

(a)

Figure 42. The first step in changing the start object in a blend is to select the entire blend group. To do this, click on any one of the blend steps with the Pick Tool. Then choose *New Start* from the ▶ menu (a).

With the arrow that appears, click on your new start object (b). (The new start object must be behind the end object.)

(b)

After clicking on the *Apply* button, the object you have clicked becomes the new start object for the blend group (c).

To create a new end object, follow the steps above, but select *New End* from the ◀ menu.

(c)

CHANGING THE BLEND PATH

Figure 43. To change the blend path with the Pick Tool, select the blend group that you want to affect. Then select *New Path* from the ↘ menu which adds the ✦ arrow (a). This deselects the blend group and you select the path for the blend steps to follow with the ✦ arrow (b).

Click on the *Apply* button to flow the blend along the path (c).

Selecting *Show Path* from the ↘ menu selects the path the blend is attached to. This is useful if you have a complex drawing and are having trouble finding the path.

Selecting *Detach From Path* separates the path and the blend group. The blend group remains where it was when it was fitted to the path.

If you attach a blend group to a path, the ↘ icon becomes black when you select the blend group.

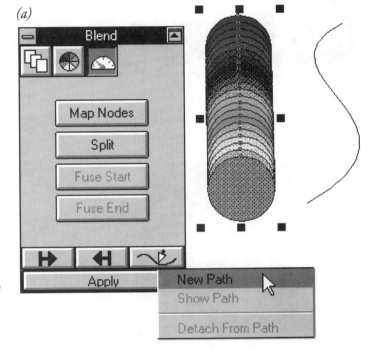

(a)

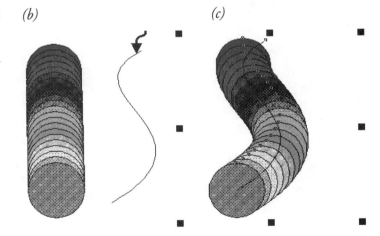

(b)   *(c)*

OTHER BLEND FEATURES

Figure 44. You can use grouped objects as the start and end objects of a blend. Make sure you have grouped the objects before you blend them.

Figure 45. You can use a single object in more than one blend group. In this example, we have blended the large circle in the background with both the circles in the foreground.

CREATING HIGHLIGHTS

Figure 46. You can use the *Blend* feature for creating highlights in objects. In this example, we have placed a small tear drop on top of a larger tear drop object (a).

Make sure you place the lighter colored object on the top, or the effect does not work.

You can see the highlight after you have done the blending (b).

If you have checked the *Rainbow* option, the highlight effect can look even more interesting (c).

You cannot blend across different layers. If you try to do this, CorelDRAW moves the objects to the same layer. See **Chapter 7, The Layout Menu** for more information on layers.

(a)

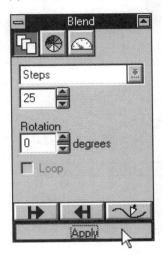

(b)

(c)

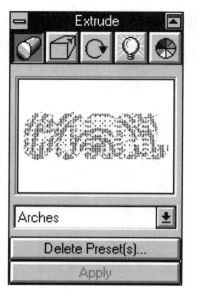

EXTRUDE ROLL-UP

Figure 47. Using the *Extrude Roll-Up* command in the **Layout** menu opens the *Extrude* roll-up. You use this option to make an object appear three dimensional.

PRESETS

Figure 48. The drop-down list in the *Extrude* roll-up allows you to access a list of preset extrusions that you can use instead of creating an extrusion for an object manually.

Choose a name from the drop-down list of extrusions to see a preview of that extrusion in the preview box above. You can then simply click on *Apply* to apply this extrusion to your object.

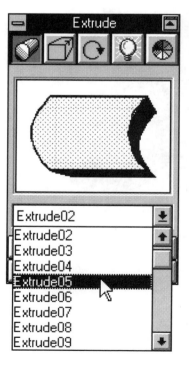

Figure 49. You can also create your own extrusion and then save it as a preset by clicking on the *Save As* button in the *Extrude* roll-up to open the *Save Extrude Preset* dialog box. Enter a name for your extrusion and click on *OK* to add it to the presets list.

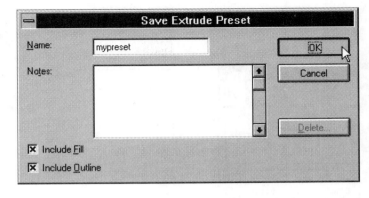

Figure 50. When no extrude object is currently selected, the *Save As* button changes to a *Delete Preset(s)* button (a). (You can delete an extrusion from the presets list by clicking on this button to open the *Delete Preset* dialog box (b) where you can choose the presets you want to delete and click on the *Delete* button to remove them.)

You can also open the *Delete Presets* dialog box by clicking on the *Delete* button in the *Save Extrude Preset* dialog box of Figure 49.

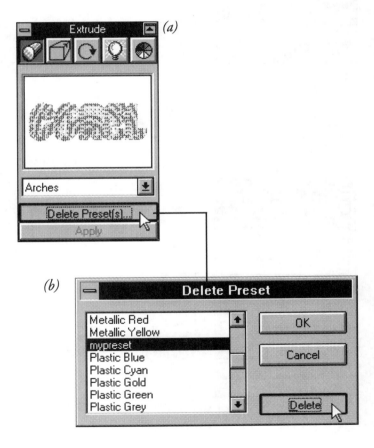

APPLYING AND EDITING AN EXTRUSION

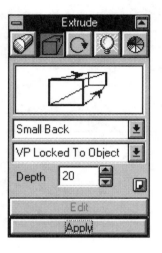

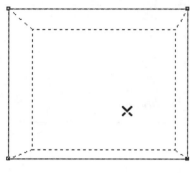

Figure 51. If you open the *Extrude* roll-up with an object selected, CorelDRAW automatically applies a wireframe extrusion to it. As you make changes in the *Extrude* roll-up, they are reflected in the wireframe extrusion.

You can also alter the wireframe extrusion by moving the ✕ icon (the vanishing point) with the mouse. You can open the *Extrude* roll-up before you select your object; select the object, then click on the *Edit* button to apply the wireframe extrusion to this object. You are then free to make any changes to the object in the *Extrude* roll-up.

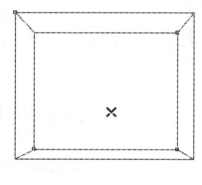

Figure 52. Clicking on the *Apply* button after you have made changes in the *Extrude* roll-up applies these changes to the object. As long as you keep the object selected, the wireframe extrusion remains and you can still edit it.

When you deselect the object after using the *Apply* button, the wireframe extrusion disappears, leaving the extrusion as it was when you clicked on *Apply*.

To edit the extrusion again, select the object and click on the *Edit* button in the *Extrude* roll-up.

Figure 53. This icon (⬡) in the *Extrude* roll-up is the *Depth* icon. The options in the drop-down list shown here determine the effect of the extrusion. You can choose either a perspective or a parallel extrusion through these options.

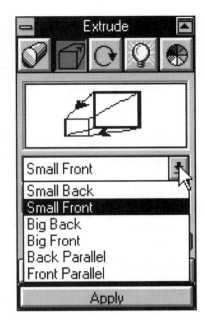

With a perspective extrusion, the extrusion always looks as though it is heading toward or away from the vanishing point. The first four options in this drop-down list are perspective extrusions. The front and back choices indicate whether the extrusion will appear in front of or behind the object you are extruding.

With a parallel extrusion, the extrusion face is the same size as the original object, and the vanishing point is always in the center of the extrusion face. The last two options in this drop-down list are the parallel extrusion options.

When you select a different option from this drop-down list, you can see how it will affect the selected object in the preview box. The arrows indicate the direction of the extrusion in relation to the Control object and the thick black square represents the Control object itself.

The higher the value in the *Depth* option below the drop-down lists, the closer the extrusion is to the vanishing point. You can change the *Depth* option only when you are working with perspective extrusions.

Figure 54. The second drop-down list allows you to set the options for the vanishing point. The *VP Locked To Object* option fixes the vanishing point in relation to your object; if you move the object, the vanishing point moves in order to remain in the same relative position. The *VP Locked To Page* option fixes the vanishing point in its position on the page, as you move the object the vanishing point stays in its position and the extrusion changes accordingly. The *Copy VP From* option allows you to copy a vanishing point from another extruded object and the *Shared Vanishing Point* option allows objects to share a vanishing point.

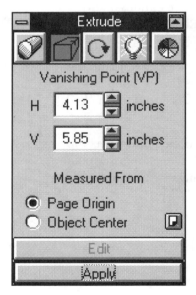

Figure 55. Click on the ▯ icon in the bottom right of the *Extrude* roll-up for the options shown here. These options let you position the vanishing point (✗) of the extrusion precisely. You do this by typing in a *H*orizontal and *V*ertical value.

You can adjust these values in relation to either the zero point of the ruler (*Page Origin*), or the middle of the object's highlight box (*Object Center*).

You can also change the vanishing point by dragging it to a new location with the mouse while in the *Extrude* editing mode.

ROTATING EXTRUSIONS

Figure 56. The third icon in the *Extrude* roll-up is the *3-D Rotation* icon (↻). Clicking on this option brings up the *3-D Rotation wireframe*. The *3-D Rotation wireframe* does not work with parallel extrusions, only perspective.

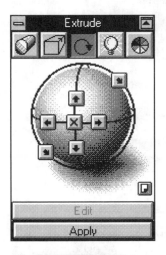

Figure 57. The two arrows around the outside of the *3-D Rotation wireframe* (◨) rotate the object five degrees clockwise or counter-clockwise when you click on them. The extrusion wireframe moves as you click on these arrows.

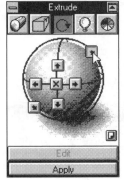
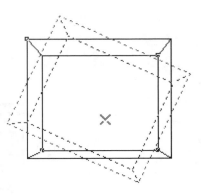

Figure 58. The four arrows on the *3-D Rotation wireframe* spin the object five degrees in the direction of the arrow you click. This example displays the spinning option using the right arrow (➡).

The up and down arrows tumble the object, end over end, either forwards or backwards.

The ✕ button at the center of the sphere removes any rotations you have applied to an object.

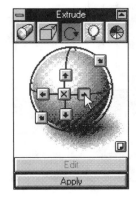
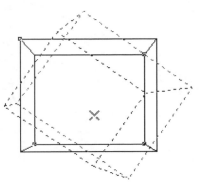

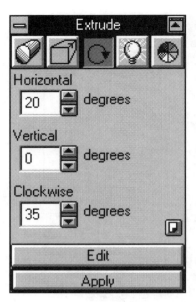

Figure 59. Clicking on the ⏻ icon at the bottom right of the *3-D Rotation wireframe* gives you these options (for perspective extrusion only). Selecting these options makes the same changes that you make with the *3-D Rotation wireframe*, except that you key in a value instead of selecting it visually as in the previous two figures. Click on the ⏻ icon to return to the *3-D Rotation wireframe*.

Once you have rotated the object the way you want, click on the *Apply* button.

CHANGING THE LIGHT SOURCE

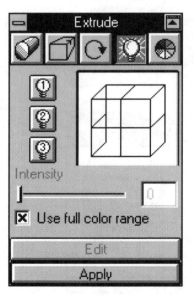

Figure 60. The *Light Source Direction* icon (♀) determines the direction of the light source shining on your object. You can include and control up to three light sources.

Figure 61. To add a light source, click on one of the three light bulb buttons. This displays a sphere, representing your object, inside a wireframe. A numbered light source marker (corresponding to the light bulb buttons) shows where the light source is in relation to the object. You can drag the numbered light source markers anywhere in the cube where two or more lines connect to change the position of the light source(s). You can only see the full

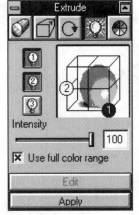

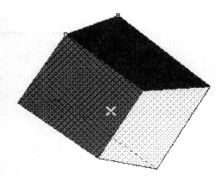

results of adding a light source when you have applied a fill to your object.

The *Intensity* option changes the strength of the highlighted light source. As you increase the number to 100, you move the object's color to white. As you decrease the value, you move the object's color to black.

A light source remains in the same place, even if you later rotate or spin the object.

CHANGING THE EXTRUDE COLOR

Figure 62. The *Extrusion Coloring* icon (⊕) determines the color of the extrusion. Selecting the radio buttons here changes the options available. Selecting *Use Object Fill* gives the extrusion the same fill as the Control object.

If your Control object has a fountain, Two-Color Pattern, texture, bitmap, or Full-Color Pattern fill, you can use the *Drape Fills* option to continue the fills to all surfaces of the object rather than creating a copy of the Control object's fill and applying it to the rest of the surfaces.

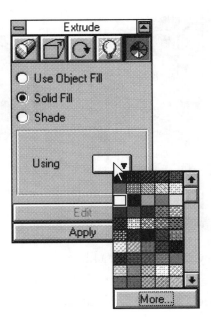

Figure 63. The *Solid Fill* option lets you choose a separate color for the extruded surfaces. Click on the color swatch to display a Color palette where you can select the color you want.

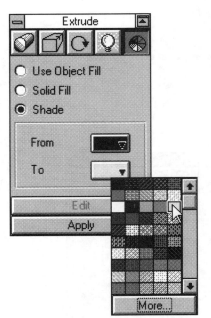

Figure 64. The *Shade* option lets you apply a linear fountain fill to the extruded surfaces. Use the *From* and *To* options to select the two colors that make up the shading.

Use the *Apply* button to apply the colors to the selected object's extrusion.

Regardless of the way you color your extrusion, the choices you make in the light source direction and intensity will influence the object's final appearance.

CONTOUR ROLL-UP

Figure 65. The *Contour Roll-Up* command from the **Effects** menu brings up the *Contour* roll-up. The options in this roll-up let you create a series of contour lines on the inside or outside of a selected object.

You can apply contours to all objects except grouped, linked, or embedded objects, and bitmaps.

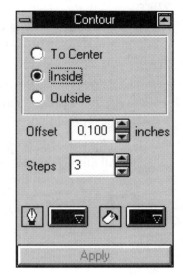

CONTOUR DIRECTION

Figure 66. The first choice in the *Contour* roll-up determines whether the contour lines appear inside or outside the object. The *To Center* option creates contour lines that go towards the center of the object (a). The *Inside* option also creates contours toward the center of the option, but you decide how many progressive shapes are included by changing the number of steps (b). The *Outside* option creates contours that appear on the outside and each shape moves further away than the previous contour shape (c). The *Outside* option can dramatically increase the size of the object, depending on the number of steps.

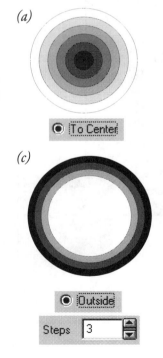

(a)

(c)

The object in all these examples is the white circle

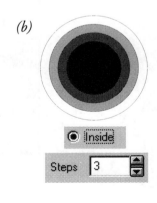

(b)

CONTOUR OFFSET AND STEPS

The *Offset* value in the *Contour* roll-up determines the amount of space between each contour step. You can enter any value between 0 and 10 inches.

The *Steps* option sets the number of contour steps. If you have the *To Center* contour direction selected, you can't select the *Steps* option.

If you have the *Inside* option selected, and all the contour steps will not fit, the contours continue to the center of the object and stop when there is no more room. The reason for this is that the *Offset* option takes precedence over the *Steps* value. You may have to reduce the *Offset* to fit all the contours inside your object.

CONTOUR COLOR

Figure 67. Clicking on the ✎ and ✐ palettes at the bottom of the *Contour* roll-up lets you select an outline and fill color that your object will blend to.

Click on the *More* button at the bottom of the palettes to see all color models.

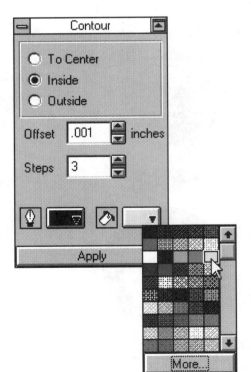

Figure 68. The original object you are contouring must have a fill for the contour effect to work. The fill and outline color of the original object will then blend with the fill and outline colors you have selected in the palettes of the *Contour* roll-up.

If the original object has no fill, the contour steps will also be empty regardless of the fill color you have selected in the *Contour* roll-up.

You can change the color of both the original object and the contour fill once you have applied the contour.

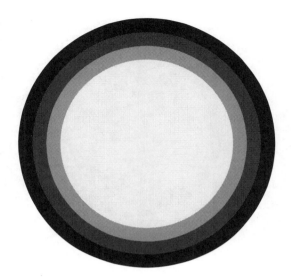

Figure 69. If you choose *Separate* from the **Arrange** menu when you have the *Contour Group* selected (the status line indicates when you do), you can then select each shape in the contour separately.

Do this by holding the Ctrl key down and clicking on the contour shape you want to select. The status line then shows you have a *Child Curve* selected, and the selection handles become circular.

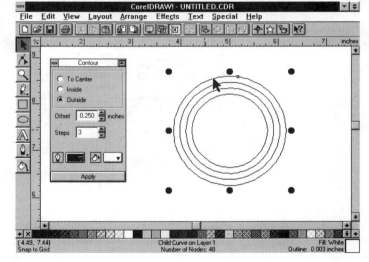

Figure 70. Following the steps in the previous figure lets you change the fill and outline of each shape in the contour individually.

The *Apply* button at the bottom of the *Contour* roll-up applies any changes you have made to the selected object.

POWERLINE ROLL-UP

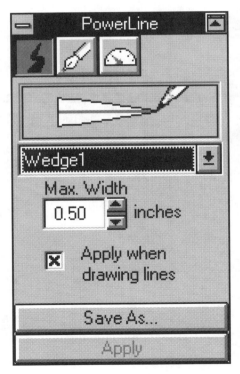

Figure 71. Choosing the *PowerLine Roll-Up* command from the **Effects** menu opens the *PowerLine* roll-up. You can use PowerLines to give your objects a hand-drawn look.

You can apply PowerLines while you are creating a drawing, or you can add them later.

PRESET POWERLINES

Figure 72. The first option in the *PowerLine* roll-up (⚡) is the *Preset* option. The drop-down list here contains 24 preset PowerLine options for you to choose from.

When you select a preset option from the list in the *PowerLine* roll-up, an example of how the PowerLine will look is displayed at the top of the roll-up.

Figure 73. These preset options work in conjunction with the *Max. Width* value below the list. If you have the *Apply when drawing lines* option checked, all lines you draw with the Pencil Tool will automatically look like the preset PowerLine with the maximum width applied to them. The *Max. Width* value can be anything from 0.01 to 16 inches.

To apply a PowerLine to an existing object, first select the object with the Pick Tool, then choose the preset option you want. Change the *Max. Width* value (if necessary) and click on the *Apply* button.

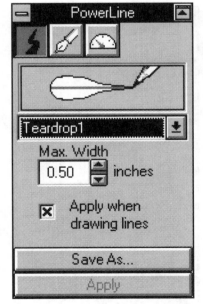

NIB SHAPE

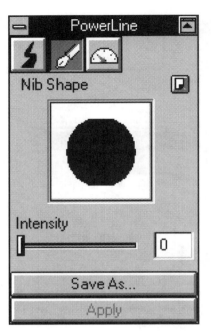

Figure 74. Click on the ✐ button in the *PowerLine* roll-up to adjust the *Nib Shape* of the PowerLines. Adjusting these options changes the shape and thickness of the PowerLine.

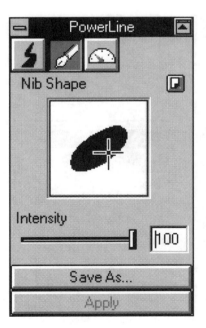

Figure 75. Hold the mouse down on the nib shape representation in the preview box and drag it around to change the shape of the nib.

The *Intensity* setting affects the width of the line along its entire length, with 100 ensuring the line (at a 90° angle) is at its maximum width. Click anywhere along the *Intensity* gauge or move the gauge marker (▯) to change this setting.

Figure 76. Clicking on the ⏻ icon in the *PowerLine* roll-up of the previous figure changes to these options which let you set the *Nib Shape* precisely.

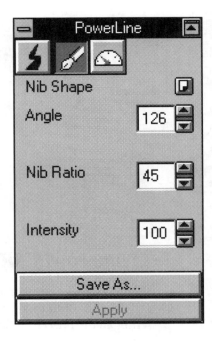

SPEED/SPREAD/INK FLOW

Figure 77. Click on the ⏢ button in the *PowerLine* roll-up to show these settings.

The *Speed* option affects the curves and changes in direction of a PowerLine. The higher the *Speed* value, the wider the PowerLine appears at a change of direction.

The *Spread* option determines the smoothness of the PowerLine. The higher the *Spread* value, the smoother the line. If the *Speed* setting is on 0, you can't change the *Spread* option.

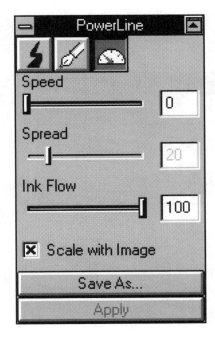

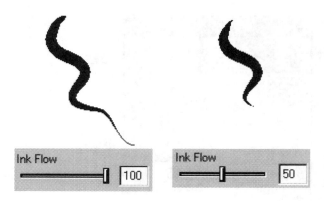

Figure 78. Decreasing the *Ink Flow* value decreases the amount of "ink" in the PowerLine. Compare the two lines in this example. One has an *Ink Flow* of *100* while the other has an *Ink Flow* of *50*.

When you check the *Scale with Image* option, the PowerLine width increases or decreases when you resize the PowerLine.

SAVING POWERLINE EFFECTS

When you make changes to the *Nib Shape, Speed, Spread,* and *Ink Flow* options, this automatically selects the *Custom* setting in the *Preset* list. You can save and name your custom PowerLine effects by clicking on the *Save As* button at the bottom of the *PowerLine* roll-up.

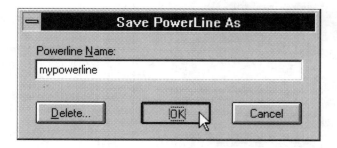

Figure 79. In the *Save PowerLine As* dialog box, type the name of your custom PowerLine in the *Powerline Name* text box and click on the *OK* button.

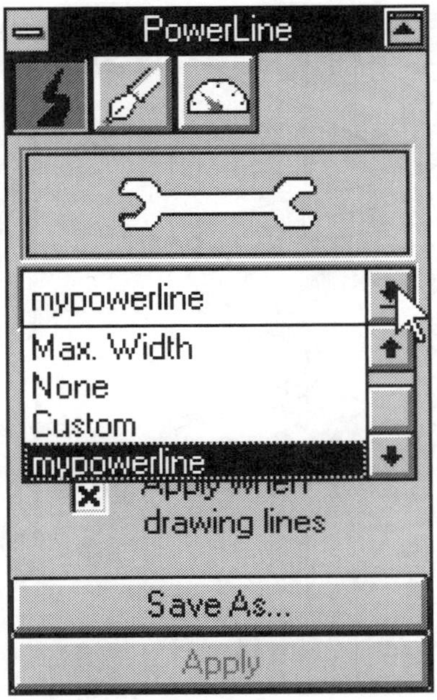

Figure 80. The name of your custom PowerLine now appears in the list of preset PowerLine effects.

You can access the *Delete* option from the *Save PowerLine As* dialog box (Figure 79) only for custom PowerLines. To delete a custom PowerLine, click on the *Delete* button in the *Save PowerLine As* dialog box to open the *Delete PowerLine Preset* dialog box where you can select your custom PowerLine and click on *Delete*.

The *Apply* button at the bottom of the *PowerLine* roll-up applies the PowerLine settings to the selected object.

EDITING POWERLINES WITH THE SHAPE TOOL

Figure 81. You can edit PowerLines with the Shape Tool just like any curved objects in CorelDRAW. The line running through the middle of the PowerLine (the core line) holds the nodes. You can see the core line and the nodes much easier in *wireframe* view.

However, the *Node Edit* roll-up contains a further option that you can access only when editing PowerLines. To open the *Node Edit* roll-up, double-click on the node of a PowerLine or anywhere along the core line.

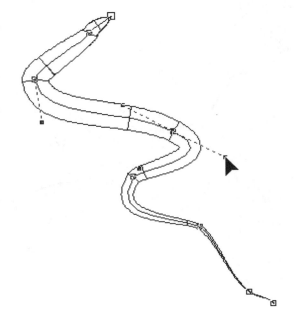

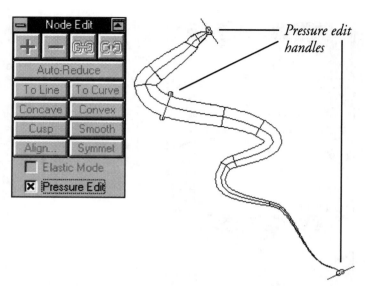

Pressure edit handles

Figure 82. Once the *Node Edit* roll-up is open, choose the *Pressure Edit* option at the bottom of the roll-up. When you select this option, sets of pressure edit handles appear at both ends of the PowerLine and sometimes at intervals along the line.

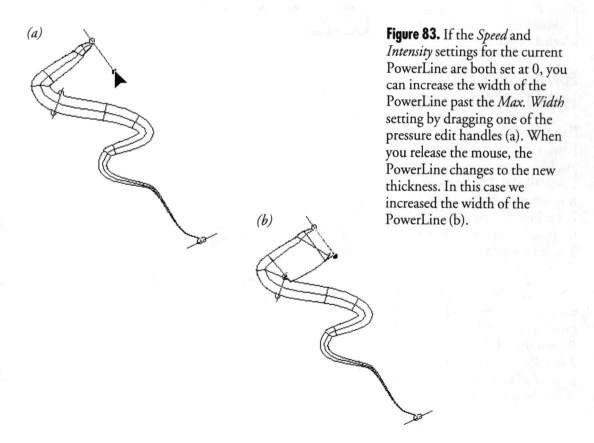

(a)

(b)

Figure 83. If the *Speed* and *Intensity* settings for the current PowerLine are both set at 0, you can increase the width of the PowerLine past the *Max. Width* setting by dragging one of the pressure edit handles (a). When you release the mouse, the PowerLine changes to the new thickness. In this case we increased the width of the PowerLine (b).

Figure 84. If the *Speed* or *Intensity* settings are greater than 0 and you want to pressure edit the PowerLine, you can't increase the width of the PowerLine past the *Max. Width* that is currently in the *PowerLine* roll-up. If this is the case, indicators appear on the pressure edit handles showing how far you can drag them (⊢—⊛—⊣).

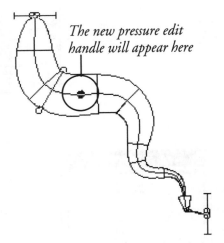

Figure 85. You can add pressure edit handles along the core line of the PowerLine by clicking wherever you want the pressure handles (this adds a ● to the line) and then choosing the + symbol from the *Node Edit* roll-up.

The new pressure edit handle will appear here

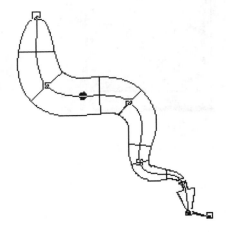

Figure 86. If you deselect the *Pressure Edit* option in the *Node Edit* roll-up, you can add nodes to the core line of the PowerLine.

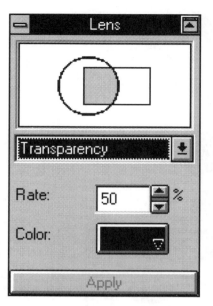

LENS ROLL-UP

Figure 87. Selecting the *Lens Roll-Up* command from the **Effects** menu opens the *Lens* roll-up as seen here. You can use this roll-up to create one object as a lens that you place over other objects to create special effects.

Using the *Lens* roll-up you can give your lens object attributes like magnification, transparency, color filtering, color adding, and infra-red imaging, that affect the objects below the lens object.

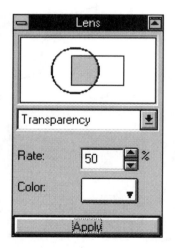

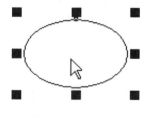

Figure 88. To create a lens, first select the object you want as your lens object, this must be a single object; grouped objects can't be used with the *Lens* effects.

If your lens object has no fill it will automatically take on the color settings of the *Color* button in the *Lens* roll-up. If you want to change the fill of your lens object, you must maintain a uniform fill for the lens effects to work.

Figure 89. Once you have selected your lens object, choose a lens type from the drop-down list of lens types in the *Lens* roll-up. Depending on the lens type, you may also be able to specify control options for your lens.

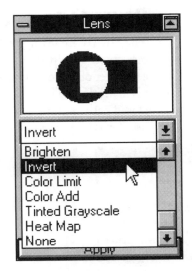

The *Transparency* option makes your lens object like a transparent piece of glass that tints the object it is over. The *Magnify* option makes your lens into a magnifying glass that magnifies objects it is over by a factor of 1 to 10. The *Color Limit* option makes your lens into a color filter, allowing only the lens color and black to appear through the lens. The *Color Add* option lets your lens act like an additive light focus for colors, any colors of objects beneath the lens are added to the color of the lens as if mixing light. The *Brighten* option adds brightness or darkness to objects beneath the lens, where the *Invert* option inverts the colors of objects underneath the lens. The *Tinted Grayscale* option changes the colors of objects beneath the lens to grayscale colors, and the *Heat Map* option gives objects underneath the lens the appearance of an infra-red image.

Figure 90. Once you have selected your lens type, click on *Apply* to create your lens object. You can then position the lens over another object to see the lens effects. A lens object can be used over other objects containing uniform, fountain, Two-Color and Full-Color Pattern, texture, or bitmap fills.

POWERCLIP

The PowerClip feature in CorelDRAW allows you to place one object within another object. When you do this, the container object constrains the object or objects that you place inside it. The container object and its contents can be a closed path, a group of objects, or Artistic Text. You can also use PowerClips to place bitmaps in container objects.

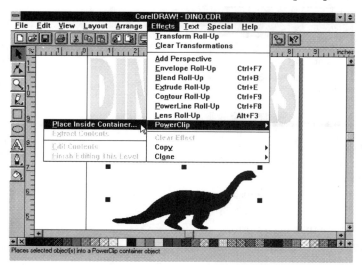

Figure 91. To create a PowerClip, first select the object(s) that you want to be the contents (i.e. the object you want to place inside another object) and then choose the *PowerClip* command from the **Effects** menu. Then select the *Place Inside Container* command from the submenu that appears.

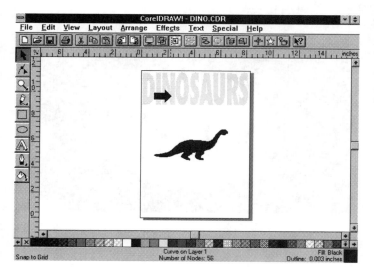

Figure 92. The mouse cursor then changes to become an arrow. You use this arrow to point to the object that you want to be the container, in this case the Artistic Text.

Figure 93. CorelDRAW then places your first object inside the container object and the two objects become a single unit.

EDITING POWERCLIPS

You can stretch, scale, rotate, skew, and mirror PowerClips just as you would any normal object. These changes apply to the PowerClip as a whole. You can also "nest" PowerClips, whereby one PowerClip contains another PowerClip. Using this "nesting" technique you can contain a maximum of five levels of PowerClips.

Figure 94. By default, the contents of your PowerClip are locked to the center of the container object. You can, however, edit both the contents, and the container's position relative to the contents.

To reposition the container over its contents you must unlock the container contents. To do this, click on the PowerClip with the right mouse button and deselect the *Lock Contents to PowerClip* command from the **Object** menu that appears.

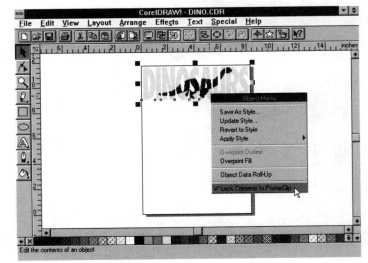

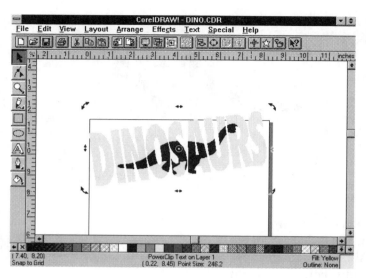

Figure 95. You can now reposition the container over its contents. When you are finished, click on the PowerClip with the right mouse button and select the *Lock Contents to PowerClip* command once again (Figure 94).

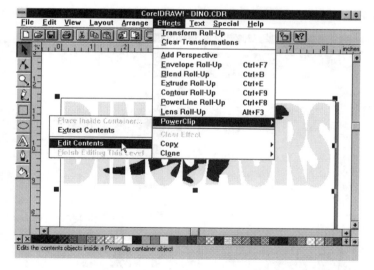

Figure 96. You can also edit the contents of a PowerClip. To do this, select the PowerClip object and choose the *Edit Contents* command from the *PowerClip* submenu of the **Effects** menu.

Figure 97. CorelDRAW then displays the container object as a blue outline. You cannot change the container object now, it appears for reference purposes only. The contents however appear in their editable form. You can move, stretch, scale, rotate, and perform any normal editing procedures on the contents.

If the contents are themselves a "nested" PowerClip (see **Editing PowerClips** earlier), you can edit either the container, as described in Figure 95, or you can edit the contents of this PowerClip by selecting it and reselecting the *Edit Contents* command from the *PowerClip* submenu of the **Effects** menu. This process can continue for up to five levels. When editing "nested" levels, the scroll bar indicates the level in which you are working.

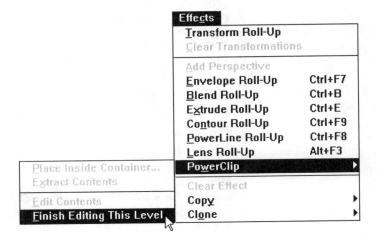

Figure 98. When you have finished editing the contents of your PowerClip, select *Finish Editing This Level* from the *PowerClip* submenu in the **Effects** menu to return to the original PowerClip object.

If you are editing a "nested" level within a PowerClip, selecting this command takes you up one level. Keep selecting this command until the editing level status information disappears from the scroll bar.

REMOVING POWERCLIPS

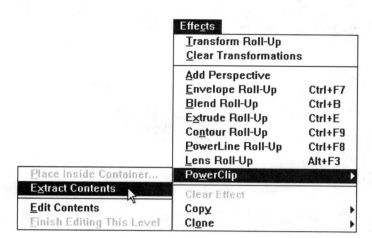

Figure 99. You can extract the contents of your PowerClip from the container object. To do this, select the PowerClip object and then choose the *Extract Contents* command from the *PowerClip* submenu of the **Effects** menu. The container and contents of the PowerClip then become separate objects. If you have "nested" PowerClips, you can repeat this process on each subsequent PowerClip that you extract from its parent PowerClip.

CLEARING EFFECTS

Figure 100. Using *Clear (Effect)* from the **Effects** menu removes the last effect you applied to the selected object.

This command changes depending on which effect you applied to the object.

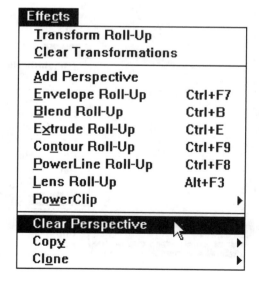

COPY EFFECT FROM

Figure 101. The *Copy* command lets you copy a range of effects from one object to another. The result of copying an effect from one object to another depends on the effect you choose. For example, copying a PowerClip from one object to another places the contents of the original PowerClip into the new object (the object you copy the PowerClip to becomes the new container object).

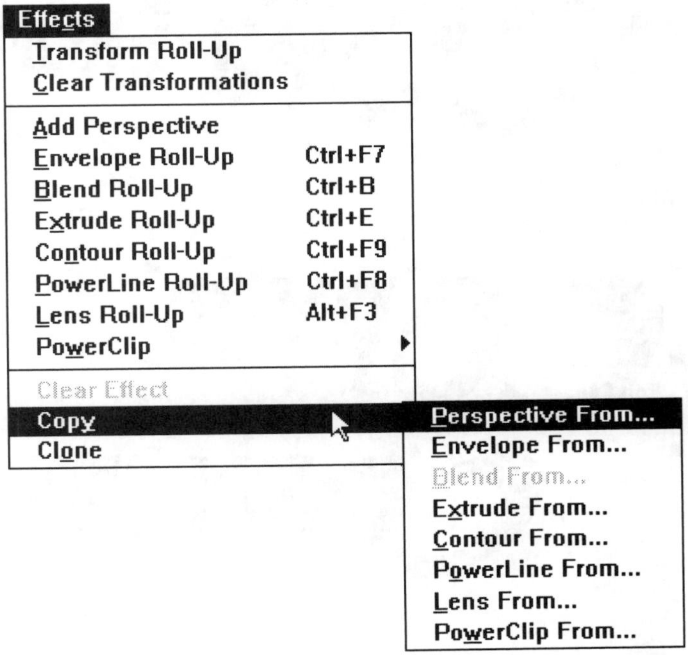

See Figure 102 for an example of copying effects from one object to another.

Effects	
Transform Roll-Up	
Clear Transformations	
Add Perspective	
Envelope Roll-Up	Ctrl+F7
Blend Roll-Up	Ctrl+B
Extrude Roll-Up	Ctrl+E
Contour Roll-Up	Ctrl+F9
PowerLine Roll-Up	Ctrl+F8
Lens Roll-Up	Alt+F3
PowerClip	▶

Clear Effect
Copy
Clone

Perspective From...
Envelope From...
Blend From...
Extrude From...
Contour From...
PowerLine From...
Lens From...
PowerClip From...

Figure 102. The first thing to do is use the Pick Tool to select the object that you want to copy the effect to.

Then choose the *Copy* command (Figure 101) and select the copy effect you want from the submenu that appears. The object you want to copy from must already have this effect applied.

(a)

(b)

Figure 103. With the arrow that appears, click on the object that has the effect you want to copy (a).

The object you selected in Figure 102 now has the effect applied to it (b).

If you click on an inappropriate object with the arrow, or you miss the object, you are alerted and then given the option of trying again.

If you choose *Copy Perspective From*, you must click on an object that you have applied a perspective to. Similarly, if you select *Copy Envelope From*, you must click on an object with an envelope and so on with each of the *Copy* effect commands.

CLONE EFFECT FROM

Figure 104. The *Clone* command in the **Effects** menu lets you clone a range of effects from one object to another. This is similar to copying effects, as described in Figures 101 through 103. However, when you clone an effect from one object to another, any changes you make to the original object are also made to the cloned object. Another difference is that you cannot edit the cloned object's effects directly, instead you must edit the original and apply the effects to both.

Effects	
<u>T</u>ransform Roll-Up	
<u>C</u>lear Transformations	
<u>A</u>dd Perspective	
<u>E</u>nvelope Roll-Up	Ctrl+F7
<u>B</u>lend Roll-Up	Ctrl+B
E<u>x</u>trude Roll-Up	Ctrl+E
Co<u>n</u>tour Roll-Up	Ctrl+F9
<u>P</u>owerLine Roll-Up	Ctrl+F8
<u>L</u>ens Roll-Up	Alt+F3
Po<u>w</u>erClip	▶
Clear Envelope	
Cop<u>y</u>	▶
Cl<u>o</u>ne	

<u>B</u>lend From...
E<u>x</u>trude From...
<u>C</u>ontour From...
<u>P</u>owerLine From...

THE TEXT MENU 10

THE TEXT MENU COMMANDS

The commands in the **Text** menu help you edit text in your CorelDRAW document.

Figure 1. This figure displays the **Text** menu and its commands.

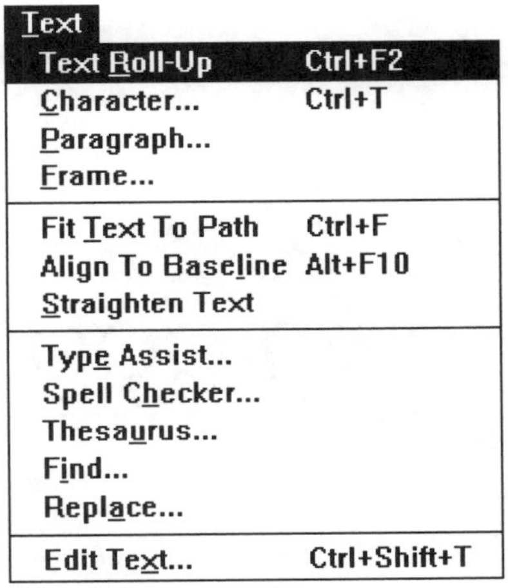

TEXT ROLL-UP

Figure 2. Clicking on the *Text Roll-Up* command in the **Text** menu opens the *Text* roll-up.

These five buttons in the *Text* roll-up govern the justification of text. The options available are *left*, *centered*, *right*, *full* (available for Paragraph Text only), and *none*.

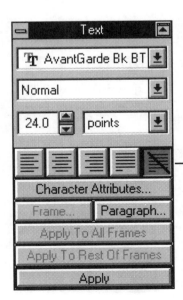

—Justification options

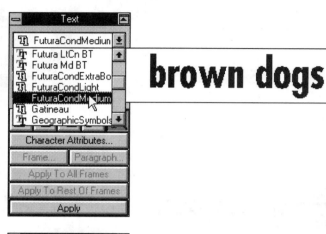

Figure 3. The drop-down list at the top of the roll-up lets you select a different font. As you drag the mouse down the list of fonts, a preview box appears to give you an indication of what the typeface looks like.

Use the scroll bar to the right of the list to access the fonts not currently in view.

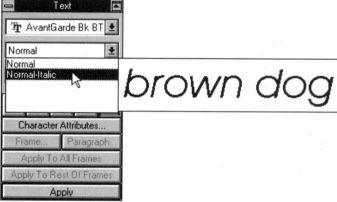

Figure 4. The next drop-down list contains the style options. Not all styles (*Normal, Bold, Italic, Bold-Italic*) are available for all typefaces. Again, a preview box lets you see what the style change looks like before you apply it.

Size is the next option in the *Text* roll-up. You can also change the unit of size by selecting a different option from the drop-down list to the right of the *Size* drop-down list.

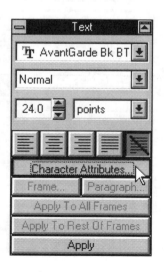

Figure 5. You can select the *Character Attributes* button to open the *Character Attributes* dialog box where you can change the attributes of your text. For more information on this dialog box, see **Character** later in this chapter.

Figure 6. You can click on the *Frame* button in the *Text* roll-up only if you have selected Paragraph Text with the Pick Tool. (The *Frame* button is grayed out for Artistic Text.) The *Frame* button opens the *Frame Attributes* dialog box.

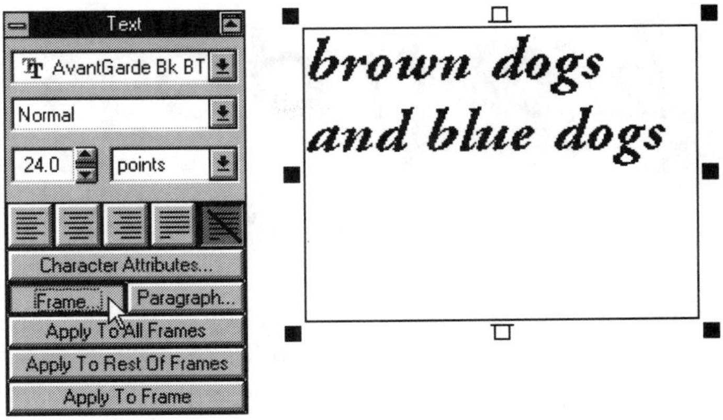

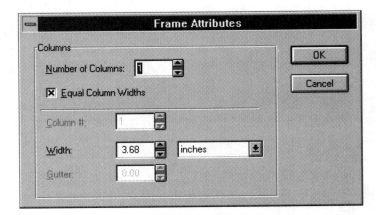

Figure 7. The *Frame Attributes* dialog box lets you apply columns to Paragraph Text. See **Frame** later in this chapter for more information on this dialog box.

Figure 8. You can click on the *Paragraph* button in the *Text* roll-up with either Paragraph or Artistic Text selected. Clicking on this button opens the *Paragraph* dialog box.

See the **Paragraph** section later in this chapter for more information on the options in this dialog box.

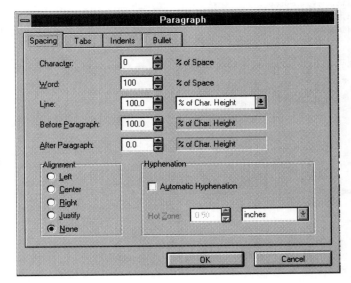

Figure 9. You can also change individual text characters (Paragraph or Artistic) through the *Text* roll-up. Select the node of one or more text characters with the Shape Tool and choose a new font, style, or size to achieve this effect.

Click on the *Apply* button at the bottom of the *Text* roll-up to apply any changes you make in the roll-up to selected text. The *Apply To All Frames* button is available only for Paragraph Text and applies your choices to all of the linked frames of your Paragraph Text, where the *Apply To Rest Of Frames* button applies your choices to the current paragraph frame and any subsequent linked frames.

CHARACTER

Figure 10. Choosing the *Character* command from the **Text** menu, when your text is selected with the Pick Tool, brings up this *Character Attributes* dialog box. Here you can change the *Font, Size, Style, Placement, Spacing* and *Alignment* of the selected text.

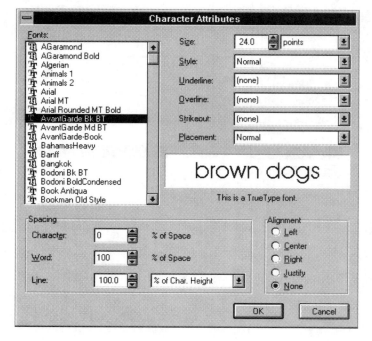

You change the *Font, Size,* and *Style* in the same way as described earlier for the *Text* roll-up window. The *Placement* options include *Normal, Superscript,* and *Subscript,* placing your text above, below, or on the text base line depending on the option you choose. The *Spacing* section allows you to add a percentage of extra space to your characters, words, or lines, while the *Alignment* section lets you align your text.

Figure 11. You can also choose the *Character* command from the **Text** menu, if your text is selected with the Shape Tool. You must select one or more of the text block's nodes with the Shape Tool to use this command. In this example, we have selected the node of the letter "f" with the Shape Tool.

Figure 12. The *Character Attributes* dialog box is now different from the one in Figure 10 as it includes three new options. These are *Horizontal Shift, Vertical Shift,* and *Angle.*

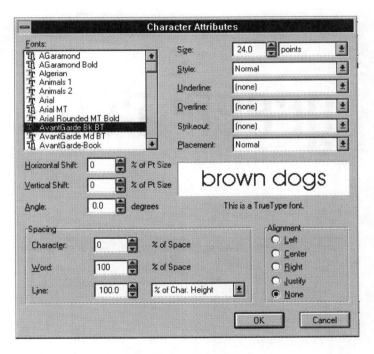

Figure 13. The *Horizontal Shift* option moves the selected text characters along the baseline by whatever percentage you insert. In this case we moved the letter "f" -15%.

The letter f was shifted horizontally -15%

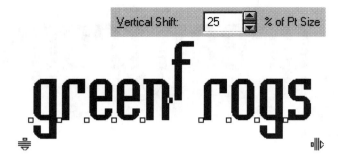

Figure 14. The *Vertical Shift* option moves the selected text characters vertically by whatever percentage you insert. We moved the letter "f," in this example, vertically 25%.

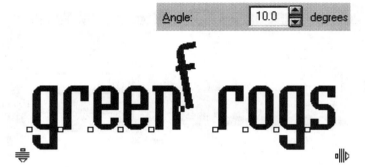

Figure 15. The *Character Angle* option shifts the angle of the selected text character by the degrees you insert. In this example, we have shifted the letter "f" 10 degrees.

FRAME

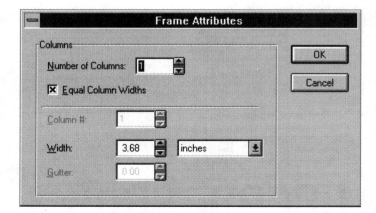

Figure 16. Choosing *Frame* from the **Text** menu opens the *Frame Attributes* dialog box. Here you can insert the number of required columns for your selected Paragraph Text. You can also specify whether you want equal column widths.

If you want to customize your column widths, deselect the *Equal Column Widths* option and enter the width for each of your columns below. The *Gutter* option determines the amount of space between each column.

PARAGRAPH

Figure 17. The *Paragraph* command in the **Text** menu brings up the *Paragraph* dialog box. You cannot access all the options in this dialog box for Artistic Text.

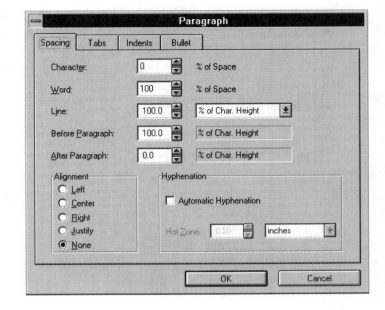

SPACING

The first tab in the *Paragraph* dialog box is the *Spacing* tab.

Figure 18. The *Character* option in the *Spacing* section of the *Paragraph* dialog box lets you select the amount of space between characters in a text block.

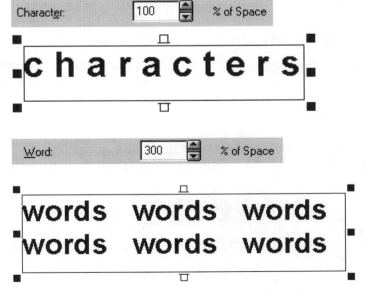

Figure 19. The *Word* option in the *Spacing* section of the *Paragraph* dialog box determines the amount of space between words in a text block.

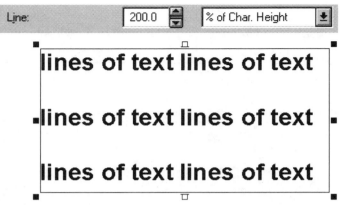

Figure 20. The *Line* option in the *Spacing* section of the *Paragraph* dialog box sets the amount of space between lines of text in a text block.

You can only access the *Before Paragraph* and *After Paragraph* options when you are working with Paragraph Text. These options let you insert space before and after paragraphs of text.

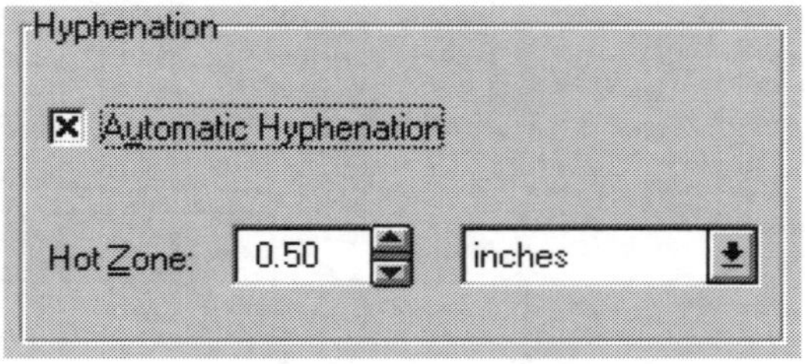

Figure 21. Clicking on the *Automatic Hyphenation* option in the *Paragraph* dialog box turns on hyphenation for the selected Paragraph Text. The *Hot Zone* determines where CorelDRAW hyphenates a word.

This zone extends left from the right of the text frame by whatever amount you insert. CorelDRAW hyphenates a word if a valid hyphenation point falls inside the *Hot Zone*. This makes your right margin less ragged. You can only use hyphenation with Paragraph Text.

You use the *Alignment* options in the *Paragraph* dialog box to change the alignment of selected text.

TABS

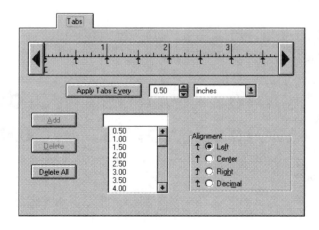

Figure 22. Click on the *Tabs* tab to access the options shown here. The options in the *Tab* dialog box let you apply tab stops to your Paragraph Text (not available for Artistic Text).

Those of you familiar with word processing and page layout programs will be familiar with tabs.

Figure 23. The *Apply Tabs Every* button adds evenly spaced tabs along the ruler in the position indicated in the adjacent box. Change this amount, then click on the button to apply the tab stops.

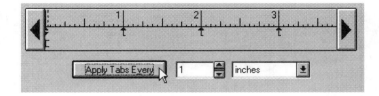

In this example we cleared all the tabs and applied tabs at every inch.

In some cases you may need to click on the *Delete All* button before you apply tabs stops along the ruler in this dialog box.

Figure 24. The *Add* button adds a tab stop to the ruler in the position indicated in the adjacent text box. The position is then added to the list of tab positions below. In this case we cleared all the tab stops (by clicking on the *Delete All* button) and then added a tab at 0.39 of an inch.

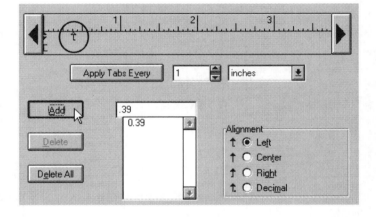

Immediately after you add a tab to the ruler it is highlighted. A highlighted tab is clear (⇑), rather than black (↑).

Figure 25. You can highlight tabs in two ways. The first way is to select the tab position number from the list by clicking on it with the mouse.

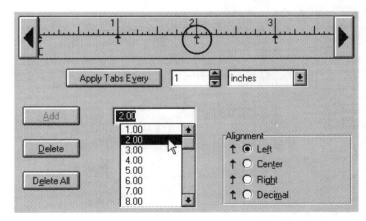

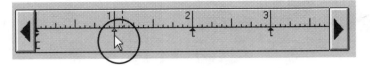

Figure 26. The second way is to click on the tab marker in the ruler in this dialog box.

Clicking on the *Delete* button removes the currently highlighted tab, while the *Delete All* button removes all the current tab stops from the ruler.

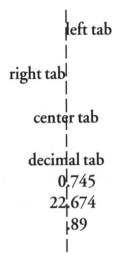

left tab

right tab

center tab

decimal tab
0.745
22.674
.89

Figure 27. The *Alignment* options affect how the text sits in relation to the tab. The dashed line in this example shows the tab stop.

To apply an *Alignment* option to a tab, choose the required *Alignment* option before applying the tab. You can also change the alignment of a tab by highlighting the tab and clicking on the new alignment option.

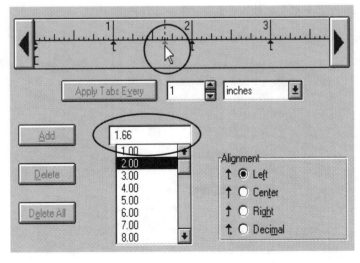

Figure 28. You can also add tabs by clicking directly on the ruler with the mouse. You can also move tab stops by holding the mouse down on them in the ruler and dragging to a new spot. You can use the text box adjacent to the *Add* button, which shows where the current tab stop is for an accurate value for your current tab position while you drag.

Figure 29. The right (▶) and left (◀) facing arrows at opposing ends of the ruler let you scroll to parts of the ruler not currently on screen.

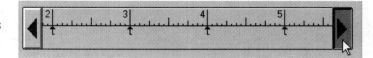

INDENTS

Figure 30. Click on the *Indents* tab to access these options. These options let you apply certain indents to Paragraph Text.

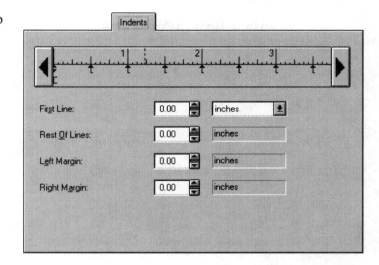

Figure 31. The *First Line* indent option indents the first line of the text by whatever value you insert. The ▲ marker on the ruler in this dialog box moves as you change the *First Line* indent setting.

The *Rest Of Lines* option applies to all the remaining lines (other than the first line). The ▼ marker on the ruler in this dialog box moves as you change the *Rest Of Lines* indent setting.

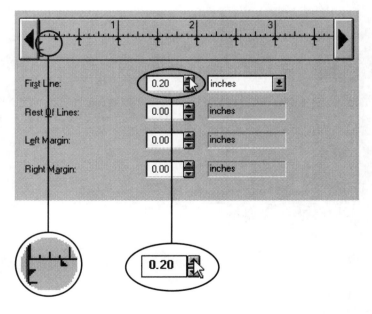

(a)

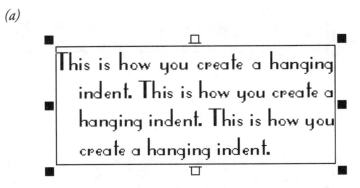

Figure 32. You can create a hanging indent (a) by making the *Rest Of Lines* indent option larger than the *First Line* option (b). Note the position of the *First Line* and *Rest Of Lines* indent markers on the ruler when you have created a hanging indent.

(b)

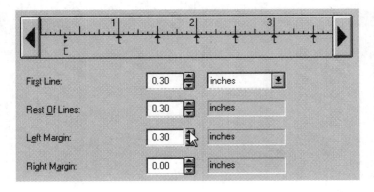

Figure 33. The *Left Margin* option lets you indent the entire text block from the left side of the text frame. All the markers on the ruler in this dialog box move as you change the *Left Margin* setting.

The *Right Margin* option indents the entire text block from the right side of the text frame.

Figure 34. You can also alter the indent settings directly through the ruler in this dialog box. By dragging the ‹ marker in the ruler, you change the *First Line* indent setting. Release the mouse on the ruler where you want your first line indent to occur.

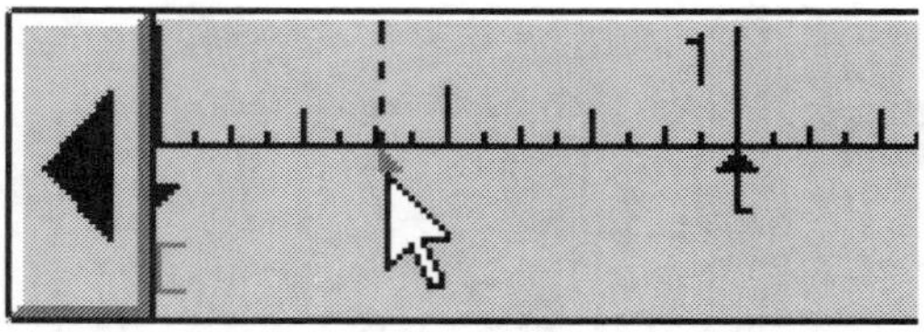

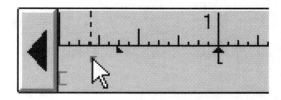

Figure 35. By dragging the › marker, you change the *Rest Of Lines* indent setting.

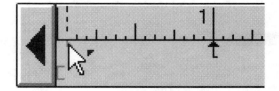

Figure 36. You can create a hanging indent by dragging the *Rest Of Lines* marker further to the right than the *First Line* marker.

If you drag the ⌐ marker, you change the *Left Margin* setting.

BULLETS

Figure 37. Click on the *Bullet* tab in the *Paragraph* dialog box to access these options. The options here let you add bullets to your Paragraph Text.

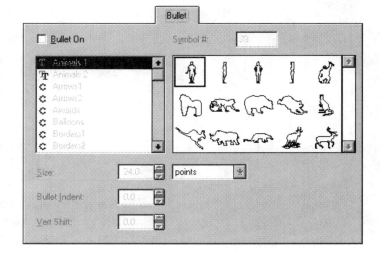

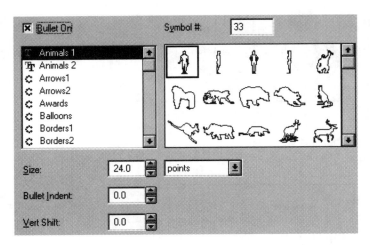

Figure 38. You must check the *Bullet On* option if you want to apply bullets to your text. You can now display a bullet at the beginning of each paragraph in your text.

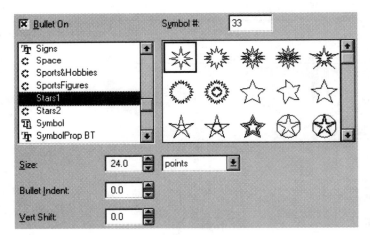

Figure 39. Below the *Bullet On* option is a list of symbol categories. These are the same symbol categories that appear in the *Symbols* roll-up. From this list you can select the symbol category that contains the symbol you want to use as a paragraph bullet.

Use the scroll bar at the right of this list to see the categories not currently in view.

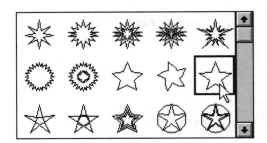

Figure 40. Once you have chosen the symbol category, click on the symbol in the list box to the right of the list. You may need to use the scroll bar to the right of this preview window to see the symbols that aren't on screen.

The *Size* option lets you set the size of the bullet. However, CorelDRAW automatically resizes the symbol in proportion to the text it is inserted into.

The *Vert Shift* option shifts the bullet up or down in relation to the text.

The *Bullet Indent* option indents the bullet from the left side of the text frame. This, of course, also affects the indent of the text.

Figure 41. The bullet we chose in the previous figure looks like this when you apply it to paragraphs of text.

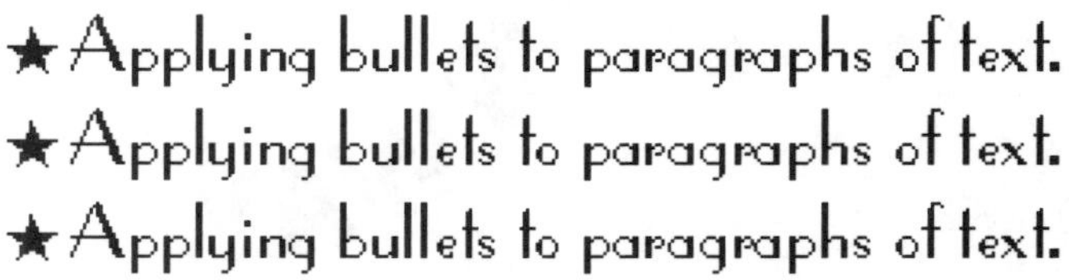

★Applying bullets to paragraphs of text.

★Applying bullets to paragraphs of text.

★Applying bullets to paragraphs of text.

Click on *OK* in the *Paragraph* dialog box to close it and apply any changes to your text.

FIT TEXT TO PATH

Figure 42. You use the *Fit Text To Path* command in the **Text** menu to open the *Fit Text To Path* roll-up. You can only fit Artistic Text to a path.

Before you can use most of the options in this roll-up, you must select your text and an object that you want to use as the path, with the Pick Tool. You can fit text to straight and curved lines, rectangles, ellipses, or even other letters.

As with all roll-ups, you must click the *Apply* button to apply the options you have selected in the roll-up.

TEXT ORIENTATION

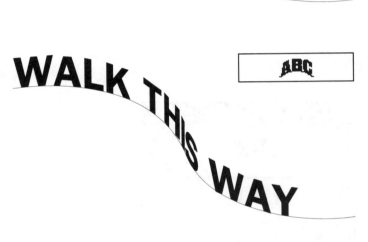

Figure 43. Selecting the first option in the drop-down list at the top of the roll-up rotates the letters to follow the curve of the path.

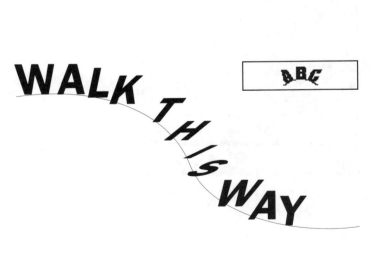

Figure 44. Selecting the second option vertically skews the text in relation to the tangential slope of the path. The more vertical the path, the more it skews the letters.

Figure 45. Selecting the third option skews the text horizontally according to the path. The more vertical the path, the more it flattens the text.

Figure 46. Selecting the last option causes the text to remain upright as it follows the path.

TEXT DISTANCE FROM PATH

Figure 47. Selecting the first option in the second drop-down list ensures that you place the baseline of the text directly on the path.

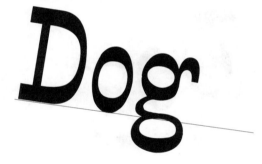

Figure 48. Selecting the second option aligns the top of your text (the ascender line) directly with the path.

Figure 49. Selecting the third option aligns the bottom of the text (the descender line) directly with the path.

Figure 50. Selecting the fourth option centers the text on the path.

Figure 51. Selecting the fifth option lets you move the text freely, above or below the path. Use the mouse to drag the text from the path after choosing this option.

A guide tells you how far you are moving the text above or below the path. Release the mouse button to reformat the text in the new position.

TEXT ALIGNMENT ON A PATH

Figure 52. The third option in the *Fit Text To Path* roll-up changes according to the type of path you have selected.

If the path is an object made up of curves, you use the drop-down list with the three options available as shown in (a).

If the object is a true ellipse or rectangle, an icon with four available selections replaces the drop-down list (b).

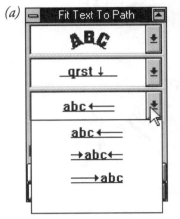

CURVED PATH

Figure 53. Selecting the first option in the drop-down list of Figure 52(a) (the default setting) places the first character of the text at the first node of the path.

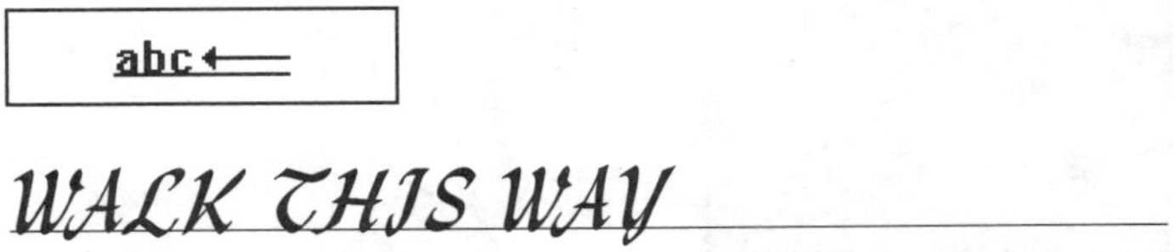

WALK THIS WAY

Figure 54. Selecting the second option centers the text between the start and end nodes of the path.

WALK THIS WAY

Figure 55. Selecting the third option aligns the last text character with the end node of the path.

WALK THIS WAY

ELLIPSE OR RECTANGLE

Figure 56. A square icon with four available selections replaces the third drop-down list if you want to fit your text to an ellipse or rectangle. From here you can click on one of four options to set which side of the object you center the text on.

Figure 57. Choose the *Place on other side* option to place the text on the other side of the path. The text is mirrored horizontally and vertically.

Figure 58. Clicking on the *Edit* button, in the *Fit Text To Path* roll-up, opens the *Fit Text To Path Offsets* dialog box. Selecting the *Horizontal Offset* option shifts the text horizontally along the path.

If you have changed the alignment of the text in relation to the path, the horizontal offset is added to this. Altering the *Distance From Path* option moves the text either above or below the path. Entering a negative value moves the text below the path.

Remember, you use the *Apply* button at the bottom of the *Fit Text To Path* roll-up to apply any changes you make to the text and path.

To edit the text on the path, hold down the Ctrl key and select it with the Pick Tool. This selects only the text. You can now select any text editing commands and apply them to the text.

For interactive kerning and character editing, select the text with the Shape Tool. You can now kern the text or select character nodes. You can also edit the path with the Shape Tool, which automatically reformats the text to the new path.

You can use the *Separate* command from the **Arrange** menu to separate the text and the path.

ALIGN TO BASELINE

Figure 59. Choosing the *Align To Baseline* command (a) shifts any text that you have moved vertically back to the original baseline as in (b). Using this command does not alter the horizontal position of text.

When you rotate text, you rotate the baseline with it. Therefore, you can return any rotated text characters that you have shifted vertically off the baseline to the rotated baseline. To do so, select the *Align To Baseline* command.

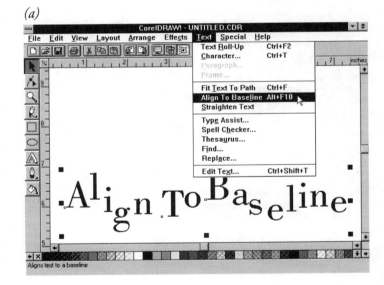

(a)

(b)

STRAIGHTEN TEXT

You use this command to straighten text that you have changed by shifting it off the baseline horizontally or vertically, altering character angle, or changing individual characters in the *Character Attributes* dialog box. Using this command does not straighten text for which you have altered the inter-word, inter-character, or inter-line spacing, or text that you have rotated, skewed, or resized with the Pick Tool.

To straighten text after you have fitted it to a path, you must first separate the text and the path with the *Separate* command from the **Arrange** menu.

TYPE ASSIST

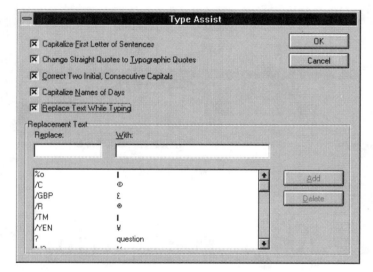

Figure 60. Selecting the *Type Assist* command from the **Text** menu opens the *Type Assist* dialog box, where you can enable options for automatic corrections to the text you enter.

Type Assist can auto-correct misspelled words like "teh" to "the." It can also change capitalization errors, replace normal quotes with typographic quotes, and convert certain letter combinations into commonly used phrases.

To enable an option, select its check box from the list of options in the dialog box. The last option, *Replace Text While Typing*, allows you to enter common mistakes or letter combinations that you want CorelDRAW to automatically correct.

Figure 61. Enter any common mistakes that you make into the *Replace* text box, i.e. "teh," and then enter the correction into the *With* text box, i.e. "the," before clicking on the *Add* button to add this combination to the *Replacement Text* list.

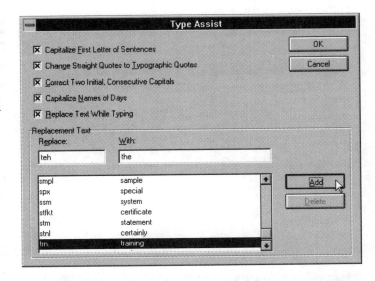

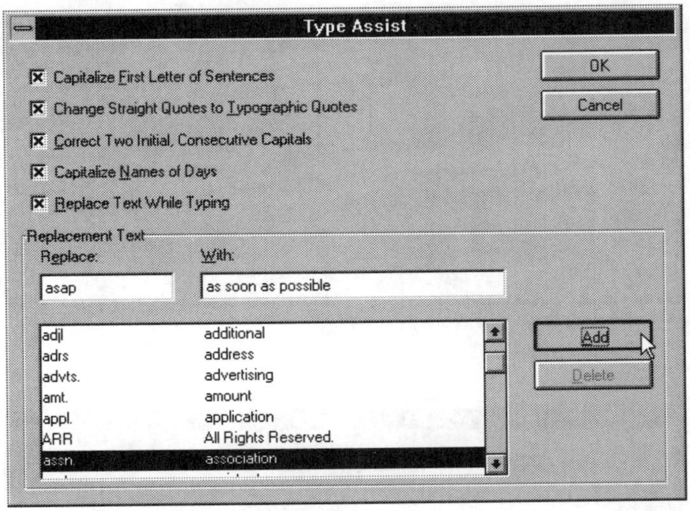

Figure 62. You can use this feature to correct common mistakes, as outlined above, or you can enter letter combinations that you want CorelDRAW to change. For example, you can have CorelDRAW change any occurrence of "asap" followed by a space with the full phrase "as soon as possible."

To do this, simply enter "asap" in the *Replace* text box and then enter "as soon as possible" in the *With* text box and click on the *Add* button. The *Replace* text box can contain up to 64 characters without spaces, and the *With* text box can contain up to 255 characters, including spaces and punctuation.

You can remove any unwanted entries in the list box by selecting them and clicking on the *Delete* button, or you can change an entry by entering new information in the *With* text box and clicking on the *Replace* button that appears instead of the *Add* button.

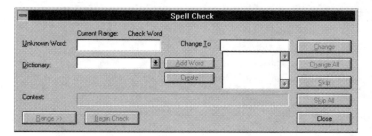

SPELL CHECKER

Figure 63. Using the *Spell Checker* command from the **Text** menu opens the *Spell Check* dialog box.

If you want to check the spelling for an entire text block (Artistic or Paragraph Text), select the text with the Pick Tool before opening this dialog box. If you want to check just a few words, highlight the words with the Text Tool before selecting the *Spell Checker* command.

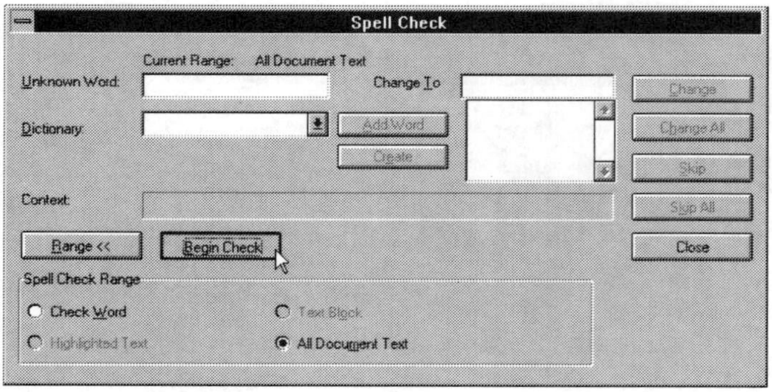

Figure 64. In the *Spell Check* dialog box, click on the *Range* button to extend the dialog box and choose a range of text for the speller to check. After selecting a text range, click on the *Begin Check* button to start the check.

Figure 65. When the spell checker comes across a word it does not recognize, it inserts this word into the *Unknown Word* field. The *Context* box displays the unknown word along with the text it occurs with in the document, to help you work out what the word should be.

CorelDRAW automatically lists suggestions for the word below the *Change To* text box and inserts the first suggestion from the list in this box. You can now scroll through the list of suggestions and select one to automatically place it in the *Change To* text box.

If there are no suggestions for the misspelled word, you can type in your own replacement in the *Change To* text box. Click on the *Change* button to replace the unknown word with the word in the *Change To* text box. Clicking on the *Change All* button replaces all occurrences of the misspelled word with the one in the *Change To* text box.

Use the *Skip* button if the spell checker has highlighted a word that you have spelled correctly, but does not appear in the dictionary, such as a name. Clicking on the *Skip All* button skips all occurrences of the word in the text.

Figure 66. You can also create a personal dictionary where you can add words that the main dictionary does not recognize (such as acronyms, names, industry jargon, etc.). To create a personal dictionary, click on the *Create* button to open the *Create Personal Dictionary* dialog box and enter a name for your dictionary.

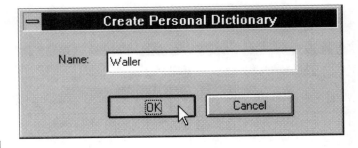

Figure 67. When you click on *OK*, CorelDRAW returns you to the *Spell Check* dialog box with your new dictionary name in the *Dictionary* list box. You can now access the *Add* button and add any unknown words to this dictionary. You can create more dictionaries in this way, which you can use for specific purposes. You can then add words to the appropriate dictionary by selecting it from the drop-down list of available dictionaries.

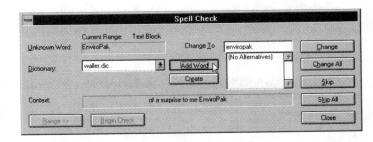

The spell checker will use your personal dictionary when spell checking your text.

THESAURUS

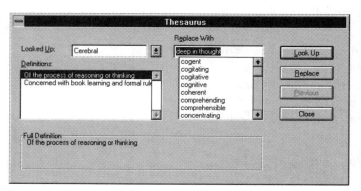

Figure 68. Choosing the *Thesaurus* command from the **Text** menu opens the *Thesaurus* dialog box. If you have selected a word with the Text Tool before selecting the *Thesaurus*, the dialog box displays this word in the *Looked Up* text box. The meanings of the word display in the *Definitions* box.

Depending on the word, there may be a number of definitions for the word, each definition having different synonyms.

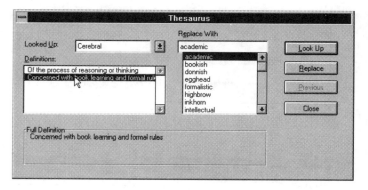

Figure 69. If there is more than one definition for the word, selecting a different one from the *Definitions* list displays a new list of synonyms.

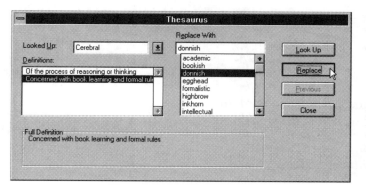

Figure 70. The list of synonyms for each meaning of your word appears below the *Replace With* text box. Select a new word from this list to display the word in the *Replace With* text box. You can then click on the *Replace* button to replace the word in the text with this word and close the *Thesaurus* dialog box.

If you choose the *Thesaurus* command with no text selected, nothing will appear in the *Looked Up* field in the *Thesaurus* dialog box. Type your own word into this field, and click on the *Look Up* button to display a list of synonyms for the word.

In this case, you cannot access the *Replace* button, because the word you typed directly into this dialog box does not exist in the document text.

Figure 71. You can at any time double-click on a synonym for it to display in the *Looked Up* box. Its meanings and synonyms then appear. The *Looked Up* drop-down list keeps a record of the words that you have looked up, and you can reselect any of these words.

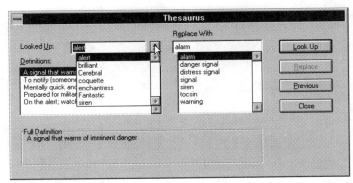

The *Previous* button takes you back to the last word you looked up and displays it in the *Looked Up* text box.

If the word in the *Looked Up* field is not in the dictionary, a message appears telling you that CorelDRAW could not find any definitions for that word.

FIND

Figure 72. You use the *Find* command from the **Text** menu to find a word, sentence, or certain characters in your Paragraph Text. The first thing to do is to insert the text cursor in the block at the point where you want to begin the search. To do this, select the *Paragraph Text* tool (▤) and click the mouse once in the text block from where you want to begin the search. In this case we inserted the text cursor at the beginning of the text block.

Whale Watchers Flock To Sydney

June 1993

Those of us interested in whales, and lets face it who isn't, have been given an unexpected treat this week with the appearance of a whale and calf off Sydney's northern beaches. This intelligent and ponderous couple have made Sydney their temporary home during their annual migration.

The best viewing spot has been from Long Reef headland, where it has been possible to see the mother and its calf frolicking together in the water. The whales have literally dwarfed the keen surfers who have been braving the cold winter waters in search of the perfect winter wave.

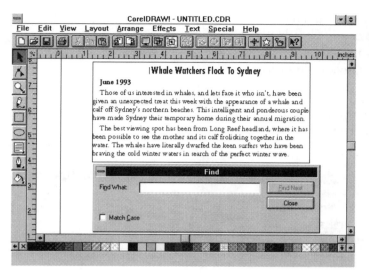

Figure 73. Following on from the previous figure, choose the *Find* command to bring up the *Find* dialog box.

You can hold the mouse button down when the cursor is on the title bar of this dialog box and drag it above or below the text you are searching. This lets you see the word once CorelDRAW has found it.

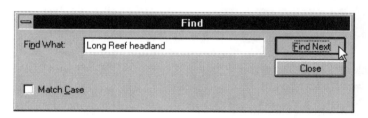

Figure 74. Type the word, sentence, or character in the *Find What* text box and click on the *Find Next* button. (You can type up to 100 characters in the *Find What* text box.)

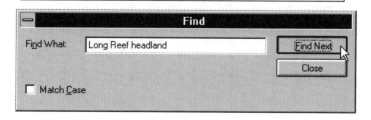

Figure 75. If the specified word (or phrase) is in the selected text, the *Find* command selects the first occurrence after the cursor. You can now click on the *Close* button to return to your document (with the relevant text still selected); or click on the *Find Next* button again to find the next occurrence of the text.

Figure 76. When the search has reached the end of the text block, CorelDRAW displays this screen prompt. You can either continue the search from the beginning of the document (*Yes*) or finish the search (*No*).

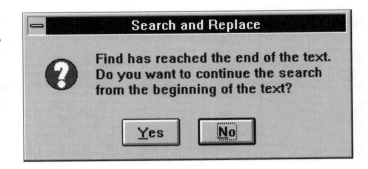

The *Match Case* option in the *Find* dialog box lets you find words that match the case (upper or lower) of whatever you insert in the *Find What* text box.

REPLACE

Selecting the *Replace* command opens the *Replace* dialog box. As with the *Find* command, you can only use *Replace* effectively if you have the insertion point in the text you want to search.

Figure 77. As with the *Find* dialog box, the *Replace* dialog box allows you to find text by looking for what is in the *Find What* text box. However, the options in this dialog box allow you to find text, and replace it as well.

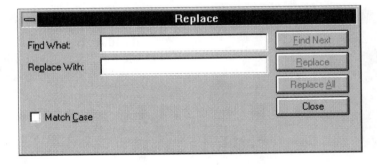

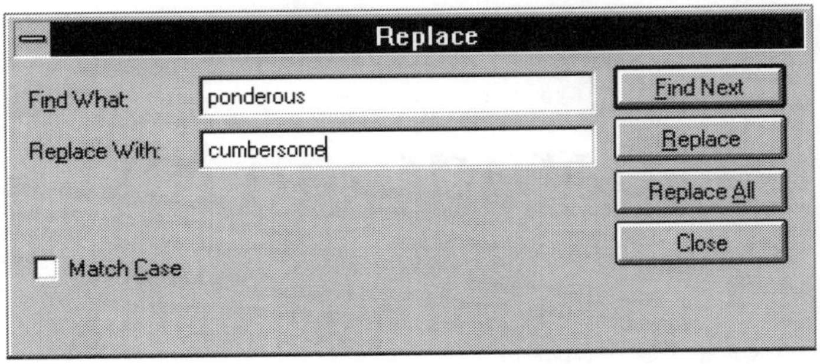

Figure 78. You enter the text you want to replace your *Find What* text within the *Replace With* text box.

As with the *Find* dialog box, you can drag the title bar above or below the text you are searching. This lets you see CorelDRAW select and replace your text once it has found it.

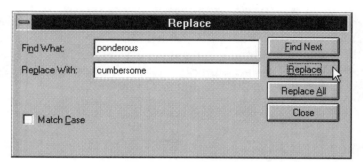

Figure 79. You can now either click on the *Find Next* button to find and select the first occurrence of the *Find What* text after the insertion point; or you can click on the *Replace* button to find, select, and replace the first occurrence of the *Find What* text after the insertion point.

Use the *Find Next* button if you want to first find the word and then decide whether you want to replace it.

You may, however, like to keep some occurrences of the word in the text; in that case you would keep using the *Find Next* button until you find the occurrence of the word you want to change. Then click on the *Replace* button to change the text.

If you want to change all occurrences of the word in the text simultaneously, click on the *Replace All* button.

The *Match Case* option in the *Replace* dialog box lets you find and replace words that match the case (upper or lower) of the word or sentence you insert in the *Find What* text box.

EDIT TEXT

(a)

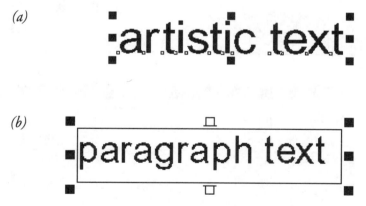

(b)

Figure 80. The *Edit Text* command opens the *Edit Text* dialog box. The dialog box that appears depends on what sort of text you have selected. If you have Artistic Text selected (a) when you choose the *Edit Text* command, you will activate the *Edit Text* dialog box with options for Artistic Text. Selecting Paragraph Text (b) activates the *Edit Text* dialog box for Paragraph Text.

ARTISTIC TEXT

Figure 81. The *Edit Text* dialog box for both Artistic Text and Paragraph Text contains a *Character* button. Clicking on this button opens the *Character Attributes* dialog box where you can change the character attributes for any text that you have highlighted in the *Edit Text* dialog box.

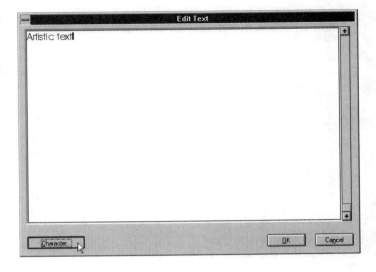

Figure 82. This dialog box operates in the same way as described in the **Character** section earlier in this chapter. You can change the *Font, Size, Style, Placement, Spacing,* and *Alignment* of the selected Artistic Text.

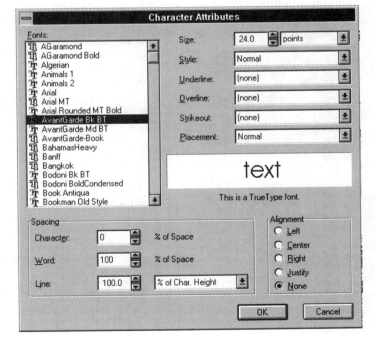

PARAGRAPH TEXT

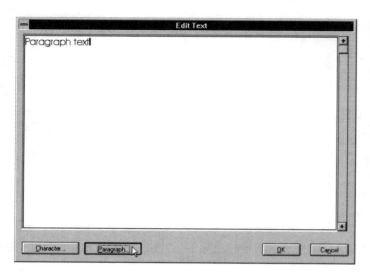

Figure 83. The *Edit Text* dialog box for Paragraph Text includes both a *Character* and *Paragraph* button.

You can change the character attributes for selected paragraph text in this dialog box through the *Character* button (see Figure 82) but you can also change the paragraph attributes for your selected text in this dialog box by clicking on the *Paragraph* button. This opens the *Paragraph* dialog box.

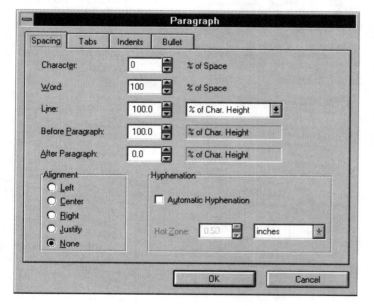

Figure 84. At the top of the *Paragraph* dialog box there are a number of tabs that allow you to view and set different paragraph attribute options. This dialog box operates in the same way as described in the *Paragraph* section earlier in this chapter.

THE SPECIAL MENU COMMANDS

The **Special** menu commands let you create patterns, arrows, and symbols, extract and merge text, as well as customize some of the features of CorelDRAW.

Figure 1. This figure displays the **Special** menu and its commands.

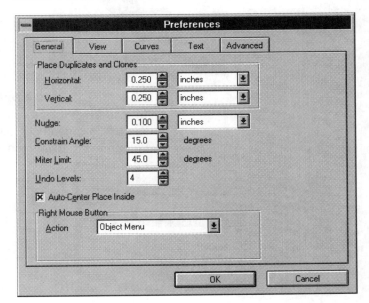

PREFERENCES

Figure 2. Selecting the *Preferences* command from the **Special** menu opens the *Preferences* dialog box.

GENERAL PREFERENCES

The *Place Duplicates and Clones* option on the *General* tab in the *Preferences* dialog box sets the offset from the original of a duplicated or cloned object when you choose *Duplicate* or *Clone* from the **Edit** menu. Using a positive value for both the *Horizontal* and *Vertical* options positions the duplicate or clone up and to the right. A value of zero, for both *Horizontal* and *Vertical,* places the duplicate or clone directly behind the original object.

The *Nudge* option lets you set the amount of space you can move a selected object using the arrow keys on your keyboard.

The *Constrain Angle* option sets the angular constraint when you use certain functions in conjunction with the Ctrl key. These include: rotating, skewing, drawing straight lines (*Freehand* mode), and manipulating control points when drawing curves in *Bezier* mode.

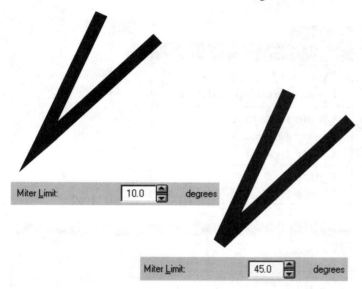

Figure 3. The *Miter Limit* sets the sharpness of a corner, or how far the vertex extends beyond the actual corner. The higher the value (between 5 and 45), the more beveled the corner. Compare the two corners in this example. CorelDRAW bevels the joint below the specified angle.

The *Undo Levels* option on the *General* tab (see Figure 2) lets you choose how many times you can undo commands. The more *Undo Levels* you have, the more memory it takes to run CorelDRAW.

Checking the *Auto-Center Place Inside* option on the *General* tab in the *Preferences* dialog box determines whether PowerClip contents are centered within the container object. For more information on PowerClips see **Chapter 9, The Effects Menu**.

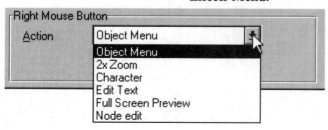

Figure 4. The *Right Mouse Button* drop-down list determines the *Action* assigned to clicking your right mouse button. By default, clicking the right mouse button on an object activates the **Object** menu (see **Chapter 12, The Object Menu**). However, you can choose a new action for your right mouse button from this drop-down list.

VIEW PREFERENCES

Figure 5. Clicking on the *View* tab activates the options for the view preferences. The *Auto-Panning* option scrolls the page when you resize, move, or drag an object past the edge of the screen.

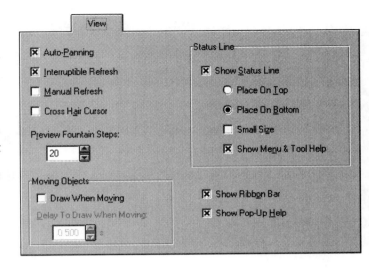

With the *Interruptible Refresh* option checked, you can interrupt redrawing on the screen if you click the mouse, press a key, or select a menu command or tool. This is useful for complex drawings, when you do not want to wait for CorelDRAW to redraw the entire graphic.

With the *Manual Refresh* option checked, the screen is not redrawn until you press CTRL+W. As with *Interruptible Refresh* this can be particularly useful for complex drawings.

If you select *Cross Hair Cursor* on the *View* tab, your mouse pointer turns into a cross-hair that covers the whole screen.

Figure 6. The *Preview Fountain Steps* option lets you set the number of sections that make up a fountain-filled object on the screen. The lower the number, the faster it is to redraw, but you may not see a very smooth transition between the two colors.

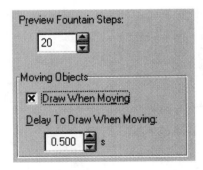

The *Moving Objects* section lets you determine viewing options for when you are moving objects. The *Draw When Moving* option allows you to see a wireframe of your object when you are moving it, instead of just its outline frame. The *Delay To Draw When Moving* option determines how long you have to pause when moving an object before CorelDRAW redraws it.

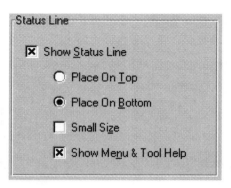

Figure 7. The *Status Line* section on the *View* tab allows you to determine how you want to display the status line in CorelDRAW. The *Show Menu & Tool Help* check box here lets the status line display a description of each menu item or tool that you place the cursor over.

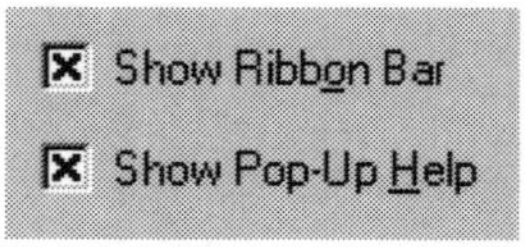

Figure 8. The last two options in the *View* tab of the *Preferences* dialog box allow you to display or hide the ribbon bar, and to choose whether or not you want pop-up balloon descriptions to appear when you place the cursor over menu items or tools. This is an alternative to the *Show Menu & Tool Help* option described in Figure 7.

CURVES PREFERENCES

Figure 9. The *Curves* tab at the top of the *Preferences* dialog box displays the *Curves* options. Most of the option settings in this dialog box range from 1 to 10, with 5 the default setting. You will find the default settings generally sufficient, but you may change them here if you wish.

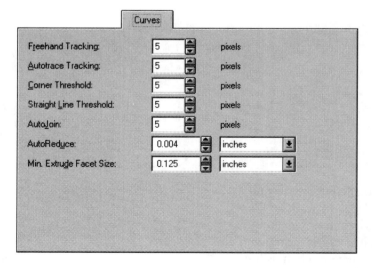

The lower the number you insert for *Freehand Tracking*, the closer the bezier curves follow the line you are drawing. This usually means more nodes and a rougher looking line. Inserting a higher number results in fewer nodes and smoother curves.

The *Autotrace Tracking* option works the same way as the *Freehand Tracking* option, but applies to the tracing of a bitmap. The lower the number, the closer the line will follow the outline of a bitmap when autotracing with the Pencil Tool. The curves appear smoother with a higher number, but they won't follow the outline of the bitmap as closely. See the **Autotrace** section in **Chapter 2, The Utility, Drawing, and Text Tools,** for more information on autotracing.

Corner Threshold applies to both freehand drawing and autotracing; it determines the sharpness and smoothness of corners. If you set a low number, the corners are more likely to be cusps, and changes of direction are more acute. Setting a high number ensures that the corners are smoother, but the line might not necessarily follow the true outline of the bitmap.

The *Straight Line Threshold* option also applies to both freehand drawing and autotracing. If you set a low number for this option, CorelDRAW is more likely to create curves when drawing or autotracing—except for definite straight lines. A higher number creates straighter lines, except for definite curved line sections.

The *AutoJoin* option determines how closely you must put an end node of a drawing to the beginning node before CorelDRAW automatically joins them. The lower the number, the closer you have to put the cursor when ending a drawing. The higher the number, the less precise you need to be.

The higher the *AutoReduce* value, the more nodes CorelDRAW removes when you *AutoReduce* an object from the *Node Edit* roll-up.

The *Minimum Extrude Facet Size* applies to the complexity of your extrusions. While you are working on a drawing, set a large facet size to speed up the redraw time. You can then set a low facet size for smooth rendering when you are ready to print.

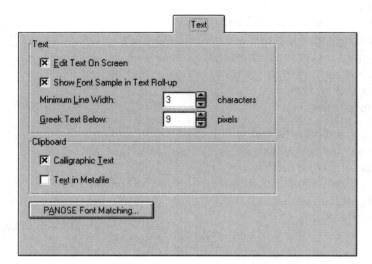

TEXT PREFERENCES

Figure 10. The *Text* tab in the *Preferences* dialog box displays the *Text* options.

The *Edit Text On Screen* option allows you to edit text directly on screen, or only through the *Edit Text* dialog box.

The *Show Font Sample in Text Roll-up* option allows you to choose whether or not you display a font preview for a selected font in the *Text* roll-up.

The *Minimum Line Width* option sets the minimum number of characters that CorelDRAW will allow to start a new line in enveloped Paragraph Text. For example, if the value is set to 3 (the default) CorelDRAW will not start a new line in an envelope without at least three characters for that line.

The *Greek Text Below* option determines at what size CorelDRAW displays gray lines instead of Paragraph Text on the screen (greeked text). When using small point sizes greeked text speeds up redrawing time.

The *Clipboard* section allows you to choose the text format you want when you copy text to the Clipboard. Selecting *Calligraphic Text* retains calligraphic pen outlines applied to text when you transfer or export that text. The *Text in Metafile* check box determines whether text that is transferred to the Clipboard is pasted as text or curves. Enabling this check box pastes text as text and disabling it pastes text as curves.

The *PANOSE Font Matching* button opens another *Preferences* dialog box. In this dialog box you can determine what font substitutions you can make for missing fonts when exporting or importing text material to or from other systems that do not have fonts that match your fonts in CorelDRAW.

ADVANCED PREFERENCES

Figure 11. The *Advanced* tab in the *Preferences* dialog box contains the *Advanced* options.

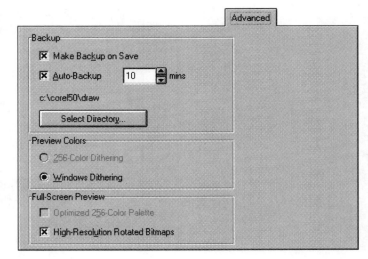

Checking the *Make Backup on Save* option creates a backup file whenever you save a file. The backup file is automatically assigned the extension *.BAK*.

The *Auto-Backup* check box creates a backup file at a specified interval (default 10 minutes). The backup files are stored in the directory shown here unless you change this using the *Select Directory* button.

The *Preview Colors* section of the dialog box determines how CorelDRAW displays colors on your screen. It automatically selects the *256-Color Dithering* option if your screen supports this. It selects the *Windows Dithering* option if your screen can't display 256 colors.

The *Optimized 256-Color Palette* in the *Full-Screen Preview* section optimizes the colors on *editable preview* so that it uses up to 256 colors with no dithering. You can access this option only if your screen driver supports it. The *High-Resolution Rotated Bitmaps* option enables the actual bitmap to display in full screen preview. When this is disabled, a thumbnail is used instead of the actual bitmap.

SYMBOLS ROLL-UP

The *Symbols Roll-Up* command in the **Special** menu opens the *Symbols* roll-up. The features in this roll-up are described in **Chapter 2, The Utility, Drawing, and Text Tools.**

PRESETS ROLL-UP

Figure 12. The *Presets Roll-Up* command in the **Special** menu opens the *Presets* roll-up, where you access a variety of visual macros that automate certain drawing tasks.

(a)

(b)

Figure 13. To apply a preset, simply select the object you want to apply the preset to, and then choose the preset you want from the drop-down list in the *Presets* roll-up (a).

A preview of the preset's result appears in the preview box to show what your object will look like, and any notes attached to the preset appear in a fly-out. When you have selected the effect you want, click on *Apply* to apply the preset to your object (b).

Because the preset is a macro, CorelDRAW sometimes takes a while to apply all of the commands that make up your chosen preset.

You can also use the *Presets* roll-up to create your own presets through the *Start Recording* button. Any actions you perform on an object when you are recording are saved as a part of your preset and you can then apply them to other objects by selecting your preset later. For details on recording a preset, see *Working with Presets* in your CorelDRAW manual.

CREATE PATTERN

Figure 14. The *Create Pattern* command in the **Special** menu lets you create patterns from an image you have drawn on your page. This image or drawing then becomes part of the patterns in the *Two-Color Pattern* or *Full-Color Pattern* dialog boxes. Selecting this command brings up the *Create Pattern* dialog box.

Your first choice is whether you want the pattern to be a *Two Color* or a *Full Color* pattern. You can select the three *Resolution* options only if you are creating a *Two Color* pattern. Click on *OK* once you have made your choices.

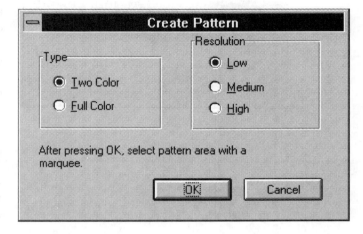

Figure 15. To create a pattern (Figure 14), you must first marquee select the area you want to include in the pattern. The mouse pointer changes to a cross-hair that covers the whole screen. This makes it easier for you to accurately select the area you want.

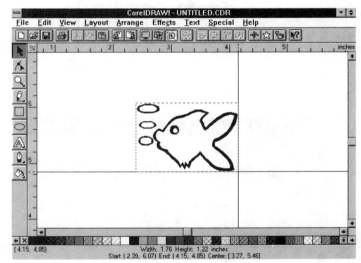

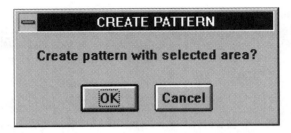

Figure 16. When you have selected the area, release the mouse; this displays a screen prompt asking you to confirm that the area you selected with the cross-hair is the area you want in the pattern. Clicking on *OK* creates the pattern.

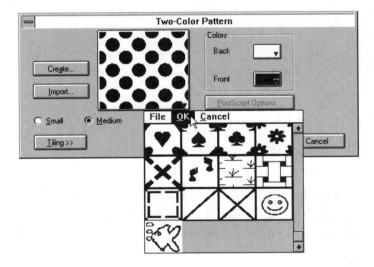

Figure 17. The *Two-Color Pattern* dialog box now shows the new graphic. If we had selected the *Full Color* option in the *Create Pattern* dialog box, the *Full-Color Pattern* dialog box would display the new pattern.

See the **Fill Tool** section in **Chapter 3, Outline and Fill Tools** for more information on applying two-color patterns and full-color patterns to objects.

CREATE ARROW

Figure 18. You can choose the *Create Arrow* command, from the **Special** menu, only if you have selected an object. The *Create Arrow* prompt then appears asking you whether you want to create an arrowhead with the selected object.

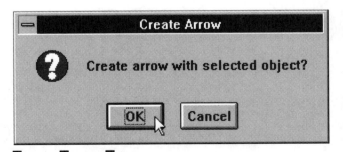

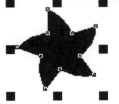

Clicking on *OK* inserts the selected object in the *Arrows* field of the *Outline Pen* dialog box. The larger you make the selected object, the larger it will appear as an arrowhead option.

Figure 19. You can now use the arrowhead you created at the beginning or end of a line. See the **Outline Tool** section in **Chapter 3, Outline and Fill Tools**, for more information on applying arrowheads to a line.

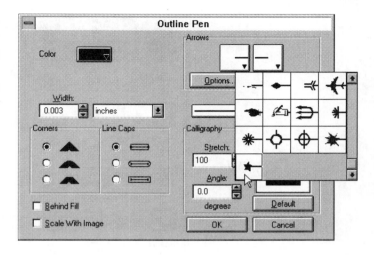

CREATE SYMBOL

You use the *Create Symbol* command to create symbols that will appear in the *Symbol* roll-up. You can create a symbol from any closed object of any size.

Figure 20. With the Pick Tool, select the object you want to use as a symbol, then choose *Create Symbol* from the **Special** menu. This opens the *Create Symbol* dialog box of the next figure.

In this example we combined the text with the object behind to make them all the one object.

Figure 21. From the *Symbol Category* list in the *Create Symbol* dialog box, choose the library you want the new symbol to appear in and click on *OK*.

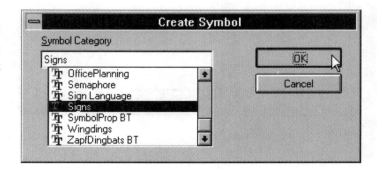

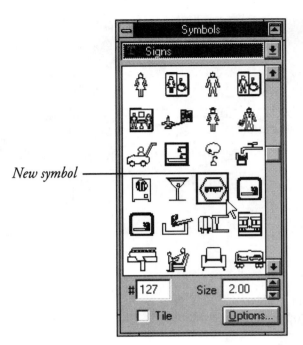

New symbol

Figure 22. Your object now appears in the *Symbols* roll-up in the category you chose in the *Create Symbol* dialog box. You can place it on the page and edit it as you can with any symbol in CorelDRAW.

EXTRACT

You use the *Extract* command from the **Special** menu to save text created in CorelDRAW in an ASCII format for editing in a word processor. You must save the file before using the *Extract* command.

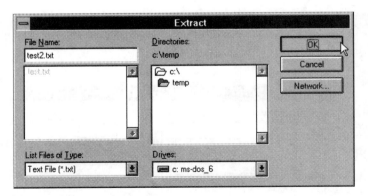

Figure 23. Select the text you want to extract and choose *Extract* to open the *Extract* dialog box. Like the *Open Drawing, Save Drawing,* and *Export* dialog boxes, you must choose the destination of the file and give it a name. Click on the *OK* button once you have done this.

Figure 24. You can now open the extracted text file in a word processing program. In this example, we have opened the file in Windows Write. If you have more than one text string, the text appears in the word processor in the order of the most recently created, to the first created.

You must not change the order of the text. You should not change the text and numbers displayed within the less-than and greater-than symbols, because CorelDRAW needs these to identify the text. Save the word processing file, once you have made the necessary changes to the text. You can then merge the text back into CorelDRAW.

MERGE BACK

Use the *Merge Back* command from the **Special** menu to put extracted text back into the file you extracted it from.

Figure 25. After opening the file that you originally extracted the text from, select *Merge Back* to open the *Merge Back* dialog box. Find the text file using the *Drives* and *Directories* lists and click on the *OK* button. This inserts the edited text file back into the CorelDRAW file.

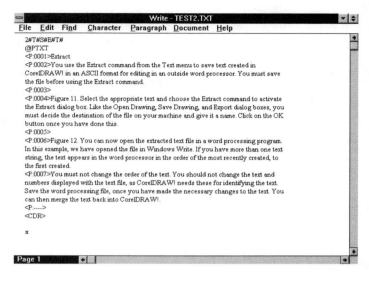

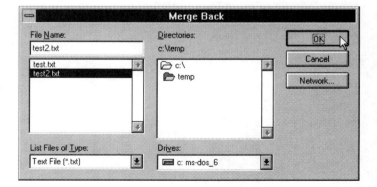

You merge the text back into the CorelDRAW document in the same format you extracted it, except for text that you blended, extruded, fitted to a path, or altered in the *Character Attributes* dialog box. The text returns to exactly the same position you extracted it from. If you added a lot more text in the word processor, it may overlap other text, however CorelDRAW will correct this.

If you made any changes to the text in the CorelDRAW file that you extracted the text from, the *Merge Back* procedure overwrites these changes.

THE OBJECT MENU 12

THE OBJECT MENU COMMANDS

The **Object** menu commands cover a range of options. You can use this menu to save, update, revert to, and apply styles, as well as assign overprint to an object's fill or outline, open the *Object Data* roll-up, and change clone objects.

Figure 1. This figure displays the **Object** menu and its commands. Not all options in the **Object** menu are always available.

Figure 2. The way you activate the **Object** menu differs slightly depending on what option you have selected in the *Preferences* dialog box.

To open this dialog box, choose the *Preferences* command from the **Special** menu and, in the *Preferences* dialog box that appears, click on the *General* tab.

If you have the *Object Menu* option selected for the *Right Mouse Button* action in this dialog box, you can click the right mouse button on an object to get the **Object** menu.

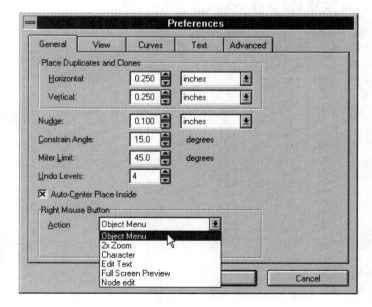

If you have checked another option for the right mouse button action in the *Preferences* dialog box, you must hold the right mouse button down on an object to activate the **Object** menu.

SAVE AS STYLE

The first command in the **Object** menu is the *Save As Style* command. This command lets you save and name the attributes applied to an object as a style. You can then quickly and easily apply these attributes to another object by assigning it that style.

Style attributes can be saved and applied to graphics, Artistic Text, and Paragraph Text. When you are saving styles, CorelDRAW recognizes whether you are working with graphics, Artistic Text, or Paragraph Text.

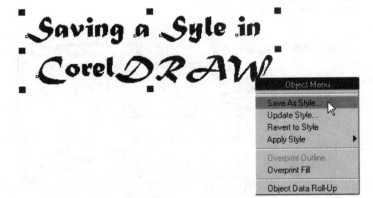

Figure 3. Once you have applied all the necessary attributes to an object (in this case Artistic Text), you click (or hold) the right mouse button down on the text and choose *Save As Style* from the **Object** menu.

Figure 4. The *Save Style As* dialog box then appears. At the top of this dialog box you type in a name for the style. This name can be up to 15 characters long.

Then, in the *Include* section, check the attributes you want to include in the style and click on the *OK* button.

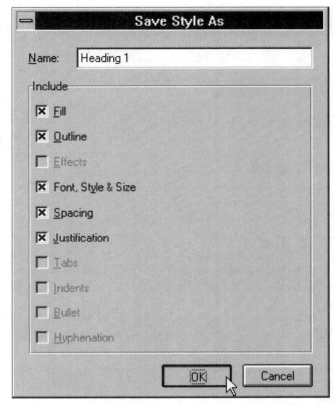

Figure 5. The style you create now appears in the *Styles* roll-up. You can apply this style to other objects or text which saves you from applying the attributes one by one to any new objects or text you want to format in the same way.

When you save styles, they are added to the current template.

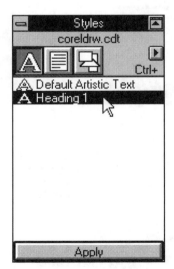

UPDATE STYLE

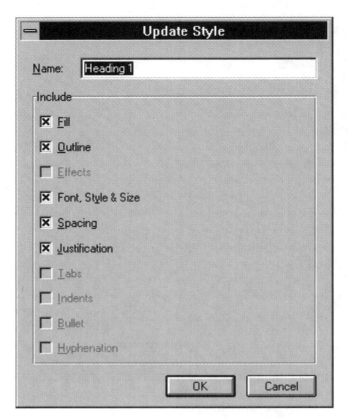

Figure 6. Choosing the *Update Style* command from the **Object** menu opens the *Update Style* dialog box. Select the *Update Style* command for an object if you have made changes to it since applying a style to it and want to add those changes to the style. In the *Include* section of the dialog box, choose the attributes you want to update and click on *OK* to add the new changes to the style.

CorelDRAW then updates all objects in the drawing that you have assigned this style to. You can also change the name of the style in this dialog box.

REVERT TO STYLE

Figure 7. You use the *Revert to Style* command in the **Object** menu if you have made changes to an object since applying a style to it. CorelDRAW then changes the object's attributes to how they were when you last applied a style to it.

APPLY STYLE

Figure 8. The *Apply Style* command brings up a submenu of styles. The styles that appear here depend on what styles (if any) you have created, what template you have loaded, and what object you have activated the **Object** menu for. These are the same styles that appear in the *Styles* roll-up.

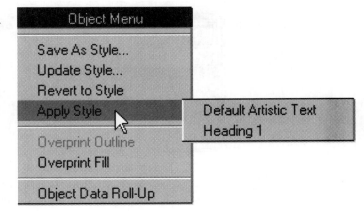

If you are applying styles to Paragraph Text, you can apply a different style to each paragraph. To apply a style to just one paragraph, insert the Paragraph Text cursor in the paragraph you want to affect and select the style. To apply a style to all the Paragraph Text, select the text block with the Pick Tool.

For more information on *Styles*, see **Chapter 7, The Layout Menu.**

OVERPRINT OUTLINE AND OVERPRINT FILL

These two commands let you apply the *Overprint* feature to an object's outline and fill. When you create color separations from CorelDRAW, colors are "knocked out" where they overlap. This ensures that a third color is not created where this overlap occurs. If, for some reason, you want the colors to overlap, you can apply the *Overprint* feature to the objects concerned and there is no knock out.

For more information on overprinting, see the *Print* command in **Chapter 4, The File Menu.**

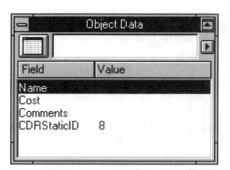

OBJECT DATA ROLL-UP

Figure 9. The *Object Data Roll-Up* command from the **Object** menu opens the *Object Data* roll-up. Use the options in this roll-up primarily for creating a database of information about your drawing.

A database is a tool for organizing, managing, and retrieving information. This information is stored in columns of information. This feature is useful, but not necessary for the day-to-day use of CorelDRAW.

Once you have set up the database and opened the *Object Data* roll-up, you can click on an object in your drawing to find out the relevant information in the *Object Data* roll-up.

Remember, to open the *Object Data* roll-up, click or hold the right mouse button on an object to first bring up the **Object** menu; then select the *Object Data Roll-Up* command. Once you have displayed this roll-up, you can move it around the screen, roll it up, or remove it as you can any other roll-up. You can also change the size of this roll-up by holding the mouse down on any edge of the roll-up and dragging it in or out.

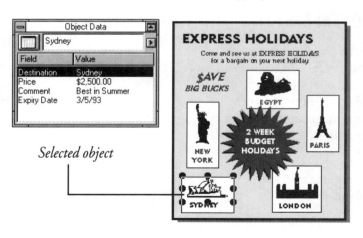

Selected object

Figure 10. In this travel flyer example you could include information in the database regarding the destination, price, general comment, and the expiry date of the offer. Here we have selected one of the destinations, and all the relevant information appears in the *Object Data* roll-up. An employee can follow this procedure to find out this information for a customer.

Notice that the object selected in this example (Sydney Opera House) is a child object. This means it is part of a group of objects and we had to hold the Ctrl key down to select it by itself. You can include information on groups of objects as well as child objects.

See the following sections on how to create such a database.

CREATING FIELDS

Figure 11. The first step in creating the database is to establish and create the fields. Choose *Field Editor* from the *Object Data* roll-up to open the *Object Data Field Editor* dialog box.

Figure 12. You create new fields in this dialog box by clicking on the *Create New Field* button at the top of the dialog box. This adds *Field0* to the text box and the list of fields below the button (a). You can type the name of your field directly over the top of the *Field0* text and press Enter to add the field (b).

Follow the same procedure to add all the fields you want. If any fields already exist that you do not want, you can simply select them from the list of fields and click on the *Delete Field(s)* button, or type a new field name directly over them.

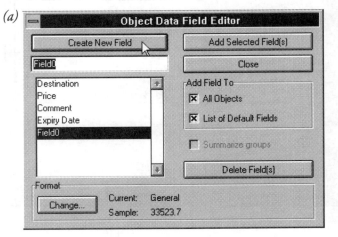

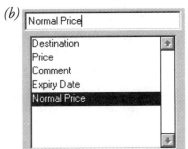

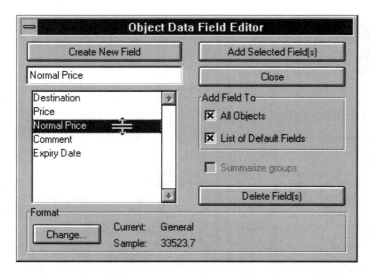

Figure 13. The order the fields appear in this dialog box is the order they will appear in the database and the *Object Data* roll-up. If you want to change the order of the fields, hold the mouse button down when the cursor is on the field label you want to move, drag it to a new position in the list, and release the mouse button.

In this example we have moved the *Normal Price* field up underneath the *Price* field.

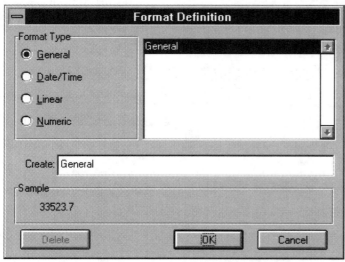

Figure 14. Once you have added all the fields and put them in the right order, you can format a field by clicking on the *Change* button at the bottom of the *Object Data Field Editor* dialog box. This opens the *Format Definition* dialog box. You have four format options.

When you choose one of the options other than *General*, you then have further formatting choices. CorelDRAW lists these options in the preview list to the right of the format choices.

Apply the *General* format option to fields that include general text.

Use the *Date/Time* format for fields that are going to contain the date. In the example of our travel brochure, we formatted the *Expiry Date* field with the *Date/Time* option.

Use the *Linear* format option for fields that are going to contain measurements, and the *Numeric* option for fields that will include currency or percentage information. We applied the *Numeric* option to the *Price* field in our travel brochure.

When you choose a new format option, the *Sample* section of the dialog box displays an example of how it will look. You can also customize your own format by typing it into the *Create* edit box in the *Format Definition* dialog box.

Choose a format separately for each field in your database.

Once back in the *Object Data Field Editor* dialog box, you must click on the *Add Selected Field(s)* button to close this dialog box and return to the *Object Data* roll-up.

Figure 15. The field names you created appear under the *Field* heading in the *Object Data* roll-up. You can now enter the information into the *Object Data* roll-up for a selected object. You then select another object to add the information for that object, and so on. Here you can see that the list of fields contains the field names already there, plus the new one we added: *Normal Price*.

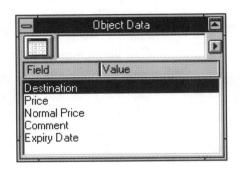

ADDING FIELD INFORMATION

Figure 16. With the Pick Tool, select the object for which you want to insert information. If the object is part of a group, you must hold the Ctrl key down to select the object separately. Then, in the *Object Data* roll-up, click on the field that you want to put the information in. In this example we selected the *Egypt* graphic.

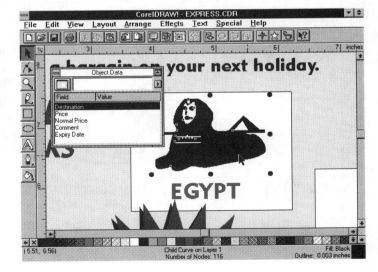

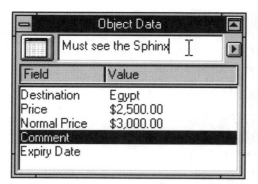

Figure 17. Next, insert the cursor in the text box at the top of the roll-up and type in the information for the selected field. Press the Enter key (or the down arrow on your keyboard) to add the information to the *Value* list in the roll-up.

You can then select the fields one by one and add the information in the same way as just described. In this example, we have added the *Destination*, *Price*, and *Normal Price* information and are about to enter the *Comment Value*.

You can edit the field value once you have entered it. To do this, select the field you want to edit from the *Object Data* roll-up, and change the text that appears in the text box of the roll-up.

THE OBJECT DATA MANAGER

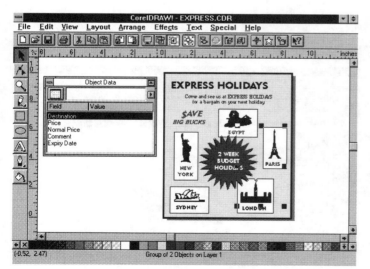

Figure 18. If you want to add information to the database—say for a group of objects—you can open the *Object Data Manager*. You do this by first selecting the relevant object or group of objects, and clicking on the [ ] button from the *Object Data* roll-up. In this example, we selected a group of objects that included the *Paris* and *London* graphics.

The status line tells us we have a group of two objects selected.

Figure 19. When the *Object Data Manager* appears, you can type in the different field information for each object in the group. If you had already typed in this data, it would be displayed in the *Object Data Manager.*

Object Data Manager					
File Edit Field Options Preferences					
3: Expiry Date 3/5/1 994					
	Destination	Price	Normal Price	Comment	Expiry Date
1					
2	London	$2,750.00	$3,500.00	Visit Buckingha	9/6/94
3	Paris	$2,500.00	$3,250.00	Must know som	3/5/94
TOTAL					

Figure 20. Here we have added a main heading in each field for the two grouped items. You can also type this directly into the database.

To enter text directly into the database, click the mouse in the cell you want, and type in the relevant text. Use the arrow keys on the keyboard to move from cell to cell. Once you have entered text into the database, you can edit it directly to update any necessary changes.

Object Data Manager					
File Edit Field Options Preferences					
TOTAL: Destination					
	Destination	Price	Normal Price	Comment	Expiry Date
1	**Europe**	**$5,000.00**	**$6,750.00**	**Two for the pr**	**9/12/94**
2	London	$2,750.00	$3,500.00	Visit Buckingha	9/6/94
3	Paris	$2,500.00	$3,250.00	Must know som	3/5/94
TOTAL					

Figure 21. You can change the size of columns in the database by holding the mouse button down when the cursor is on the bar between the columns, and dragging the column edge to a new position and releasing the mouse.

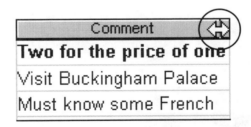

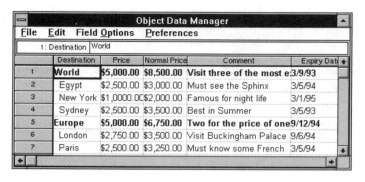

Figure 22. If you have two or more separate groups in the drawing, you can view all the information by selecting both groups and activating the *Object Data Manager* through the ▣ button in the *Object Data* roll-up.

In this example, the first group (*World*) contains the *Sydney*, *Egypt*, and *New York* graphics. The second group (*Europe*) contains the *Paris* and *London* graphics. In this way, you can view the entire database of information.

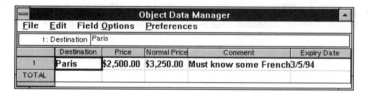

Figure 23. If we want to view any of these graphics individually, we first have to select the graphic with the Ctrl key held down. The information in the *Object Data* roll-up and, subsequently the *Object Data Manager,* applies to this selected object only.

OBJECT DATA ROLL-UP FLY-OUT

FIELD EDITOR

Figure 24. The ▶ icon in the *Object Data* roll-up pops-up this fly-out.

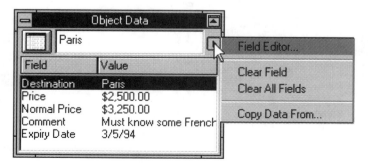

Figure 25. The *Field Editor* command in the *Object Data* roll-up fly-out opens the *Object Data Field Editor* dialog box. You use this dialog box to create and format new fields. For information on creating and formatting fields see **Creating New Fields** earlier in this chapter.

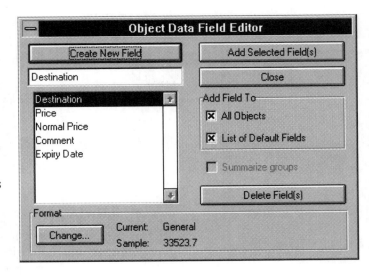

The *Add Field To* options in this dialog box let you apply the fields to all objects. Additionally, if you check the *List of Default Fields* option, you can add the fields in this dialog box to a list of default fields for all new CorelDRAW documents.

If you change the default list with the *List of Default Fields* option active (by adding or deleting fields) in one document, it will affect all the documents that contain the same fields.

To select multiple fields in this dialog box, hold the Ctrl key down and click on the fields you want to select from the list.

Check the *Summarize groups* option to summarize the totals of a group of fields. The subtotals for each selected group then appear when you open the *Object Data Manager*.

Click on the *Delete Field(s)* button in the *Object Data Field Editor* dialog box to remove the selected fields. When you do this you are prompted to confirm your decision.

The *Change* button in the *Object Data Field Editor* dialog box opens the *Format Definition* dialog box. Here you can choose or customize a format type for each of the fields in the database.

CLEAR FIELD

The *Clear Field* command in the *Object Data* roll-up fly-out (Figure 24) removes all the information from the selected field.

CLEAR ALL FIELDS

The *Clear All Fields* command deletes all the database information from the fields in the *Object Data* roll-up.

COPY DATA FROM

The *Copy Data From* command lets you copy all the information associated with one object to another object, saving you from retyping it. This command works in the same way as the *Copy Attributes* command from the **Edit** menu in CorelDRAW.

OBJECT DATA MANAGER MENU COMMANDS

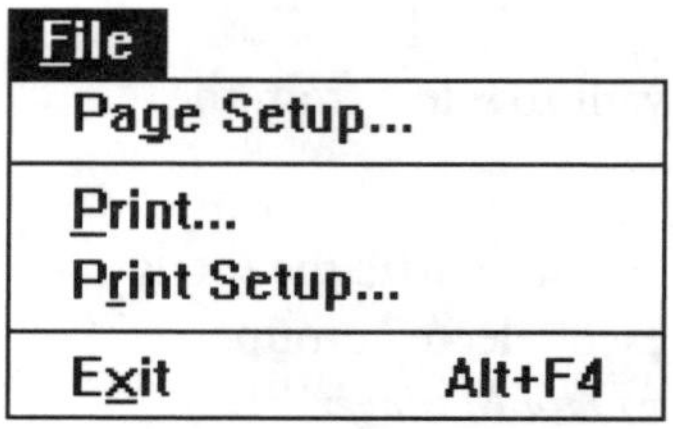

```
File
   Page Setup...
   Print...
   Print Setup...
   Exit            Alt+F4
```

Figure 26. The first menu in the *Object Data Manager* is the **File** menu.

The *Page Setup* command lets you set up the database for printing.

The *Print* command lets you print the database.

The *Print Setup* command allows you to set up the printer before you print the database.

The *Exit* command closes the *Object Data Manager* and returns you to the *Object Data* roll-up and your drawing.

Figure 27. The **Edit** menu in the *Object Data Manager* contains these commands.

```
Edit
  Undo
  Redo

  Cut
  Copy
  Paste
  Delete
```

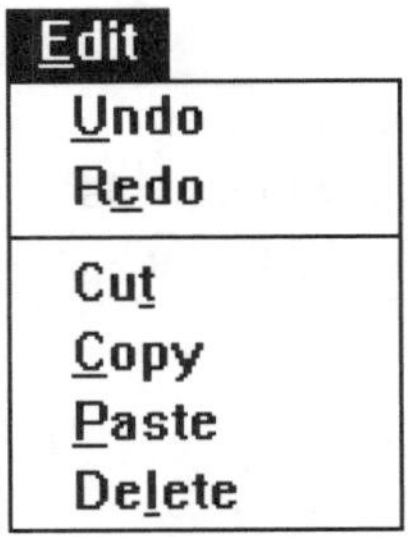

The *Undo* command reverses previous actions. For more information, see the **Undo** section in **Chapter 5, The Edit Menu.**

The *Redo* command reverses the action of the *Undo* command.

The *Cut* command removes information from selected cells and places it in the Windows Clipboard.

The *Copy* command makes a copy of the information in the selected cells and places it in the Windows Clipboard.

The *Paste* command pastes the contents of the Windows Clipboard into selected cells of the database.

The *Delete* command removes the contents of selected cells.

Figure 28. The **Field Options** menu in the *Object Data Manager* contains these commands.

```
Field Options
  Change Format...
  Summarize Groups
  Show Hierarchy
  Show Totals
  Field Editor...
```

The *Change Format* command opens the *Format Definition* dialog box (see Figure 14).

The *Summarize Groups* command displays the subtotals of individual groups when a field shares a multiple group.

The *Show Hierarchy* command indents objects within each group.

The *Show Totals* command adds the totals of a selected field.

The *Field Editor* command opens the *Object Data Field Editor* dialog box.

Preferences
   Show Group Details   ▶
√ Highlight Top-level Objects
√ Italicize Read-only Cells

Figure 29. The **Preferences** menu in the *Object Data Manager* contains these commands.

The *Show Group Details* command expands the datasheet to include all objects in a group of selected objects.

The *Highlight Top-level Objects* command emboldens the first level of a group.

The *Italicize Read-only Cells* italicizes cells you cannot edit directly, e.g. the *TOTAL* cell.

GRAPHICS DATABASE DYNAMIC DATA EXCHANGE LINKS (DDE)

The graphics database feature in CorelDRAW also supports dynamic data exchange (DDE) links to other spreadsheet programs. This allows you to set your graphics database as a source file that you link to a destination spreadsheet file. Then any changes you make to the source file are updated in the linked destination file automatically. CorelDRAW maintains these links through the CDRStaticID field. This field appears by default in the *Object Data Field Editor*, but you can delete it like any other field (we deleted this field for all of our examples as it was an unnecessary field). However, if you delete this field, and later need to use it, you have to recreate it.

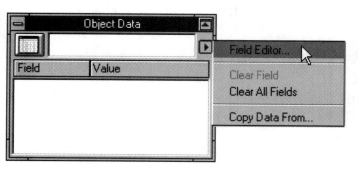

Figure 30. To recreate the CDRStaticID field, select the object or group of objects that you deleted the field from and then select the *Field Editor* command from the *Object Data* roll-up.

Figure 31. Then in the *Object Data Field Editor* dialog box that appears, click on the *Create New Field* button and name the new field "CDRStaticID" paying close attention to the capitalization. When you click on *Close*, CorelDRAW automatically assigns a value to the field for each object.

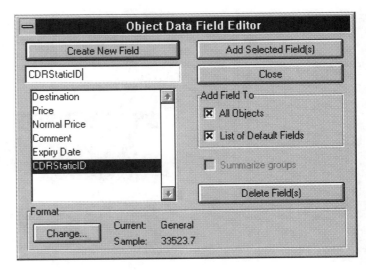

SELECT CLONES AND SELECT MASTER

Figure 32. You can access the *Select Clones* command in the **Object** menu only when you have used the *Clone* command from the **Edit** menu. If you use the **Object** menu on a master object (the object a clone derives from), choosing the *Select Clones* command (a) selects the cloned objects.

Conversely you can access the *Select Master* command only when you use the **Object** menu on a cloned object (b). Choosing this command selects the master object that the clone was derived from.

For more information on clones, see **Clone** in **Chapter 5, The Edit Menu.**

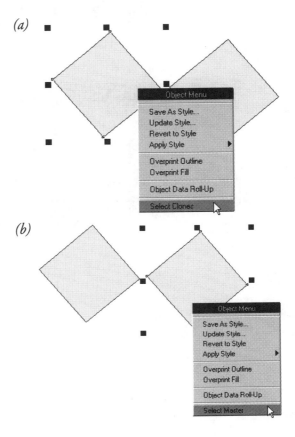

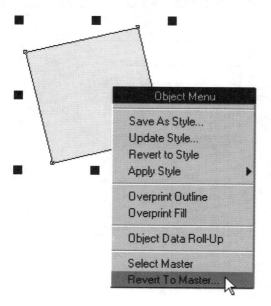

REVERT TO MASTER

Figure 33. You can access the *Revert To Master* command in the **Object** menu only when you have changed the cloned object independently of the master object.

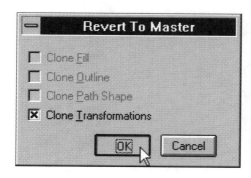

Figure 34. The *Revert To Master* command opens the *Revert To Master* dialog box. Here you select the option you have changed in the cloned object and click on *OK*. The cloned object then reverts to match the master object.

Index

More from Peachpit Press. . .

101 Windows Tips and Tricks
Jesse Berst and Scott Dunn

This power-packed, user-friendly survival guide gives you power-user tips to make Windows faster, easier, and more fun. Icons and illustrations lead your eye to the key points, and friendly explanations get you up to speed in a hurry. $12.95 *(216 pages)*

Dr. Daniel's Windows Diet
Daniel Will-Harris

Put Windows on a high-performance diet! This little book offers simple solutions to a universal problem—Windows can be slow. These easy-to-follow prescriptions cover the essentials of making Windows work faster—from autoexec.bat to virtual memory. It helps you work faster too, with keyboard shortcuts, file tips, and more. $8.95 *(107 pages)*

The Little DOS 6 Book
Kay Yarborough Nelson

A quick and accessible guide to DOS 6. This book is packed with plenty of tips as well as an easy-to-use "cookbook" section on DOS commands. It also covers DOS basics, working with files and directories, disk management, and more. $13 *(232 pages)*

The Little PC Book
Larry Magid

There are two ways to get started with PCs: trial by fire or friendly tutoring in non-technical, bite-size pieces. *The Little PC Book* is clearly the latter: a painless way to become PC literate, without being buried in details. This book won rave reviews from *The Wall Street Journal, Business Week,* and dozens of other publications. $17.95 *(376 pages)*

Mastering CorelDRAW 4
Chris Dickman

Packed with field-tested tutorials, this book leads you through the inner workings of this top-rated graphics program. In addition to teaching Corel's sophisticated drawing and paint tools, the book also covers creating slides, making signs, using scanners, working with service bureaus; and it offers tips on other software. A disk of utilities, templates, and fonts is included. $34.95 *(776 pages)*.

PageMaker 5 for Windows: Visual QuickStart Guide
Webster and Associates

Provides a fast, highly visual introduction to desktop publishing in PageMaker 5 for Windows. Packed with hundreds of illustrations, the book shows how to set up a publication, work with text, import graphics, use Aldus Additions, and more. $14 *(256 pages)*

The PC is not a typewriter
Robin Williams

PC users can now discover secrets from Robin Williams on how to create beautiful type. Here are the principles behind the techniques for professional typesetting, including punctuation, leading, special characters, kerning, fonts, justification, and more. $9.95 *(96 pages)*

Photoshop 2.5 for Windows: Visual QuickStart Guide
Elaine Weinmann and Peter Lourekas

The author of our award-winning *QuarkXPress for Windows: Visual QuickStart Guide* does it again. Here's an accessible way to learn how to use masks, filters, colors, tools, and more. $18.95 *(264 pages)*

The Photoshop Wow! Book, Windows Edition
Linnea Dayton and Jack Davis

Full color throughout, this books shows how professional artists use Photoshop to manipulate scanned images and create astonishing special effects. Each chapter deconstructs an actual piece of art and shows step-by-step how it was created. The companion disk contains a variety of Kai's Power Tools and other Photoshop filters and utilities. $34.95 *(208 pages with disk)*

QuarkXPress for Windows: Visual QuickStart Guide
Elaine Weinmann

QuarkXPress for Windows takes an easy, visual approach to learning the basics of QuarkXPress. This handy *QuickStart Guide* covers everyday features from one of the most popular and powerful desktop publishing programs around. $15 *(224 pages)*

The QuarkXPress Book, 2nd Edition for Windows
David Blatner and Bob Weibel

Better than the user manual, this book teaches you how to work with Quark's sophisticated type tools, import graphics, modify pictures, work with color, prepare files for a service bureau, and more. The inside cover features three panels of useful keyboard shortcuts. $29.95 *(704 pages)*

Real World Scanning and Halftones
David Blatner and Steve Roth

Master the digital halftone process—from scanning and tweaking images on your computer to imagesetting them. You'll learn about optical character recognition, gamma control, sharpening, PostScript halftones, Photo CD, Photoshop and PhotoStyler. $24.95 *(296 pages)*

The Windows 3.1 Bible
Fred Davis

Compiled by one of America's leading Windows experts, this book is a wall-to-wall compendium of tips, tricks, warnings, shortcuts, reviews, and resources that will inform, entertain, and empower Windows users of every ability level. It details the software's general principles, such as managing programs and files, multitasking, and working with fonts. Thoroughly indexed, the book also contains information on how to install and configure Windows 3.1 for optimal performance. $28 *(1,154 pages)*

The Windows Bible CD-ROM
Fred Davis

Get interactive while saving time and money! Now the complete guide to Windows 3.1 is available on CD-ROM. Point, click, and search for any topic covered in the 1,154-page *Windows 3.1 Bible* much faster than flipping through its pages. Provides the most comprehensive online help available for Windows, plus over 500 megabytes of fonts, sounds, images, icons, utilities, games, shareware, freeware, and more. $34.95 *(CD-ROM)*

How soon will I get my books?

UPS Ground orders arrive within 10 days on the West Coast and within three weeks on the East Coast.

UPS Blue orders arrive within two working days anywhere in the U.S., provided we receive a fax or a phone call by 11 A.M. Pacific Time.

For a full listing of Peachpit Press titles, call 1-800-283-9444 and request our full-color catalog.

Order Form

to order, call:
(800) 283-9444 or (510) 548-4393 or (510) 548-5991 (fax)

Qty	Title	Price	Total

Shipping	First Item	Each Additional		
UPS Ground	$ 4	$ 1	Subtotal	
UPS Blue	$ 8	$ 2	8.25% Tax (CA only)	
Canada	$ 6	$ 4	Shipping	
Overseas	$14	$14	**TOTAL**	

Name

Company

Address

City   State   Zip

Phone   Fax

❏ Check enclosed   ❏ Visa   ❏ MasterCard   ❏ AMEX

Company purchase order #

Credit card   Exp. Date

What other books would you like us to publish?

Please tell us what you thought of this book:

Peachpit Press • 2414 Sixth Street • Berkeley, CA • 94710